understanding **phenomenology**

Understanding Movements in Modern Thought
Series Editor: Jack Reynolds

This series provides short, accessible and lively introductions to the major schools, movements and traditions in philosophy and the history of ideas since the beginning of the Enlightenment. All books in the series are written for undergraduates meeting the subject for the first time.

Published

Understanding Empiricism
Robert G. Meyers

Understanding Phenomenology
David R. Cerbone

Understanding Existentialism
Jack Reynolds

Understanding Poststructuralism
James Williams

Understanding German Idealism
Will Dudley

Understanding Psychoanalysis
Matthew Sharpe & Joanne Faulkner

Understanding Hegelianism
Robert Sinnerbrink

Understanding Rationalism
Charlie Heunemann

Understanding Hermeneutics
Lawrence K. Schmidt

Understanding Utilitarianism
Tim Mulgan

Understanding Naturalism
Jack Ritchie

Understanding Virtue Ethics
Stan van Hooft

Forthcoming titles include

Understanding Ethics
Tim Chappell

Understanding Feminism
Peta Bowden & Jane Mummery

understanding **phenomenology**

David R. Cerbone

ACUMEN

First published in 2006 by Acumen
Reprinted 2007, 2008, 2010 (twice), 2012

Acumen Publishing Limited
4 Saddler Street
Durham
DH1 3NP
www.acumenpublishing.co.uk

ISBN: 978-1-84465-054-5 (hardcover)
ISBN: 978-1-84465-055-2 (paperback)

British Library Cataloguing-in-Publication Data
A catalogue record for this book is available from the British Library.

Typeset in Minion Pro.
Printed by Ashford Colour Press Ltd, UK.

Contents

Acknowledgements

Over the course of writing this book, I have incurred many debts. Indeed, many of these debts extend well back before work began on this project. I must acknowledge Hubert Dreyfus, with whom I first studied Heidegger's *Being and Time* (and phenomenology more generally) and from whom I continue to learn and draw inspiration. Randall Havas has been a mentor and friend for roughly twenty years. Randall's influence on my thinking has been immeasurable and his support has been unwavering; he is also to be thanked for taking the time to provide detailed comments on previous drafts of this work. Another friend, Wayne Martin, also provided incredibly detailed, sometimes daunting, comments that I have tried to accommodate in the course of making revisions. Ed Minar also deserves special mention for reading the manuscript in its entirety and offering both criticism and encouragement. I should also like to thank the many people with whom I have discussed phenomenology over the years and from whose work I have learned more than I could ever have discovered on my own: Steven Affeldt, William Blattner, Taylor Carman, Steven Crowell, Charles Guignon, John Haugeland, Sean Kelly, Rebecca Kukla, Cristina Lafont, Jeff Malpas, Mark Okrent, Joseph Rouse, Ted Schatzki, Joseph Schear, Hans Sluga and Mark Wrathall. (And although it is very likely that the word "phenomenology" has never passed between us, I must acknowledge the tremendous influence of Barry Stroud on my thinking.) Some parts of the book were presented at an annual meeting of the International Society for Phenomenological Studies, and I am grateful to my fellow members for their insightful comments and criticisms. Thanks go as well to the people at Acumen connected with this project: Steven Gerrard and Tristan Palmer, and the series editor, Jack Reynolds, as well as two anonymous referees, who provided detailed, extremely helpful comments and criticisms. Thanks as well to Kate Williams for her easygoing expertise in preparing the manuscript for publication. I should also like to acknowledge Humanity Books, for allowing me to use bits and pieces of my paper, "Phenomenology: Straight and Hetero" in my discussion of Dennett and Husserl in Chapter 5.

A great deal of what is now this book began as lecture notes for courses I have taught over the past several years, and I am grateful to the many students who have allowed themselves to be subjected to my various fumbling attempts to understand and explain phenomenology. I have learned from them far more than they probably realize. The philosophy department at West Virginia University (WVU) has provided me with a happy and supportive environment in which to teach and continue my research, and I am grateful to my colleagues, especially to Richard Montgomery and Sharon Ryan, who have each served as department chair during the writing of this book. I am also grateful to WVU for granting me sabbatical leave in order to complete this project.

On a more personal level, I should like to thank my parents, Anne and Ralph, for their many years of love and support. My wife Lena and my two boys, Henry and Lowell, deserve the greatest thanks; without their love, understanding and inspiration, writing this book, like so much else, would not have been possible.

David R. Cerbone

Abbreviations

Translations have been modified where appropriate.

BN   J.-P. Sartre, *Being and Nothingness*
BP   M. Heidegger, *Basic Problems of Phenomenology*
BPW   E. Levinas, *Basic Philosophical Writings*
BS   D. C. Dennett, *Brainstorms*
BT   M. Heidegger, *Being and Time*
BW   M. Heidegger, *Basic Writings*
CE   D. C. Dennett, *Consciousness Explained*
CES   E. Husserl, *The Crisis of the European Sciences*
CM   E. Husserl, *Cartesian Meditations: An Introduction to Phenomenology*
FTL   E. Husserl, *Formal and Transcendental Logic*
HCT   M. Heidegger, *The History of the Concept of Time: Prologomena*
HE   J.-P. Sartre, *The Humanism of Existentialism*
HSHC   D. C. Dennett, "How to Study Human Consciousness Empirically, or Nothing Comes to Mind"
Ideas I   E. Husserl, *Ideas Pertaining to a Pure Phenomenology and to a Phenomenological Philosophy: First Book*
Ideas II E. Husserl, *Ideas Pertaining to a Pure Phenomenology and to a Phenomenological Philosophy: Second Book*
IM   M. Heidegger, *Introduction to Metaphysics*
IOP   E. Husserl, *The Idea of Phenomenology*
LI   E. Husserl, *Logical Investigations*
OTB   M. Heidegger, *On Time and Being*
PCIT   E. Husserl, *On the Phenomenology of the Consciousness of Internal Time (1893–1917)*
PCP   E. Husserl, *Phenomenology and the Crisis of Philosophy*
PP   M. Merleau-Ponty, *Phenomenology of Perception*

introduction

Opening exercises

Introducing a book on phenomenology, indeed introducing phenomenology, is no easy matter, in part because there are so many ways to begin and no one way is ideal. The difficulty is compounded by the fact that, as will become apparent in the chapters to follow, there is a great deal in the way of technical vocabulary and concepts associated with phenomenology, but to begin by making use of such terminology will only add to whatever confusions arise from reading the primary texts. Since phenomenology has a relatively well-defined history, commencing at the start of the twentieth century (with some nineteenth-century premonitions), along with a generally agreed on set of central figures, a book introducing phenomenology could begin historically, with a recitation of various names, dates and places. Lacking, however, would be any sense of why select just these names to the exclusion of others, and what it is that is holding them all together. The historical development of phenomenology will be one of the themes of this book, and so there will be ample opportunity for names and dates as we proceed.

There is, of course, the word "phenomenology" itself, but its meaning, the study or science of phenomena, only raises more questions: phenomena as opposed to what, and what does it mean to study, or have a "science" of, phenomena (whatever they turn out to be)? Equally unhelpful is attending to the history of the word, whose use extends back a few hundred years and has well-established uses in both philosophy (e.g. in the philosophy of Hegel) and science (e.g. in thermodynamics) that are often only loosely related to how the term is used in the twentieth-century phenomenological movement. Accounting for these various uses thus does little to illuminate what is special and significant about this movement.

I begin instead by inviting you to engage in a very simple exercise, which can be developed so as to indicate, in very broad outline, both the subject matter and philosophical importance of phenomenology. This exercise involves little more than continuing to do what you are doing right now, which at least includes looking at the words printed on the page of this book. (If you wear glasses, it might prove helpful to take them on and off as we proceed; if you do not wear glasses, you can squint or in some other way "screw up" your eyes.) That you are looking at the words on this page, that you are reading, means, among other things, that you are engaged in the act of seeing, or, to be a bit fancier but perhaps no less awkward, that you are currently having or enjoying visual experience. Now, suppose you are asked to describe *what* you see. In response, you may note such things as the page before you, along with the words and letters, and perhaps also the shape of the page, the shape and colour of the letters. You may even read aloud the words that are occupying you at the moment the request is entered. You may also, if you are being especially careful and attentive, say something about the background that forms a field on which the page appears. That you say such things is something we shall return to shortly, but first I want you to consider a slightly different request. Instead of being asked to describe what you see, the "objects" of your visual experience, suppose you were asked to describe your *seeing* of the objects. Here, you are being asked to shift your attention away from the things you see to your visual experience of these things, and here you may find the request a little less straightforward. Nonetheless, a moment's thought may serve to get such a description going. (If you wear glasses, this might be a good time to take them off and put them back on a few times.)

I happen to wear glasses. If I were to take them off while looking at the page of the book held at the usual half-arm's length away, the letters, words and page would, as I might put it, become blurry, while restoring my glasses would render them sharp once again. Of course, I do not for a moment think that the blurriness characterizes the things I am look-ing at in and of themselves, as though my removing my glasses had the magical power to soften the actual ink, paper and so on. (Think here of the difference between removing your glasses and taking your wet hand and rubbing it across the printed page. Doing the latter, wetting the paper and smearing the print, really does affect the object.) That there are descriptions that apply to visual experience without necessarily applying to the objects of that experience helps to make vivid the distinction we are trying to delineate between what we see and our seeing of it. To concentrate on the latter, to focus one's attention not so much on what one experiences out there in the world but on one's experience of the world, is to take the first step in the practice of phenomenology. The word "phenomenology" means "the study of phenomena", where the notion of a phenomenon coincides, roughly, with the notion of experience. Thus, to attend to experience rather than what is experienced is to attend to the phenomena.

Considerable care is needed in spelling out this talk of "attending to experience", since there are directions we could go in that would very quickly take us away entirely from the domain of phenomenology. Let us stick for a moment with the example of the blurriness brought on by the removal of my glasses. One way I might attend to that experience is to begin to investigate the causes of the change in the character of my visual experience. I may begin to wonder just why it is that my vision becomes blurry, just what it is about the structure of my eye, for example, that is responsible, or what it is about the glasses I wear that removes the blurriness. Such an investigation, while no doubt interesting and extremely important for some purposes, would lead us away from the experience itself, and so away from phenomenology. Phenomenology, by contrast, invites us to stay with what I am calling here "the experience itself", to concentrate on its character and structure rather than whatever it is that might underlie it or be causally responsible for it. But what might we learn or discern by staying with the experience itself? What kind of insights might we glean and why might they matter philosophically? Of course, the answers to these questions will be canvassed in considerable detail throughout this book, but for now a sketch will suffice.

Let us resume our exercise, now concentrating on the description of our experience. In doing so, we may begin to notice a few things. First of all, and as has already been noted, your current visual experience is of something: a page of this book, the words on the page and so forth. These objects are an integral part of your experience in the sense that it would not be the experience it is were it not to involve these objects. (Although phenomenology asks us to concentrate on our experience, on how things "appear" to us, to remain faithful to the character of that experience, we must not neglect or distort the idea that such "appearances" are largely appearances *of* things.) At the same time, these objects are not literally a part of your experience in the way that the pages of the book are a part of the book. (This observation indicates that the relation between experience and its objects requires special attention, as it cannot be accommodated by the usual understandings of "part" and "whole".) For the moment, we will content ourselves with noting that talk of the book, page, words and letters being a part of the visual experience indicates that these are the objects of the experience: that the experience is of or about them. To introduce some rather technical vocabulary that will occupy us considerably in this book, this notion of experience being "of" or "about" its objects signals its having what the phenomenological tradition calls "intentionality". The phenomenological tradition has seen intentionality to be the defining, and even exclusive, feature of experience, and so phenomenology can be characterized as the study of intentionality. (Other schools of philosophy have likewise been concerned with understanding and explaining the notion of intentionality, so this kind of interest alone does not serve to pick out phenomenology uniquely.)

To return to your experience, although it is true that the book, page, words and letters are the objects of your current visual experience, at the same time it is not the case that you see the entirety of the book or even the entirety of the page at any given time. The object is presented to you perspectivally, in the sense that you see only one side of the object and from a particular angle. At the same time, it is not as though even your momentary experience is like looking at something flat, as though you were looking at a picture of the book, nor would it be correct to say that what you are "really" aware of is some kind of mental image that represents the book (phenomenology emphatically rejects the idea that attending to experience be construed as a kind of "introspection"). In a certain sense, even your momentary experience includes more than what you momentarily see, more, that is, than what you are currently seeing. What I mean here is that your current experience intimates that there is more to be seen: that the book can be seen from other angles; that it has other sides to be seen. This lends your current experience more in the way of "depth" and "density" than the experience of a flat image has. All this talk of perspective, intimation, depth, and density indicates that our visual experience, even in the simple case of looking at this book, has a rich and complex structure, which can be delineated and described in considerable detail. Moreover, if we reflect on this structure, we might begin to appreciate that it is far from arbitrary or idiosyncratic; on the contrary, we might begin to think that this structure indicates something essential with respect to having any visual experience of objects such as books. And here we begin to get a sense of the kind of interest phenomenology takes in our experience. By describing our experience, of which visual perceptual experience is but one example, one can delineate the "essential structures" of experience.

That is, one can delineate those structures experience must have in order to *be* experience (of that kind). In this respect, and here we introduce more technical vocabulary, phenomenology aims to be a transcendental enterprise, concerned with articulating the "conditions of the possibility" of experience or intentionality (unpacking just what this means will occupy us in the chapters to come).

To begin to name names, I have so far developed our opening introductory exercise primarily along the lines of the phenomenologist Edmund Husserl (1859–1938), who initiated the kind of phenomenological philosophy we shall be examining throughout this book. Phenomenology begins with Husserl, but it by no means ends there. Although its subsequent practitioners are collectively inspired by, and indebted to, Husserl, many branch off in different directions, sometimes in ways that complement his original vision, and sometimes in ways that more properly amount to rejection or repudiation. The details of both Husserl's project and its development and criticism by some of those who inherit phenomenology from him will occupy us in the chapters to come. For now, I want to continue with our exercise in ways that sketch out some of these continuations.

In reflecting on the perceptual experience of the book, we have thus far been concentrating on that experience as it unfolds from moment to moment, noting how the particular moments "hang together" by pointing towards other possibilities of experience (e.g. the page and book from other angles). All of these moments are bound together by, among other things, their all being "of" or "about" one particular thing: the book that is the object of this visual experience. One way we can continue the exercise is by broadening the horizons of our reflection, by locating both the object of this experience and the activity in which you were, and still are (I hope!), engaged: reading. To say that a book is the object (or content) of your perceptual experience is to ascribe to your experience a particular meaning or significance, that is, your experience has the meaning "book" or perhaps "book here in front of me" (we need not worry about the completeness of any of these specifications). Now, just as any given moment of experience intimates further possibilities of experience beyond that moment, so too the fact that your current experience has this significance points beyond the confines of this current experience. That is, your current experience is not of or about a mere object, something whose sole description is that it takes up space or manages to take up just this much of your field of vision; rather, it is a thing charged with a very particular, determinate significance – it is a book. That it is a book signifies, among other things, its having a particular use or purpose (reading, introducing phenomenology and so on). These uses and purposes further signify other things (reading glasses, bookshelves, paper, ink and so on) and activities (such as studying philosophy, perhaps attending university courses), as well as *others* (the author of the book, other readers, the bookshop assistant, the friend who recommended it). In other words, the particular significance your experience has ultimately intimates what Martin Heidegger (1889–1976) would call a "world". As we shall see, one of the principal tasks of phenomenology, for Heidegger, is to illuminate the phenomenon of world.

I said before that one of the ways in which the moments of your experience throughout our exercise hang together is that they have as their content one and the same thing, namely the book from whose pages you are reading. There are other ways in which the various moments hang together: they are united not just by means of a common object, but also by a common *subject*, that is, all of these experiences are had by someone whose experiences they are, namely you. At the same time, the subject whose experiences they are often does not figure centrally in the content of the experience, at least it probably did not until I asked you to reflect more closely on your experience. When you are absorbed in reading, the words, sentences and paragraphs are the focus of your experience, and it is only a reflective, often disruptive, move that introduces the element of "Here I am reading" into your ongoing experience. Until that point, there was little in the way of an "I", subject or self as part of the experience. The notion of the subject plays a prominent role in phenomenology, both as one of the "unifiers" of experience and as a "phenomenon", that is, as something that figures in the content of experience, but there is considerable disagreement, for example between Husserl and Jean-Paul Sartre (1905–80), over the proper characterization of the subject of experience.

Let us consider a final direction in which to take our opening exercise, which incorporates elements from both of the last two sketches. If we consider further the object of your experience, the book, it will no doubt be noticed that books are designed and constructed with the aim of reading in mind. To that end, books are designed and constructed so as to accommodate various aspects or dimensions of your body. If books were too large, the size of an automobile for example, or too small, say the size of a sugar cube, then you would have considerable trouble putting them to their proper use; in other words, such books would be unreadable, regardless of the quality of the prose they contain. Similar observations apply to other aspects of the book: the size and shape of the print, the spacing of the words, the dimensions of the pages and so on. Your bodily existence is not just intimated in your experience of the book, but is more directly manifest. In looking at the page, you are probably peripherally aware of your hands holding the book; you may also dimly discern the outlines of your glasses or the tip of your nose. Your attention may shift, gradually or abruptly, if you feel a sudden twinge or if your fingers gripping the book begin to fall asleep. Your body is not just present as a further object of perception, but is also manifest as active and perceiving: when you pick up the book, your hands take hold of the book and bring it into position to be read more or less automatically; periodically, you reach down (or up, if you are reading lying down, with the book above your head) to turn the page, your fingers gripping the corner of the page without awaiting a cue from an active intellect (like waiters who quietly refill your glass before you have noticed its emptiness). The bodily character of experience is a principal concern of Maurice Merleau-Ponty (1908–61), although as we shall see, many of his insights trace back to ideas already being worked out by Husserl.

If we take stock of the various ways in which we have developed our opening exercise, we may note a number of underlying points of commonality that serve to unite the four figures mentioned. Most prominent is the common concern with the notion of *experience*, of things "showing up" or being "manifest". Phenomenology is precisely concerned with the ways in which things show up or are manifest to us, with the shape and structure of manifestation. Perception, on which we have been concentrating, is one form of manifestation, but not the only one (some things, such as numbers and equations, are most genuinely manifest purely intellectually). A guiding claim of phenomenology is that the structure of manifestation, of intentionality, is neither arbitrary nor idiosyncratic; rather, the claim is that there is an essential structure, irrespective of whatever the causal underpinnings of experience turn out to be. A further commitment at work in phenomenology's concern to delineate the essential structures of experience is that these structures must be delineated in such a way that they are themselves made manifest in experience. This additional commitment further underscores the point that the interest phenomenology takes in experience is markedly different from the kind that proposes hypotheses about the causes of our experience.

Phenomenology's general disregard for causes is symptomatic of a further point of agreement: its opposition to what is perhaps the most dominant trend in contemporary philosophy (which was also a heavy hitter at the time of Husserl), namely "naturalism". Such a view, which gives pride of place to the findings of the natural sciences, tends to be preoccupied with precisely the kinds of causal structures phenomenology disregards. One of the dangers of scientific naturalism, according to the phenomenological tradition, is that such a preoccupation makes one lose sight of (and sometimes actively deny) the idea that things are manifest at all. Potentially lost as well is any appreciation of the kinds of essential structures that are definitive of the kind of beings we are.

We can get a sense of the opposition between phenomenology and naturalism by attending to a passage from one of the latter's most famous advocates, the twentieth-century American philosopher, W. V. Quine. In the opening passage of his essay, "The Scope and Language of Science", Quine can be seen as articulating, in broad brushstrokes, the point of view adopted by naturalism:

> I am a physical object sitting in a physical world. Some of the forces of this physical world impinge on my surface. Light rays strike my retinas; molecules bombard my eardrums and fingertips. I strike back, emanating concentric air waves. These waves take the form of a torrent of discourse about tables, people, molecules, light rays, retinas, air waves, prime numbers, infinite classes, joy and sorrow, good and evil.   (Quine 1976: 228)

Although one of the prepositions most closely associated with the notion of intentionality ("about") makes an appearance in the last sentence of the quotation, what is most striking in Quine's characterization of himself and his experience is the absence of intentionality. Quine's talk of light rays, retinas, molecules and eardrums, all of which figure prominently among the causes of our experience, ignores the content of the experience so caused. Recall our exercise in its opening development. A description of your visual experience involved both the objects of that experience (the book, page, words) and the way those objects were experienced (angle or aspect, sharp or blurry and so on). Were we to have extended the exercise to auditory experience, we might have included the slight rustling of the pages as they were turned, the ambient noises in the background, and so on. It would have been very artificial, however, to include in those descriptions any of the things that Quine appeals to. When you see, you see the book, for example, not light waves striking your retina; when you hear, you hear the music being played, not molecules bombarding your eardrums.

Although Quine's description is written in the first person, beginning as it does with "I am", nonetheless his characterization of himself as a "physical object" appears to overlook entirely the idea that the "I" picks out a subject of experience: a being to whom the world is present and who is present to himself. Again, recall our exercise. When you reach to turn the page of the book, you are not present to yourself as one more "physical object" among others; you experience yourself as actively engaged with the world, and, with suitable reflection, you experience yourself as having experience. That is, you can become reflectively aware of the fact that the world is manifest to you in various ways. Moreover, that you encounter a book, an item whose significance intimates a whole array of purposes and activities, belies the idea that the world manifest in experience is merely the physical world, the world that can be exhaustively characterized in the terms of the physical sciences.

Where Quine, and thus scientific naturalism, begins is altogether different from the starting-point of phenomenology. The disparity can be further documented by comparing the passage I cited from Quine with one from Husserl, where he offers a description of what he calls "the natural attitude", by which he means our ordinary conscious awareness of ourselves and the world around us. Husserl begins as well with the first-person declarative "I am …", but how he continues is markedly different. Notice in particular the differences between Husserl's description and that provided by Quine, especially how Husserl's description seeks to capture the content and quality of his own experience, while Quine's simply passes it by. Notice also that nothing Husserl says contradicts or repudiates any of Quine's claims (the differences and disagreements between phenomenology and naturalism are more subtle). Husserl writes:

> I am conscious of a world endlessly spread out in space, endlessly becoming and having endlessly become in time. I am conscious of it: that signifies, above all, that intuitively I find it immediately, that I experience it. By my seeing, touching, hearing, and so forth, and in the different modes of sensuous perception, corporeal physical things with some spatial distribution or other are *simply there for me*, "*on hand*" in the literal or the figurative sense, whether or not I am particularly heedful of them and busied with them in my considering, thinking, feeling, or willing. Animate beings too – human beings, let us say – are immediately there for me: I look up; I see them; I hear their approach; I grasp their hands; talking with them I understand immediately what they mean and think, what feelings stir within them, what they wish or will.   (*Ideas* I: §27)

Over the course of this book, we shall have occasion to return to the differences between these two passages, and between the respective philosophies they initiate, both to bring the specific contours of phenomenological philosophy into sharper focus and to measure the significance of phenomenological philosophy. Given that naturalism is one of the dominant philosophical outlooks today, any success on the part of phenomenology in undermining naturalism attests to its lasting importance.

The four philosophers I have introduced over the course of our opening exercise – Husserl, Heidegger, Sartre and Merleau-Ponty – are without doubt the most famous figures in the phenomenological movement. Accordingly, a chapter will be devoted to each of them, and the final chapter will canvass several critical responses to phenomenology. There are many other significant figures in the phenomenological tradition, such as Max Scheler, Eugen Fink, Alfred Schutz, Edith Stein and Paul Ricoeur, who will not receive much in the way of further mention in this book. Their omission is in no way meant to suggest that their contributions to phenomenology are uninteresting or unimportant, although understanding their contributions very often presupposes some grasp of the works and ideas we shall be considering in this book. Getting a grip on the thought of these four main figures serves to lay the foundation for further study, which is, after all, what an introductory text ought to do. Even by so restricting our attention and even by devoting an entire chapter to each figure, we shall really only be scratching the surface of these complex and comprehensive philosophical views. The primary texts of phenomenology are, for the most part, rather massive tomes (my edition of Heidegger's *Being and Time* comes in at over 500 pages, and Merleau-Ponty's *Phenomenology of Perception* is nearly that long as well; Sartre's *Being and Nothingness* is around 800 pages, and Husserl's *Logical Investigations* alone is nearly 1000), and their length is matched by the density of their prose. When I teach phenomenology, I never fail to notice the looks of shock and incomprehension on students' faces after the first reading of Husserl has been assigned. My hope is that this book, by providing an overview of each figure and by working through some of their main ideas, will help to relieve some of this stress.

one

Husserl and the project of pure phenomenology

Husserl: life and works

Edmund Husserl was born in 1859, in Prossnitz, in what is now the Czech Republic. He was educated at the University of Leipzig, where he concentrated primarily on mathematics, eventually earning a doctorate in the subject. It was not until the 1880s that his interests became more exclusively philosophical. At that time, he encountered the psychologist and philosopher Franz Brentano, whose work revived the medieval notion of "intentionality". Attending Brentano's lectures in Vienna profoundly altered the course of Husserl's intellectual development, setting him on the path to phenomenology. However, Husserl's work in the late 1800s still reflected his primary interests in mathematics and logic: in 1887, he published *On the Concept of Number*, which was followed by the *Philosophy of Arithmetic* in 1891. At the turn of the twentieth century, Husserl's first monumental work appeared, his *Logical Investigations*, wherein he describes himself as achieving his "break-through" (LI: 43) to phenomenology. *Logical Investigations* begins with a "Prologomena to Pure Logic", which contains a sustained attack on empiricist and psychological conceptions of logic. As such, the work forms a cornerstone of Husserl's anti-naturalism, which we shall consider in more depth shortly. The "Prologomena" is followed by six "investigations", devoted variously to such interrelated concepts as meaning, intentionality, knowledge and truth, as well as a theory of parts and wholes.

Already in *Logical Investigations*, Husserl conceived of phenomenology as a kind of pure, non-empirical discipline that "lays bare the 'sources'

Brentano's lectures in the 1880s exerted an enormous influence on Husserl's philosophical development. Husserl would later recall: "at a time when my philosophical interests were increasing and I was uncertain whether to make my career in mathematics or to dedicate myself totally to philosophy, Brentano's lectures settled the matter" (SW: 342). And: "Brentano's lectures gave me for the first time the conviction that encouraged me to choose philosophy as my life's work" (SW: 343). (Brentano's influence extended well beyond Husserl: Sigmund Freud and the Austrian philosopher Alexius Meinong were also among his students in Vienna.) In his *Psychology from an Empirical Standpoint*, first published in 1874, Brentano characterized the mind and consciousness in terms of "mental phenomena", which are distinguished by the "intentional in-existence" of the objects they are about. Husserl later rejected Brentano's conception of intentionality, arguing that since the objects most intentional states are about "transcend" those states, the idea of intentional in-existence is incorrect.

from which the basic concepts and ideal laws of *pure* logic 'flow', and back to which they must be traced" (LI: 249). "*Pure* phenomenology represents a field of neutral researches" (*ibid.*), which means that phenomenology is to proceed without the aid of any unexamined assumptions; phenomenology is to be a "presuppositionless" form of enquiry (see e.g. LI: 263–6). Around 1905, however, Husserl described his conception of phenomenology as undergoing radical dramatic changes. At this point, Husserl began to think of phenomenology in transcendental terms, and emphasized to an even greater degree the idea of phenomenology as a pure discipline. The meaning and import of the two key terms "transcendental" and "pure" will occupy us considerably over the course of this chapter, as they serve to underwrite what he saw as his principal methodological innovation: the "phenomenological reduction" (which is foreshadowed in *Logical Investigations*, but only explicitly articulated following Husserl's "transcendental turn"). Husserl's revised conception of phenomenology is evident in his 1907 lectures, published as *The Idea of Phenomenology*, as well as in his 1911 manifesto, "Philosophy as Rigorous Science", which contains another attack on naturalism in philosophy. In 1913, Husserl published the first volume of *Ideas Pertaining to a Pure Phenomenology and to a Phenomenological Philosophy* (hereafter *Ideas*). There would eventually be two further volumes, although neither of them would be published during Husserl's lifetime.

The remainder of Husserl's philosophical career was spent developing, refining and reconceiving transcendental phenomenology. Husserl repeatedly characterized himself as a "beginner" in phenomenology, and many of his works reflect this, not by being amateurish but by their willingness to reopen the question of just what phenomenology is and how it is to be practised. Husserl's perpetual rethinking of phenomenology translated also into hesitation and delays with respect to publication. Following the publication of *Ideas* in 1913, other works appeared only sporadically. Among them are *Formal and Transcendental Logic* in 1929, *Cartesian Meditations* in 1931 and *The Crisis of the European Sciences* in 1936.

Husserl died in 1938. His final years following his retirement from a chair in philosophy at Freiburg were rather unhappy ones. The rise of the Nazis in Germany meant that Husserl, owing to his Jewish ancestry, was barred from any kind of official academic activity. Carried along by the wave of Nazism was one of Husserl's most promising followers, Martin Heidegger, who joined the party in the early 1930s (in the early 1940s, the dedication to Husserl in Heidegger's *Being and Time* was quietly deleted, only to be restored in the 1950s). The political situation was not the sole cause of Husserl's unhappiness, however. As he grew older, Husserl lamented both the incompleteness of his own achievements in phenomenology and the lack of any obvious successor (Heidegger, among others, having clearly failed to take up the banner, or at least not in the right way).

Although Husserl did not publish a great many works in the last twenty-five years of his life, this was not from lack of writing. Husserl left nearly 30,000 pages (in shorthand!) of manuscripts. Slowly these are being edited and published, both in their original German and in English translation. These include the second and third volumes of *Ideas*, as well as *Experience and Judgment*, a companion to his *Formal and Transcendental Logic*. When one combines the manuscripts with the published works, Husserl's philosophy becomes nearly unsurveyable, and certainly not something that can be adequately accounted for in one chapter of an introductory work. We shall concentrate, as Husserl often does, on a small handful of examples. In doing so, I hope to capture the overall "feel" of Husserl's phenomenology, thereby conveying its principal methods, aspirations and achievements.

From anti-naturalism to phenomenology

From this brief synopsis of Husserl's life and works we can extract two concerns that, especially when combined with a third, account for the particular character of his phenomenology, both in its methods and aspirations. One concern, present in one way or another from the beginning of Husserl's intellectual–academic life, is with the notions of logic and mathematics. A second concern, stemming largely from the influence of Brentano, is with the notions of consciousness and intentionality. Throughout his philosophical career, Husserl is concerned both to understand the nature and status of logic and mathematics, and account for our grasp or comprehension of them. Moreover, when we consider our third concern, we can get a better feel for how such an account looks, or at least how it ought *not* to look. The third concern, which emerges in Husserl's thinking in the late-nineteeth century and becomes a guiding theme in his *Logical Investigations* and later works, is that of anti-naturalism: a rejection of the idea that the natural sciences can provide a complete or exhaustive account of reality. This is not perhaps the best way to put Husserl's claim, since "reality" might be taken to be coextensive with "nature", and certainly the natural sciences have pride of place in understanding the latter. Better put, Husserl's opposition to naturalism amounts to the claim that there are truths and principles that the natural sciences presuppose, but for which they themselves cannot account; not every truth is a natural scientific truth.

Rather than reality, then, what the natural sciences cannot account for is "ideality": the ideal truths and principles of logic and mathematics. Any attempt to "naturalize" these truths and principles has disastrous consequences, according to Husserl, resulting ultimately in the self-refutation of naturalism itself. That is, naturalism tries to account for logical principles entirely in terms of psychology: logical principles are psychological principles; the laws of logic are natural laws of psychology, that is, laws that generalize how human beings and perhaps other sentient beings think. The problem for this account is that such natural laws are descriptive, much like the laws of motion for planets and other celestial bodies, whereas the relation between logic and any actual psychological processes is "normative": the laws of logic govern thinking by prescribing how sentient beings ought to think. By rendering logical laws entirely in psychological terms, the naturalist, according to Husserl, blurs this distinction, indeed destroys it entirely. The result is "relativism": there will be, at least in principle, different logical laws and principles, different laws and principles of truth, depending on the character of the psychological processes found in any kind or population of creatures. To say that something is true or that one thing follows logically from another means, on the naturalist's rendering, that this or that kind of being characteristically holds that thing to be true or generally believes one thing when it believes the other.

Now consider even these sorts of claims concerning the characteristics and behaviour of populations of sentient beings: when the naturalist makes these claims, he typically puts them forward as *being true*, but what does this mean? It is obvious, Husserl thinks, that the naturalist intends more than to claim that this is how he and perhaps his fellow naturalists happen to think; indeed, the naturalist does not intend to say anything about his psychological states and processes at all. Rather, the naturalist intends to discover, and put forward, what is ultimately the truth about such things as psychological states and processes, without reference to any of his own psychological states and processes whatsoever, but this means that the notion of truth itself cannot be understood in terms of psychological states and processes. In this way, the naturalist, in his official position, courts self-refutation by depriving himself of the very notion of truth that guides his scientific aspirations. (Unofficially, we might say, the naturalist can be seen to be guided by such a notion of truth after all, and Husserl's arguments are primarily designed to make this clear to the naturalist himself.)

One aspect of Husserl's anti-naturalism, then, is his rejection of the idea that logic can be understood psychologically; the doctrine commonly known as "psychologism" is ultimately self-refuting, and in so far as naturalism traffics in psychologism, it too totters on the brink of absurdity. What, though, does this concern with the nature and status of logic have to do with the notions of consciousness and intentionality? After all, the latter two notions, especially that of consciousness, appear to be psychological notions, and so any rejection of psychologism with respect to logic would appear irrelevant to arriving at a proper understanding of them. While there are other, relatively independent aspects of Husserl's anti-naturalism that play a role in his particular way of approaching the notions of consciousness and intentionality, there is a connection between his rejection of psychologism in logic and his conception of how consciousness and intentionality ought to be studied. Although logic is independent of thinking in the sense that logical laws bear a normative relation to any actual thought processes, at the same time the very category of *thought* is bound up with the idea of logical structure. That a particular psychological process merits the label "thinking" or that a particular psychological state the label "thought" indicates its having a logical structure: the state or process involves "ideal contents" that can be logically related, for example inferentially, to other states and processes with such contents. In so far as psychological states and processes partake of such ideal structures and contents, that is, in so far as they achieve the status of thinking and thoughts, then there is, paradoxical as this sounds, a non-psychological dimension of psychology. In other words, there are fundamental, definitive aspects of psychological states and processes that cannot themselves be adequately characterized in psychological terms.

An example at this point might be of assistance. Suppose I have the thought: "Plato was the teacher of Aristotle". It is easy to imagine someone else simultaneously having that very same thought, that is, a thought with the same *content*. Although my and the other person's having that thought involve numerically distinct psychological processes – that is, there is whatever process is going on in my mind and there is whatever process is going on in the other person's mind – there is still one thing that we think, namely that Plato was the teacher of Aristotle. What we think, the particular thought that both of us have, stands in various kinds of logical relations to other (possible) thoughts. For example, the thought "Someone was the teacher of Aristotle" follows logically from the first thought, and this is so whether the second thought ever happens to occur to me or the other person; that the second thought follows from the first holds regardless of what I or the other person (or anyone else) then go on to think. I may, after having the first thought, forget all about Aristotle and Plato, occupy myself with something else entirely, and so never draw the conclusion that someone was the teacher of Aristotle.

We can push this example further in the following way. What I have been calling the ideal content, in this case the content "Plato was the teacher of Aristotle", specifies the particular thought in question in a way that the particular psychological processes involved in my having the thought do not. What I mean here is that it is at least conceivable that another kind of creature, whose material structure is radically different from mine, could come to have the thought "Plato was the teacher of Aristotle", even though the various empirical details of that creature's psychological processes and states are thoroughly different from mine. The causal underpinnings of this imagined creature's having that thought might differ dramatically from the underpinnings of my having that thought, and yet we can each be understood to be having that one identical thought. What our thought episodes have in common, then, is not an empirical, causal structure, but an ideal content, which specifies something essential about the thought, something essential to its being the particular thought that it is, in a way that all the particular characteristics of the psychological states and processes do not.

Regardless of the empirical differences between me and this imagined creature, it is conceivable that we have the same thought, that is, that we each have thoughts that exhibit the same intentionality: each of our thoughts is *about* Plato and Aristotle (and about the former being the teacher of the latter). For Husserl, following Brentano, intentionality is "the mark of the mental", and so we can see him as generalizing these remarks about thought to the notion of conscious experience in its entirety. All conscious experience, in so far as it exhibits intentionality, has an essential structure that is independent of the empirical particulars of any being whose experience it is. Given this independence, the essential structure of experience cannot be understood naturalistically, that is, in terms of the empirical psychological states and processes that might be causally responsible for beings having such experience.

The role played by this notion of essential structure for Husserl indicates another aspect of his anti-naturalism. The essential structure of experience is the structure that experience has in virtue of which it *is* experience, which for Husserl means in virtue of which experience exhibits intentionality. As such, the notion of essential structure plays a distinctive explanatory role that cannot, Husserl thinks, be taken over by the natural sciences. This role can be discerned in a question raised by Husserl in his manifesto-like essay of 1911, "Philosophy as Rigorous Science", the lion's share of which consists of a polemic against what he sees as the prevailing naturalism of his day. The question Husserl raises is: "How can experience as consciousness give or contact an object?" (PCP: 87). Husserl's appeal to the notions of "giving" and "contacting" indicates that the question concerns the possibility of the intentionality of experience: how does experience come to be *of* or *about* objects? Such how-possible questions are transcendental questions, and Husserl thinks that such questions are beyond the scope of the natural sciences. This is so because the natural sciences, no matter how sophisticated, still operate within what Husserl calls the "natural attitude": our ordinary stance with respect to the world that takes for granted or presupposes the givenness of objects. Science, in its attempts to locate the most basic constituents of reality and delineate their causal structure, partakes of such presuppositions, just as much as we do in everyday life. As Husserl puts it, the natural sciences, and the natural attitude more generally, are "naive". To say that the natural sciences and the natural attitude are naive does not mean that there is anything wrong with them. (Husserl is no opponent of the natural sciences, nor of the natural attitude, but only of naturalism, which is, we might say, a metaphysical interpretation of the natural attitude.) The charge of naiveté only indicates a limitation, not an error, on the part of the natural attitude and the natural sciences; the charge indicates that there are questions that are in principle beyond their reach.

What the charge of naiveté implies, in this context, is that any attempt to answer Husserl's how-possible questions from the standpoint of the natural sciences is hopelessly circular. Since the natural sciences presuppose a world of objects, any answers they might provide to Husserl's how-possible questions make use of the very things whose givenness is to be explained. In other words, the natural sciences (and the natural attitude more generally) cannot account for how consciousness succeeds in "contacting" objects, since any possible explanation offered by them will be couched in terms of objects, and that, from Husserl's perspective, is no explanation at all. Transcendental questions are in principle beyond the reach of the natural sciences, and so naturalism, which sees the natural sciences as the be all and end all of enquiry, amounts to little more than wilful blindness with respect to the idea of transcendental enquiry (see IOP: esp. 3–4, 13–21, 29–32).

One can find in Husserl another line of argument that challenges the viability of a natural scientific account of consciousness and, in doing so, tells against naturalism as an adequate philosophical perspective. This argument turns on what Husserl sees to be a radical disanalogy between the kinds of things with which the natural sciences concern themselves and the kinds of things of which consciousness consists. Consider first the domain of the natural sciences. Here we have, among other things, what we shall simply call "physical objects". We can discern something important about the nature of physical objects even if we confine ourselves to ordinary perceptual experience. One thing that is true about physical objects (or at least the ones that are large enough to see) is that they can be seen from more than one side. If I hold a rock in front of me, I can turn it around in various ways and, in so turning, the rock presents different sides for my viewing pleasure. There is, moreover, no way of turning the rock so that I see it in its entirety at any given time, and indeed it is not clear what a *complete* perceptual experience of the rock might involve; there are always more angles from which to look at the rock, more distances from the rock that I might stand, more variations in lighting conditions and so on. Implicit in the perceptual experience of physical objects is a notion of infinity or, perhaps, limitless possibility (this is an idea to which we shall return later in the chapter). If we consider the variety of possible presentations of the rock in ordinary perceptual experience, we can discern a further idea that tells us something about the nature of physical objects. That is, there are, we might say, some presentations that are better than others with respect to revealing the rock in and of itself. There are better and worse distances from which to get a look at the rock, better kinds of lighting and so on. What makes some conditions worse is that they are misleading or inaccurate. Under these conditions, the rock only seems to be one way or another, whereas it really is some other way. For example, if I view a whitish-grayish rock under a red light, it will appear to be more pink than it really is. The point of these considerations is that in the case of physical objects a distinction between *is* and *seems* is both readily available and generally applicable.

Husserl argues that when it comes to consciousness, these essential features of physical objects can be seen to be lacking (see PCP: 103–7). If we shift from the rock I am perceiving to my perceiving of it, it becomes apparent that we cannot transfer many of the things we noted about the rock to my experience of it. Start with the notion of perspective. Although the rock presents itself from one side or another, this is not the case with my perception of it. The rock, we might say, appears in my experience of it, but my experience is not presented to me in a further appearance. My experience just *is* the presentation of things such as the rock, and nothing more. Unlike the rock, my experience is not available from a variety of perspectives. I cannot "turn around" my experience in the way that I can turn the rock, seeing it now from one side, now from another. Indeed, my experience, unlike the rock, does not have "sides" at all. Unlike the rock, which admits of endless possible presentations or appearances, the appearance is exhausted by its appearing. If this is so, then the phenomena of which consciousness consists do not admit of the is–seems distinction. There is nothing more to the appearance than its seeming the way it is; there is no way it might really be in contrast to how it appears. While the rock might look blurry, but really have sharp, smooth edges, this is not the case with my blurry experience of the rock (when I restore my glasses, I have a *new* experience, rather than a new perspective on the old one).

The collapse of the is–seems distinction in the case of conscious phenomena points to a further disanalogy between physical objects (and the natural world more generally) and consciousness. This further disanalogy is "epistemological" in nature: it concerns the differences with respect to knowledge and certainty that are available in these respective domains. I said before that the rock was something that, as a physical object, admitted of an endless series of possible presentations. This means, among other things, that no one experience presents or takes in the rock in its entirety: there is always something further to see, some other way to see it. To use Husserl's terminology, any perceptual experience of things like the rock will always be "inadequate", which means that there will always be "sides" that may be intimated by the experience but are not part of the experience in the sense of being presented *in* that experience. Another way to put this is to say that the rock, and physical objects more generally, transcends my experience of it, which is just as it should be. Since my experience of the rock is an experience of a transcendent entity, which admits of the is–seems distinction, then there is always room for error in my experience. It is always conceivable that future experience will give the lie to my current and past experience: what I took to be a rock may turn out to be a Styrofoam prop or, worse, a figment of my imagination. To use more Husserlian terminology, my experience of the rock is not "apodictic": it does not admit of complete certainty.

Shifting again from the rock to my experience of it, the epistemological situation changes dramatically. Since my experience of the rock does not admit of the is–seems distinction, that is, my experience does not have hidden "sides" in the way that the rock does, then if I make the experience, rather than the rock, the "object" of my experience, I can grasp it in its entirety in a way that I can never do in the case of the rock. An experience whose "object" is a phenomenon, rather than a physical object, is one that admits of the possibility of "adequacy": the phenomenon can be completely present as the object of that experience. Unlike the rock, which is a transcendent entity in relation to my conscious experience, my experience of the rock is immanent to my conscious experience and so does not, in principle, exceed my experience of it. Moreover, the absence of the is–seems distinction in the case of my experience means that I can achieve a level of certainty or apodicticity when the "object" of my experience is itself a conscious phenomenon. Even if it turns out that the rock only appears to be blurry but really has sharp edges, or even does not really exist, I can still be certain that I am currently having a blurry-edged rock experience. The existence of the rock is always open to doubt, even if such doubts may begin to sound rather hysterical, but this is not the case with respect to my experience, that is, with respect to *its* content and qualities. Phenomenology, as a discipline whose "objects" are precisely conscious phenomena, admits of a level of certainty that is different in kind from what is attainable within the natural sciences.

The natural sciences proceed by gathering data, proposing hypotheses that explain the data, devising tests for the proposed hypotheses and so on. In this way, the natural sciences work by going beyond what is given in experience, always searching for laws and principles that bear an explanatory relation to the objects and processes that are observed. The sciences will thus tolerate appeal to objects, states and processes that are unobservable, for example in the domain of microphysics. It is not surprising, then, that scientific hypotheses are always proposed as tentative, open to revision and defeasible by alternatives. Phenomenology, by contrast, focuses precisely on what is given in experience, eschewing entirely the method of formulating hypotheses and drawing inferences from what is given to what lies behind or beyond it. For Husserl, phenomenology is to adhere strictly to what he calls "the principle of all principles":

> No conceivable theory can make us err with respect to the *principle of all principles*: *that every originary presentive intuition is a legitimizing source of cognition*, that *everything originarily* (so to speak, in its "personal" actuality) *offered* to us *in "intuition" is to be accepted simply as what it is presented as being*, but also *only within the limits in which it is presented there*.
>
> (*Ideas* I: §24)

The phenomenological reduction

Our examination of Husserl's anti-naturalism has revealed several guiding interests and aspirations of his phenomenology, namely:

- discerning and describing the essential structure of experience;
- asking and answering transcendental questions about experience; and
- achieving epistemological certainty.

Moreover, Husserl's anti-naturalism underwrites the status and significance he ascribes to phenomenology. That is, the arguments Husserl gives in support of his anti-naturalism are meant to establish the autonomy of phenomenology with respect to the natural sciences, as well as its priority with respect to the natural sciences. The former is established by his arguments for the difference in kind between conscious phenomena and the objects and processes studied by the natural sciences. The latter is established by his arguments concerning the natural sciences' in-principle limitations when it comes to transcendental, how-possible questions; what this means is that the natural sciences (and the natural attitude more generally) must take something for granted that stands in need of philosophical explanation. For Husserl, phenomenology is the way to supply that explanation.

But how does Husserl proceed in trying to supply such an explanation? The answer to this question is already implicit in the claims and concerns that have emerged in our examination of his anti-naturalism. We saw before that the essential structure of experience is not to be confused with the causal structure of experience. It is perfectly conceivable, Husserl would contend, that two creatures have the same experience in terms of "ideal content" even though the underlying "machinery" that produces the two creatures' respective experiences is entirely different. If we want to focus on that essential structure, we must suspend or exclude all questions and claims concerning whatever might be causally responsible for conscious experience. By excluding any consideration of the causes of experience so as to focus on the essential structure of experience, Husserl is at the same time preparing the way for asking and answering transcendental questions about the possibility of experience. We saw before that the natural sciences, and the natural attitude more generally, cannot answer transcendental questions without incurring the charge of circularity; the stance of the natural attitude takes for granted that consciousness has made "contact" with objects, and so it cannot account for the possibility of that contact. This suggests that properly answering such questions requires again that one suspend or exclude the presuppositions and commitments of the natural attitude. In order to engage in transcendental philosophy, we must not take for granted that objects are indeed given in experience; instead, we must allow that it is at least conceivable that our experience never reaches anything beyond itself at all.

Questions concerning the sources and the success of experience are entirely irrelevant to the kind of investigation Husserl wants to conduct. Accordingly, his investigation begins by excluding those questions: by "bracketing" them or, as Husserl sometimes puts it, putting them "in parentheses". To begin with this act of exclusion (or *epochē*, which is Greek for "abstention") is to perform what Husserl calls the "transcendental-phenomenological reduction": "transcendental" because it makes available the possibility of asking and answering how-possible questions with respect to the intentionality of experience; "phenomenological" because the performance of the reduction directs the investigator's attention towards conscious phenomena, thereby making possible the discernment and description of their essential structure. Husserl sometimes refers to the reduction as a kind of "purification", characterizing it as an act of "meditation". We must not be misled by these labels into conjuring images of New Age mysticism, complete with closed eyes and crossed legs, nor should we seek out sensory deprivation tanks, thereby isolating ourselves physically from the environing world. Any of these manoeuvres will, for the most part, deprive the would-be phenomenologist of much of the raw material for his investigation for which the flow of experience must continue unabated. Rather than an alteration in the flow of experience, the principal change heralded by the performance of the reduction is a shift in attention on the part of the one whose experience it is. When I perform the reduction, I no longer attend to the worldly objects of my experience, nor do I wonder about the causal underpinnings of that experience; instead, I focus my attention on the experience of those worldly objects. I pay attention to the presentation of the world around me (and myself), rather than to what is presented. The reduction is thus a kind of reflection: for Husserl, the realm of reflection is "the fundamental field of phenomenology (*Ideas* I: §50).

Phenomenological description

The performance of the reduction is only the first step in Husserl's phenomenology, as it prepares the way by focusing the phenomenological investigator's attention exclusively on the "flow" of his experience. (We have, in the phenomenological reduction, the more formal and rigorous articulation of the "shift" sketched out in our opening exercise in the Introduction.) Once the standpoint of the reduction has been attained, the investigator can then set about answering the kinds of questions Husserl considers phenomenology ideal to answer. Again, these questions concern the essential structures of experience. What structure must experience have in order to *be* experience? How is it possible for conscious experience to "reach" or "contact" an object? How, in other words, is intentionality possible?

I want to approach Husserl's answers to these sorts of questions by working carefully through a particular example. We have so far confined ourselves to cases that centre on visual experience (reading this book, looking at a rock), but I should like now to consider an example centred on auditory experience. The example will be developed along the lines of Husserl's own discussion in *On the Phenomenology of the Consciousness of Internal Time*, much of which is devoted to carefully describing and dissecting the experience of hearing a melody. Following Husserl's more elaborate description and analysis, I want us to explore the experience of hearing a melody with an eye towards answering the following questions, which can be understood as instantiating the general questions enumerated above:

(a) What sort of structure must experience have in order to be *of* or *about* a melody?
(b) What sort of structure must experience have in order to have the content *hearing a melody*?
(c) How is it possible for conscious experience to be *of* or *about* a melody?

For our purposes, (a)–(c) can be viewed as different formulations of the same question.

Before we proceed any further, it is important to block a certain way of responding to these sorts of questions that Husserl would regard as entirely unsatisfactory. Suppose one were to try to answer (c) by saying that in order for conscious experience to be of or about a melody, one must be suitably placed with respect to a melody that is playing, for example in a concert hall or next to a radio broadcasting a concert. What such an answer specifies is nothing that is either necessary or sufficient for having this particular kind of experience. It is perfectly conceivable that one have that experience without being suitably placed; that is, it is conceivable that one have an experience that is "qualitatively identical" to the one had by someone who is sitting in the concert hall or next to the radio (hence being suitably placed is not *necessary*); it is also perfectly conceivable that one be suitably placed and yet fail to have that kind of experience (hence being suitably placed is not *sufficient*). In short, such an answer leads us away from the experience itself, and it is primarily for this reason that the performance of the phenomenological reduction screens off this avenue of response.

Having foreclosed what Husserl would regard as an unfruitful way of handling our guiding questions, let us continue with our new exercise. So as to focus our attention, let us concentrate on a particular melody, one that is probably familiar to you even if you are not particularly well-versed in classical music: the opening four notes of Beethoven's Fifth Symphony. The opening consists of three identical eighth notes, followed by a longer note that is a tone and a half lower than the opening three. To make a first, rough pass at the experience of hearing the opening of Beethoven's Fifth, such an experience involves, at the very least, hearing all four of these opening notes. While this is correct, it is only the very beginning of a description of this particular experience: the notes must not just be heard, but they must be heard in a particular way or in a particular pattern.

One aspect of such a pattern is that the notes must be heard in succession. One must hear the first note at t_1, the second note at t_2, the third note at t_3 and the fourth note at t_4. If one were instead to hear all four notes all at once, one's experience would be not of or about Beethoven's Fifth, but of a slightly dissonant chord. Successiveness would thus appear to be an essential aspect of one's experience in order to have this particular kind of experience. (We shall return to this idea of successiveness and what it involves after we have pressed on a bit further.)

Hearing one note after the other, rather than all at once, is not, however, sufficient for having an experience with the content "hearing the opening of Beethoven's Fifth". As one hears each succeeding note, one's experience of the preceding note(s) must, in one sense, cease: if one continues to hear the previous notes, then the succession will amount not to a melody, but to a slowly building cluster of sounds, one on top of the other, much like the effect of holding down the right-most pedal on the piano while striking the notes. It is crucial, then, that with the experience of the sounding of each successive note in the opening, the experience of the sounding of the preceding note must cease. However (and here things get a bit more slippery), the experience of the previous notes must not be erased entirely. If, with the experience of each successive note, the experience of the previous notes was forgotten (and no experience with respect to upcoming notes was in any way expected), then one's experience would not "add up" to a melody. It would be an experience of a note, then an experience of another note, then an experience of yet another note, and then an experience of yet another note after that. Even this characterization is somewhat misleading, since from the point of view of the one whose experience it is, the notes would not even be experienced as "one, then another" or as "one after another". To the extent that we can comprehend it, the experience would be an even more radical version of the condition suffered by the main character in the film, *Memento*: a note would sound, only to be immediately forgotten.

To "add up" to a melody, the experience of each note must in some way be remembered as further notes are experienced. "Remembered" is not quite right here, and for a number of reasons. First, remembering has connotations of calling something to mind: reproducing a prior experience in one's memory for further inspection and contemplation. But that is not a fair characterization of what happens in the case of hearing a melody. If one called to mind the previous notes with the sounding of each note, then the experience would again be a slowly building cluster, and so the previously experienced notes would "get in the way" of the one being experienced as currently sounding. A second connotation of remembering also indicates its inappropriateness here.

Remembering is often active, something we deliberately do, as when we try to remember where we left a particular item or recall a holiday recently enjoyed. When we hear a melody we typically have no such relation to the notes that are sounding; we make no effort whatsoever to recall the previous notes or bring them to mind in any particular way. Rather than remembering, Husserl prefers to use a slightly more technical sounding term: "retention". As each note is experienced as "sounding now", the previous notes are retained. What this means is that they are still experienced in a sense, not as continuing to sound but as having just sounded, that is, they are experienced as fading into the past. (In his lectures on time-consciousness, Husserl uses a lovely image to characterize the retentional structure of experience: the "now-apprehension is, as it were, the head attached to the comet's tail of retentions relating to the earlier now-points of the motion" (PCIT: §11).)

Each note is heard at a different moment, so that each note is experienced as currently sounding at a different "now": at t_1, the first note is experienced as currently sounding; at t_2, the second note is experienced; and so on. As each new note is heard, at each new "now", the previous now-points of experience are retained as having been experienced (and as having been experienced in that order). Moreover, as one hears each note, the notes not yet heard, but are still to come, are also, in a sense, part of the experience. They are part of what is currently being experienced, not in the sense of currently sounding along with the presently experienced note, but as *expected*. Husserl's term for this is "protention". We can get a sense of the protentional dimension of experience by considering a case where the fourth note is struck incorrectly, two tones down, say, or only one. We experience a momentary shock in that case; we feel our experience to be disrupted. We might laugh or grimace, depending on our stake in the performance going off as planned, or we may just silently note to ourselves that the wrong note sounded. What all of this indicates is that with the sounding of the first notes we were already prepared for the fourth note sounding a particular way, and that expectation was already latent in our experience of the first three notes.

For a stretch of one's auditory experience to be of or about Beethoven's Fifth Symphony turns out to involve a number of complex structural elements. It is not just a matter of hearing one note, then another note and so on. There must be, in addition, a network of retentional and protentional relations holding the moments of experience together. Indeed, these relations constitute those moments *as* those particular moments; the experience of hearing, for example, the second note in isolation is very different from hearing it within the larger melody. In the latter case, the experience of the other notes is part of the experience of that one note as currently sounding, whereas this is not so in the case where the single note is struck with nothing surrounding it. That any given moment of experience involves more than what is being experienced as currently present indicates the "horizonal" structure of experience. As one note in the melody is experienced as currently sounding, the just-experienced and the still-to-be-experienced notes are part of the horizon of that moment of experience; the current moment of experience "points to" those further notes as retained or expected.

These moments of experience, with their respective horizons, "add up" to a melody. When the last note sounds, we say not just that we heard some notes, but that we heard one particular melody, such as the familiar opening of Beethoven's Fifth Symphony: *the* melody informs or governs the experience of the particular notes. As one experiences each passing note, retaining them as one goes and expecting further notes, the moments of experience are joined together, their respective horizons fused through what Husserl calls "synthesis". Through synthesis, the various moments of experience are united as being of or about, in this case, one melody.

Let us pause to take stock. Our examination of the example of hearing the opening notes of Beethoven's Fifth Symphony has revealed a perhaps surprising number of structures and structural relations – retention, protention, horizon and synthesis – that provide at least preliminary answers to our guiding questions. Recall that those questions concerned the conditions of the possibility of a particular kind of experience. How can experience be of or about a melody? What sort of structure must experience have in order to be of or about a melody? According to Husserl, experience must at least have a retentional–protentional, synthetic–horizonal structure. Without that kind of structure one could never experience a melody, no matter how many melodies happened to be playing nearby. These structures are *essential* structures, Husserl claims, since to imagine their absence is to negate the possibility of that kind of experience. (More will be said about the role of the imagination in Husserl shortly.)

Although we cannot do it justice here, there is another crucial structural feature of experience that deserves mention, as it serves to underwrite all the others mentioned thus far. In building up our characterization of the experience of the opening of Beethoven's Fifth Symphony and the structures and relations that experience involves, we began with the bare idea of "succession": the experience of each note following the preceding one in time. In many places Husserl claims that time is the most fundamental structure of conscious experience: the moments of experience are most fundamentally temporal moments. As one experiences the melody, hearing each note in turn, time is "running off", and one's experiences are indelibly indexed as occurring at their particular moments in time. Even if the melody begins to play backwards all the way back to the first note again, that will not bring about a recurrence of what we labelled t_1. On the contrary, a new moment in time, a new "now", occurs that has a qualitatively similar content in many respects to the content of t_1. The various moments of time are throughout "synthesized" as standing in an unchangeable order that is irreversible and unstoppable: one's conscious experience is always "flowing"; time is always "running off". Even an experience of everything ceasing to move, a world "frozen in time", as it is often put, has its own duration, so that one moment of experiencing this frozen world is followed by another, and then another and so on.

Noesis and noema: constitution

The structural features discerned in our example obtain more generally. They are essential not just with respect to the hearing of melodies, but play a fundamental role in the various modalities of experience. Indeed, we have discerned these structures already, as early as our opening exercise in the Introduction, although without yet availing ourselves of Husserl's technical terminology. Consider again the visual experience of material objects, for example the pages of this book, the rock discussed above and so on. Just as the melody is not heard "all at once", but rather note by note in a way that "adds up" to a melody, any material object is not seen all at once. When I hold the rock out in front of me, I see one side of it only. As I turn it slowly around while holding my gaze fixed, new sides come into view and the previously seen sides disappear. To use Husserl's terminology, the rock is presented via "adumbrations" (the same is true, in its own way, for the melody: we hear it note by note, although it sounds awkward to call the sounding notes "sides" of the melody). The adumbrational presentation of objects in visual experience is inescapable, even in the imagination. When I only imagine myself looking at a rock, it is still presented in my imagination via adumbrations: I always see the rock, even in my mind's eye, from a particular angle and from a particular distance. "It is neither an accident of the own peculiar sense of the physical thing nor a contingency of 'our human constitution,' that 'our' perception can arrive at physical things themselves only through mere adumbrations of them" (*Ideas I*: §42). Adumbrations, it should be stressed, are not isolated units of experience. As was the case with the melody, the sides that are no longer seen or are yet to be seen are still part of the current experience of the side that I can see. That the rock has sides-to-be-seen contributes to the horizon of the experience of the side facing me. As the rock turns, there is a constant change in my visual experience, and yet there is a kind of unity as well in so far as all of the presented sides are of the one rock: here again, we can see the work of synthesis, holding together the different individual moments of experience.

In *Cartesian Meditations*, Husserl calls the unifying of the adumbrational moments of experience the synthesis of "identification": all of the various adumbrational presentations are united as presentations *of* the one rock, the one melody and so on. The process of synthesizing the various moments of experience Husserl calls "noesis". The rock in the one case, the melody in the other, are, as synthetic unities, the *meanings* of those respective stretches of experience. Husserl sometimes refers to this meaning as the "apprehension-form" governing the successive moments of experience making up the experience of the melody; another term he uses is "noema". The kind of work we have been doing with respect to our various examples, exploring the process of synthesis and its hori-

---

Noema

The noema of a mental process (what Husserl also calls the "sense" or "meaning" of the mental process) is that in virtue of which the process is directed to an object, regardless of whether or not the object exists (my thoughts about Santa Claus are as much about something (i.e. Santa Claus), as my thoughts about Winston Churchill). The noema is thus to be sharply distinguished from the object itself. To any given object there correspond myriad noemata, depending on just how the object is meant, and there can also be noemata that direct consciousness towards non-existent objects (such as Santa Claus). This sharp distinction is essential to the efficacy of the phenomenological reduction, whereby "noematic structures" can be examined in isolation from any questions concerning the real existence of whatever objects these structures direct consciousness towards. For readers approaching phenomenology from the perspective of analytic philosophy, Husserl's conception of the noema, with its sharp distinction between the sense or meaning of a mental process and the object meant, is akin to Frege's famous distinction between sense (*Sinn*) and reference (*Bedeutung*). For Frege, two expressions may differ in sense while having the same referent, as in his example of "the morning star" and "the evening star", both of which refer to the planet Venus.

---

zonal counterpart, is thus what Husserl calls "noetic–noematic analysis". The appeal both to noesis and noema indicates the structural complexity of experience, involving the process of experiencing (noesis) and the content experienced (noema). (There is also a third element, the subject whose experience it is, but we shall defer discussion of that.) Along with the concepts of noesis and noema, a third comes into view that affords us further insight with respect to our guiding questions. A passage from *Cartesian Meditations* will be helpful here (by "cogitatum" in the first sentence, Husserl means the current content of experience, e.g. the side of the rock that is currently presented to me in my perceptual experience; what is "non-intuitively co-intended" are all the other sides that can be experienced, but are currently hidden from me):

> [P]henomenological explication makes clear what is included and only non-intuitively co-intended in the sense of the cogitatum (for example, the "other side"), by making present in phantasy the potential perceptions that would make the invisible visible .... Thus alone can the phenomenologist make understandable to himself *how*, within the immanency of conscious life ... anything like *fixed and abiding unities* can become intended and, in particular, how this marvelous work of "constituting" identical objects is done *in the case of each category of objects* – that is to say: how in the case of each category, the constitutive conscious life must look, in respect of the correlative noetic and noematic variants pertaining to the same object. (CM: §20)

Notice in particular the emphasis in this passage on "how", as it indicates an answer to our how-possible, transcendental questions. The process of synthesis and the correlative notion of horizon together supply the answer to our questions. Conscious experience reaches or contacts objects by "constituting" them within the flow of experience itself. Husserl's discussion of noetic–noematic analysis thus culminates in the notion of "constitution", but what exactly does it mean to talk of objects being constituted in the flow of experience? A proper understanding of this concept requires that we stay squarely within the perspective of the phenomenological reduction. In particular, we must be careful to avoid thinking that this notion of constitution applies to actual, worldly objects. The rock that I hold in my hand is not made out of adumbrations; rather, it is composed of molecules, which in turn are composed of atoms, and so on. The notion of constitution applies to the *appearing* of the rock in my perceptual experience: the appearing of the rock is, and must be, via adumbrational presentations united by the synthesis of identification. Only in this way can my perceptual experience be of or about a rock; only in this way can my experience "intend" a rock; only in this way can my experience have the content or meaning "rock". Constitution thus applies at the level of sense, that is, it applies with respect to how my experience makes the kind of sense it does, by being, for example, about enduring objects.

Phenomenology brings into view the systematic nature of objects at the level of appearance or experience: objects are constituted as systems of adumbrational presentations. The adumbrations form a system in the sense that they are not arranged haphazardly. If I currently see one side of the rock, then slowly turning it will reveal further sides in an orderly, smoothly continuous way (provided I do not blink). If I turn the rock slowly, I do not see the front side and then, immediately, the back side, followed immediately again by the bottom side, followed immediately by the presentation of the front of, say, my coffee cup. If my experience were like that, then my experience would never reach or be about objects; at best, my experience would be a chaotic play of images, lacking entirely any sense of stability or predictability. There would be, in Husserl's words, no "fixed and abiding unities".

There are distinctive notions of constitution "in the case of each category of objects", in the sense that different kinds of objects will be constituted differently. The constitution in experience of melodies, for example, is different from the constitution of material objects (the latter, for example, involve visual adumbrations and often olfactory ones, whereas heard melodies involve neither). There is also what Husserl sometimes calls a "more pregnant" notion of constitution, and this concerns the distinction in experience between real and unreal objects. We might begin to get a feel for this distinction by returning to the idea of objects understood at the phenomenological level as systems of actual and possible adumbrational presentations. If we consider the extent of such systems, we can begin to recognize that there are no easily drawn limits. When I consider the adumbrational presentation of the rock in my hand, there seems to be no end to possible ways that it might present itself in my experience. Just consider the different distances from which the rock might be viewed, or the different angles; either of these is infinitely divisible. We can also multiply indefinitely the possible times at which the rock may be viewed, the variety of lighting conditions, and so on, so that there is a distinct lack of finality with respect to our experience of even as mundane an object as a rock. One consequence of this is that whenever I take it that my current perceptual experience is of a *real* rock, I commit myself precisely to these countless possibilities of experience. When I see the rock from one side and posit that what I am seeing is a real rock, that means, among other things, that the rock can be seen from other points of view: that it has other, currently hidden, sides to be seen. These possibilities span different modalities of experience. A real rock is one that can be touched, scratched, smelled and even tasted. Various pathways among these possibilities can be traced out, continually vindicating my commitment: as more and more possible presentations are "actualized", I can feel more confident about my taking the rock to be real. At the same time, the course of my experience might not go as expected. Reaching out my hand to touch the rock I had taken to be real, the horizonal possibilities might not be actualized. Where I had expected the sensation of resistance, what I took to be the rock yields to my grip in spongy surrender. In the wake of such an experience, I find myself compelled to retract my confident declaration of the reality of the rock. My experience was, instead, of a clever imitation, a piece of foam artfully carved and coloured so as to be virtually indistinguishable, at least visually, from a genuine rock. (When, from that point on, I turn my gaze towards the sponge-rock, there is a very distinct sense in which it will now look different. The horizon of possibilities has henceforth changed.) Experience can also go awry in more extreme ways. The rock before me may turn out not even to have hidden sides to be seen. Rather than a real rock, what I see is but a clever hologram or even a momentary hallucination. Hallucinatory experience, and even deliberately imagined experiences, make up what we might call "degenerate" systems of possible experiences. In the case of objects that prove to be unreal (imagined, hallucinated) the infinite possibilities afforded by real objects break off abruptly, thereby negating all previous experiences of them. Husserl refers to this dramatically as the "explosion" of the noema (see *Ideas* I: §138).

The constitution of the ego

Husserl's notions of noesis and noema make up two fundamental structural elements of experience. All conscious experience having intentional content consists of a correlated noetic–noematic pair. There is, however, a third fundamental element of experience: the one whose experience it is, what Husserl refers to as the "ego".

Even at the outset of Husserl's phenomenology, discerned within the performance of the reduction, the ego is manifest as a constitutive element of experience, but considerable care is required, Husserl thinks, to characterize the appearing ego properly. That is, the phenomenological reduction is not intended to be a mere psychological reduction, focusing attention on my experience where "my" refers to a flesh-and-blood human being (phenomenology, for Husserl, is not a matter of introspection). The performance of the reduction applies equally to the subject of experience as it does to the objects. When I suspend any questions concerning the relation between conscious experience and the environing world, that suspension extends all the way to questions concerning whose experience it is. I bracket the assumption or presupposition that I am a worldly, materially real human being just as much as I do the assumption that my experience is taking place within a materially real world. (And by suspending any commitment to my materiality, I do not thereby conceive of myself as an immaterial being either. Despite his general admiration for Descartes, Husserl criticizes him for failing to make the "transcendental turn" by treating the ego revealed by the *cogito* as "a little *tag-end of the world*" (CM: § 10).)

Although my existence as an empirically real being is bracketed, the performance of the reduction does not render the stream of experience subjectless. The reduced experience is still very much owned but only by what Husserl calls the "pure" or "transcendental" ego, the subject of experience considered only as a subject of experience. Such an ego is always intimated by the ongoing flow of experience; the stream of experience always refers, however implicitly, to a subject whose experience it is, even if the features of that subject are exhausted by the bare fact of its having this particular stream of experience. We must be careful here not to misconstrue Husserl's talk of the revelation of the pure ego within the performance of the reduction. The pure or transcendental ego is not a *second* self or subject over and above my worldly subjectivity, as though that worldly subjectivity were in some way inhabited by the pure ego in the way that a hand inhabits a glove. Rather, the pure ego is the very same subject, only considered in abstraction from all of the features that contribute to my empirically real existence. The pure ego, we might say, is what is left over as given or manifest in experience, even if all of my beliefs about my empirically real existence were false. Even in that extreme case, my experience would still carry with it a sense of ownership, a sense of its being "had" by a subject. It is this pure or abstract sense of having that Husserl intends to explore within his phenomenology.

Just as objects are "constituted" within the flow of experience, so too is the ego. As experience continues, moving in particular directions, having its variously changing contents, the ego is built up precisely as the subject of *that* experience. If, for example, I now have the experience of seeing a rock in front of me, then from this point on it remains true of me that I had this experience; the identity of the ego or "I" includes the having of this particular experience at this particular time. In this way, the ego's identity or content accumulates with the passage of time. The ego is thus "*not an empty pole of identity*, and more than any *object* is such" (CM: §32), but a continuously self-constituting subject of experience. Such self-constitution is both passive (as is largely the case with the ever-accumulating history of perceptual experience) and active, since the ego's history includes various acts, such as judgements, decisions and commitments. That is, the ego's history will include the declaration and abandonment of convictions, the making and cancellation of decisions and so on: the ego "constitutes himself as *identical substrate of Ego-properties*, he constitutes himself also as a 'fixed and abiding' *personal ego*" (*ibid.*). These self-constituting activities ultimately display what Husserl calls "an abiding style" on the part of the ego. None of this, however, should be understood as lending to the ego any kind of substantiality, as though it were a further entity or substance over and above the stream of experience. Such a substantial conception of the ego would flout the requirements of the reduction, which abstains from any commitments concerning the make-up of reality. A substantive ego is one for which a place would have to be found:, a particular location in objective time, and perhaps objective space. These are issues about which Husserl's phenomenology must remain steadfastly neutral.

A second reduction

Husserl's phenomenology is guided throughout by the idea of "essence". We have seen this in the way in which Husserl investigates conscious experience and in the kinds of questions he raises about it. His phenomenology seeks to delineate the essential, rather than the empirical, structure of experience. Throughout this chapter, however, we have (following Husserl) proceeded by means of particular examples, attentively reflecting on our perceptual experience of things such as rocks and melodies, so as ultimately to discern their "constitution" in experience. It would be overly hasty, to say the least, to draw from our consideration of these examples any conclusions about the essential structure of experience. How can we be sure that we have not just located an idiosyncratic, variable feature of experience, mistaking it for an ineliminable structure? How can we know, for example, that what holds for seeing a rock holds for seeing any material object? Might it not be possible that some material objects are not given adumbrationally in perception? Might there not be a creature that could take in a melody all at once? Husserl himself no doubt feels the force of these questions, distinguishing as he does between two stages of phenomenological investigation (see e.g. CM: §13). The first stage involves the investigation of the field of experience opened up by the phenomenological reduction. At this point, the phenomenologist is primarily concerned to describe attentively the flow of this experience, noting its features and locating promising structures. There is, however, a second stage – what Husserl refers to as "the criticism of transcendental experience" (CM: §13) – and it is at this second stage that claims concerning essences can be fully adjudicated.

Whereas at the first stage the phenomenological investigator plays the role primarily of an observer with respect to his own experience, at the second stage he more actively intervenes. That is, the investigator "freely varies" his experience, using his imagination to introduce series of changes in the course of his experience. Husserl calls this method of free variation the "eidetic reduction", from the Greek *eidos*, which means "idea" or "form". This second reduction is a kind of distillation, removing any of the arbitrary or contingent features of the experience so as to isolate the necessary form or structure of experience. The investigator can in this way delineate the essential categories of experience, for example perception, memory, desiring and so on.

To get a feel for how the eidetic reduction is supposed to work, let us start, as Husserl does, with a particular example, returning again to the perceptual experience of a rock. The rock is given in experience as having a particular shape, colour, texture and so on. The rock shows forth precisely as one particular thing, with its various features already determined as actually being one way or another. The eidetic reduction proceeds by treating all of these actualities as mere possibilities. The investigator freely varies the colour of the rock, imagining it as blue, green, magenta, yellow and so on, and similarly with the shape, texture, size and other features. Since these variations are freely imaginable, they all show themselves to be possibilities with respect to objects of perceptual experience: material objects may vary with respect to size, shape, colour, texture, and so on. There will, however, be limits on these variations introduced into the perceptual experience, transitions where the experience will break down entirely. Such transitions might occur when the investigator tries to delete shape altogether or to imagine the rock's having two colours covering the same area at the same time. The points where the experience breaks down are the key for delineating essential structure, since they mark the passage from possibility to impossibility and so fix the necessary parameters on experience.

The investigator can introduce variations not just with respect to the objects of experience, but also with respect to the subject. That is, the investigator can freely vary his own particular make-up in terms of the particular history of his experience, particular kinds of associations, beliefs, likes and dislikes, and so on. Applied in this domain, the method of free variation is meant to allow a separation between what are only the idiosyncratic features of the investigator's experience, how he just happens to experience things, and what is necessary in order to be a subject of experience at all. In this way, the results arrived at by the investigator are applicable universally, and not just with respect to his own experience. Here we can see quite clearly the distance between Husserl's conception of phenomenology and the kind of psychologism he

---

Transcendental idealism
Husserl conceives of phenomenology as a transcendental investigation, whose guiding question is one of how it is possible for consciousness to reach or contact an object. Often, this question is understood as a question of "transcendence", that is, a question concerning how consciousness manages to gain access to, and knowledge of, objects lying "outside" its boundaries. In some of his writings, such as *Cartesian Meditations*, Husserl argues that phenomenology, fully thought out, reveals the question concerning the possibility of transcending the sphere of consciousness to be a bogus one. That is, if we consider the two possible standpoints from which the question might be raised, we shall see that there is no question about transcendence worth asking. From the standpoint of the natural attitude, the question of how I, David Cerbone, get outside my sphere of consciousness in order to reach the "outer" world is nonsensical. In so far as I understand myself as one more human being, I have already conceived of myself as amid a realm of objects and other sentient beings whose independent existence I take for granted. If, however, I adopt the standpoint of the transcendental attitude, that is, the standpoint of the phenomenological reduction, there again is no genuine question of transcendence. From this standpoint, actually existing objects are constituted *immanently*. With the performance of the eidetic reduction, the standpoint of transcendental subjectivity encompasses all possible sense, and so there is, strictly speaking, nothing "outside" the realm of transcendental subjectivity. Husserl thus thinks that phenomenology ultimately establishes the truth of transcendental idealism. He does not, however, view his idealism as equivalent to the original Kantian variety. For example, Husserl rejects Kant's idea of a thing-in-itself as something beyond the bounds of sense.

attacks. Whereas the naturalist could only see laws of thought as applying to particular kinds of beings and varying as the empirical features of the beings under investigation vary, whatever laws the eidetic reduction yields apply universally and necessarily, regardless of the empirical make-up of the beings whose thought is under consideration.

Phenomenology after Husserl

For reasons that should be evident by this point, Husserl calls his phenomenology "pure" or "transcendental" phenomenology. The qualifier "pure" indicates the role of the phenomenological reduction as the all-important first step in isolating the stream of conscious experience; the purity of that stream is a function of the suspension of any questions regarding the relation between experience and the environing world, including, as we saw, even questions concerning the identity of the subject understood as a flesh-and-blood creature.

The most famous of the practitioners of phenomenology after Husserl (Heidegger, Sartre and Merleau-Ponty) are often collectively referred to as "existential", as opposed to pure or transcendental, phenomenologists. The change in the modifier indicates many more profound changes in their respective conceptions of phenomenology. Despite the many differences among their respective conceptions, the commonality of the qualifier "existential" indicates a shared suspicion concerning the legitimacy of the phenomenological reduction, at least as understood by Husserl. Perhaps, this suspicion runs, something goes wrong when one tries to isolate experience in this manner, to attend to it without at the same time attending to the way in which that experience is situated more broadly; perhaps one needs to consider the question of whose experience it is in the sense of a "concrete" subject of experience, rather than something abstract and anonymous. Heidegger, for example, inveighs against Husserl's attempt at purification, complaining that it misconceives and then overlooks precisely what is most crucial to phenomenology, what Husserl calls the "natural attitude", which the reduction suspends. Heidegger charges that "man's natural manner of experience … cannot be called an attitude" (HCT: 113), indicating that this "natural manner" is not something one freely adopts or suspends. According to Heidegger, "man's natural manner of experience" is not a set of assumptions or presuppositions at all.

In his critique, Sartre focuses on Husserl's conception of the ego or self, challenging the validity of his phenomenological descriptions, wherein the ego or self appears *within* conscious experience. Instead, Sartre aims to demonstrate "that the ego is neither formally nor materially *in* consciousness: it is outside, *in the world*. It is a being of the world, like the ego of another" (TE: 31). And in the Preface to his *Phenomenology of Perception*, Merleau-Ponty, in revisiting Husserl's phenomenology, notes that "the most important lesson which the reduction teaches us is the impossibility of a complete reduction" (PP: xiv). That we exist not as "absolute mind", but instead as worldly, embodied beings, precludes the kind of purification Husserl demands. If it is to be faithful to our experience, phenomenology must attend to its situated and embodied character, in contact with, and acting on, an environing world.

Summary of key points

- The laws and principles of logic cannot be understood as psychological laws, but are "laws of thought" in a non-psychological, ideal sense.
- Consciousness consists of "phenomena", which cannot be understood by analogy with material objects.
- To isolate phenomena, consciousness must be "purified" by bracketing any considerations concerning the sources and success of conscious experience.
- Phenomenological description concerns the noetic and noematic structures, in virtue of which experience is intentional.
- Phenomenology reveals how meanings or senses are constituted in experience.
- Even when I bracket any commitment to my existence as a worldly being, my "pure ego" remains as an essential feature of consciousness.
- The eidetic reduction uses the method of "free variation" in order to sort out essential and non-essential aspects of consciousness.

two

Heidegger and the existential turn

Heidegger: life and works

Martin Heidegger was born 1889 in Messkirch, Germany. Heidegger's early education was with the Jesuit order, during which time he steeped himself in classical studies, especially Greek culture, language and philosophy. In his early years, Heidegger entered the Seminary of the Archdiocese of Freiburg with the intention of joining the priesthood. He briefly became a novice in the Jesuit order, but left after only two weeks for reasons of poor health. In 1907, Heidegger received a copy of Franz Brentano's *On the Manifold Meaning of Being in Aristotle*, a work that steered him in the direction of "the question of being" that would occupy him for the entirety of his philosophical career. However, it was not until after he left the seminary, following a brief period where he studied theology, that Heidegger devoted himself exclusively to philosophy. He received his PhD in 1913 and his *Habilitation* in 1915, at which time he became a lecturer at the University of Freiburg.

At Freiburg, Heidegger met Husserl (by then he had already made an extensive study of Husserl's phenomenology). Heidegger's relationship with Husserl, which included an assistantship from 1919 to 1923, had a profound effect on the shape of his philosophy, inaugurating what some have called his "phenomenological decade". After a short stint as an associate professor at Marburg, Heidegger eventually succeeded Husserl as professor of philosophy at Freiburg when Husserl retired in 1928. Husserl had hand-picked Heidegger as his successor, viewing him as the means by which his phenomenological investigations might be continued in his eventual absence.

Alas for Husserl, the prospects for collaboration and continuation in phenomenology quickly soured. Published in 1927 as part of his effort to merit Husserl's chair at Freiburg and dedicated to "Edmund Husserl in friendship and admiration", Heidegger's masterpiece of phenomenology, *Being and Time*, represented, from Husserl's point of view, a profound misunderstanding of what phenomenology was all about. As Husserl saw it, Heidegger had abandoned entirely phenomenology's aspirations to raise and answer transcendental questions, to become a "rigorous science", and had settled instead for a kind of puffed-up anthropology, contributing another trendy entry into the burgeoning field of "*Lebensphilosophie*" (Life-philosophy). An attempt at collaboration for an Encyclopaedia Brittanica article on phenomenology likewise proved a failure and served to underline the growing philosophical disagreements between the two. By 1929, Heidegger's falling out with Husserl was complete.

In the early 1930s, Heidegger became involved with the Nazi Party. From April 1933 until April 1934 he briefly served as the Rector at Freiburg, during which time he became a member of the Party and used his position to reorganize the university to reflect the newly dominant Nazi ideology. He never resigned his Party membership and continued to retain some allegiance to the Nazi cause. For example, in his 1935 *Introduction to Metaphysics*, he refers, notoriously, to the "inner truth and greatness" of National Socialism (IM: 213). Heidegger was subject to "de-Nazification" after the war and banned from teaching until 1950. He continued to write and lecture throughout his long life, which ended in 1976.

I mentioned above that Heidegger's most explicit engagement with phenomenology lasted roughly a decade, until the end of the 1920s. Scholars of Heidegger generally distinguish between "early" and "late" (or "later") Heidegger, with the division occurring at around this time (what Heidegger himself refers to as "the turning"). The central work of his early period is *Being and Time*, although it does not stand entirely alone. Heidegger published the book-length study *Kant and the Problem of Metaphysics* in 1929, as well as essays and addresses such as "What is Metaphysics?" and "The Essence of Ground"; he also offered numerous lecture courses, including *The History of the Concept of Time*, *The Basic Problems of Phenomenology* and *The Metaphysical Foundations of Logic*, which have been published and translated over the years as part of the production of a standard edition of Heidegger's works, known as the *Gesamtausgabe*. As might be expected, the precise nature of the relation between Heidegger's early and later work is something on which scholars disagree. In some respects, Heidegger came to repudiate the project embarked on in *Being and Time*, seeing his early claim that ontology must begin with an account of human existence as still mired in the subjectivism and anthropocentrism of the Western philosophical tradition. One can also see both his sustained reflections on works of art and his ruminations on the essence of technology as ways of questioning the adequacy of his earlier philosophical views. At the same time, *Being and Time* sets the course for all of Heidegger's later thinking, serving as a kind of touchstone and point of orientation. The "question of being" is one that Heidegger never really abandons, and his later works, although not called by him works of phenomenology, still bear the traces of phenomenological philosophy. In his 1947 "Letter on Humanism", for example, he appeals to "the essential help of phenomenological seeing" in order to think "the truth of being" (BW: 235). Moreover, his later attempts to call to things in their "nearness", his attempts to articulate the "fourfold" in which human beings might strive to dwell, and his efforts to alert us to the levelling effects of our reigning technological understanding of being, among others, can be seen as echoes of his phenomenological concern with "that which shows itself" (BT: §7).

For the remainder of this chapter, we shall attend almost exclusively to *Being and Time*, drawing occasionally on some of the surrounding lecture material. Although I shall not be offering anything like a commentary on the work, my discussion will nonetheless follow roughly the order of Heidegger's presentation in *Being and Time*.

Ontology, phenomenology and understanding

For Heidegger, phenomenology is subservient to what he calls "fundamental ontology", which is centred on the "question of being". That is, Heidegger's guiding question in *Being and Time* is that of what it means for anything to *be*. Heidegger considers this question both the most basic philosophical question and at the same time one that the Western philosophical tradition has had a shameful tendency to neglect: the question of being "provided a stimulus for the researches of Plato and Aristotle, only to subside from then on *as a theme for actual investigation*" (BT: §1). Such neglect has been fostered in part by a tendency to treat the question of being as one whose answer is in some way already settled; being is treated as "the most universal concept", as "indefinable" or even as "self-evident" (see BT: §1). By raising the question anew, Heidegger takes himself to be challenging the entirety of Western philosophy from the ground up (no small undertaking, to say the least).

Heidegger is well aware that the question of being is a peculiar question, liable to induce little beyond an uncomfortable feeling of confusion in those to whom it is addressed (Western philosophy's neglect of the question is no doubt partly responsible for this discomfort). Indeed, on hearing the question, it is not at all clear just where to begin in trying to answer it. However, Heidegger argues that we have far more to go on than this initial sense of bewilderment would suggest. The place to begin is precisely with ourselves, with what Heidegger calls "Dasein", his name for the kind of beings we are. Heidegger uses this idiosyncratic locution, which is composed of "*Da-*", meaning "there", and "*-sein*", meaning "being", in order to exclude as many assumptions and prejudices as possible concerning the kind of beings we ourselves are. Other terms, such as "man", "human being", "*Homo sapiens*" and so on, already carry connotations from years of circulation in philosophy, theology, anthropology, psychology and biology, to name a few, that may prove problematic (here we see a continuation of Husserl's desire to avoid any presuppositions in the practice of phenomenology). Dasein is the place to begin in answering the question of being because it, unlike other kinds of entities, always has an understanding of being: human beings are beings to whom entities are manifest in their way of being. This does not mean that we already have a worked-out conception of what it is to be (if we did, there would be little for Heidegger and *Being and Time* to accomplish), but rather that our understanding is largely implicit and taken for granted, what Heidegger calls "pre-ontological". Since Dasein has an understanding of being, however implicit and non-thematic, Heidegger argues that fundamental ontology must begin with the task of spelling out or articulating this pre-ontological understanding of being. Doing so will provide a first pass at answering the question of being in general, since understanding Dasein, that is, what it is to be the kind of beings we are, involves understanding what we understand, namely being.

The claim that Heidegger wishes to explicate Dasein's pre-ontological understanding of being needs to be carefully understood. Heidegger is not particularly interested in what we happen to believe, or even think, about the notion of being, to the extent that we think or believe anything at all. Heidegger is emphatically not a philosopher of "common sense". The understanding of being is not so much something we think, but instead is manifest in how we act. Our activity, Heidegger thinks, displays a sensitivity to the categorical distinctions with respect to being that our explicit thoughts (again, in so far as we have them on these matters) have not really managed to comprehend.

As an example, consider the following pair of instructions:

(a) Find the toy surprise in the box of cereal.
(b) Find the prime numbers between fifteen and twenty.

Despite the surface similarities, very few, if any of us, will confuse these two instructions. By this, I do not mean only that we are unlikely to run together toy surprises and prime numbers, but something further: very few, if any of us, will so much as treat this pair of instructions as asking us to do the same kind of thing. Looking for prime numbers and looking for toy surprises are very different kinds of activity. An indication of this is the puzzlement that would greet the following instruction:

(c) Find the prime numbers in the box of cereal.

Indeed, it is not immediately clear just *what* is being asked for in (c), and if someone were to issue such an instruction, he or she would owe us an explanation. Perhaps the person wants to know if the number of pieces of cereal is a prime, or whether the total number of pieces can be divided into prime numbered groups; perhaps the person is merely joking around. The instruction need not be considered nonsensical, but what sense it has does not register with the immediacy of the first two instructions.

Leaving aside (c), consider how we might respond to each of the first two instructions. In response to (a), we might rummage around in the cereal box, dump out the contents and sift through them and so on. The searching is directed towards something concretely located in space and time. In response to (b), we might avail ourselves of paper and pencil, but the numbers we are looking for are not to be found there, on the paper. Indeed, trying to specify the "location" of the numbers is bound to lead to just the kind of philosophical discomfort that makes evident the gap between pre-ontological and ontological understanding. We may become entangled in interminable disputes as to what prime numbers are, where they are and how their "way of being" differs from things like toy surprises (this history of Western philosophy is littered with such debates), but the fact that we do not confuse such things in practice shows that we have a competence with respect to such things that outstrips our theorizing. This competence is precisely what Heidegger wants to investigate and explicate in order to begin to answer the question of being.

I said before that for Heidegger phenomenology is subservient to the project of fundamental ontology. At the same time, Heidegger claims that "*only as phenomenology, is ontology possible*" (BT: §7). We can begin to see why Heidegger thinks this is so by considering further his strategy for answering the question of being, namely explicating Dasein's understanding of being. Again, that Dasein has an understanding of being means that entities are manifest to it, that various kinds of beings show themselves in their various ways of being, and for Heidegger, the task of phenomenology is to "let that which shows itself be seen from itself in the very way in which it shows itself from itself" (BT: §7). As we saw already with Husserl, phenomenology is precisely concerned with these notions of manifestation and showing: phenomenology strives to render explicit the structures of manifestation, on the basis of which entities are manifest. For Heidegger, these "structures" are nothing other than the being of beings: "that which determines entities as entities, that on the basis of which entities are already understood" (BT: §2). Notice in this last formulation the seamless transition from the determination of entities to the notion of understanding. Our pre-ontological understanding of being, as an ongoing engagement with, and responsiveness to, the entities we encounter, cannot be detached or understood in isolation from those very entities. Our understanding of being is always "situated", and phenomenology cannot, on pain of distortion and falsification, fail to attend to the ways in which our understanding is located in a broader context (again, our understanding of being is not so much something we think or "have in mind", but our ways of dealing with entities in our ongoing activity). Thus, despite their shared concern with the notions of showing and manifestation, Heidegger does not simply take over or continue Husserl's phenomenological investigations. On the contrary, Heidegger's conception of phenomenology differs considerably from Husserl's, both in terms of methods and outcomes. If phenomenology's task is to explicate the structure of Dasein's pre-ontological understanding, then it must focus on Dasein's activity, which means in turn that phenomenology cannot proceed by bracketing or excluding entities. In other words, Heidegger emphatically rejects the phenomenological reduction as the appropriate starting-point for phenomenology.

Understanding and world

We have seen thus far that Heidegger's phenomenology is directed at what he calls Dasein's pre-ontological understanding of being and that pre-ontological understanding is not so much contained in consciousness as it is manifest in Dasein's (our) everyday activity. Hence, Heidegger's phenomenology, at least in its preliminary stages, is a "phenomenology of everydayness". A phenomenology of everydayness is squarely opposed to Husserl's pure phenomenology. Any attempt to isolate conscious experience will, Heidegger thinks, distort or elide the phenomena that are most fundamental, that is, those phenomena within which the world and our own existence are manifest. Rather than isolating conscious experience, Heideggerian phenomenology seeks to interpret our everyday activity ("the meaning of phenomenological description as a method lies in *interpretation*" (BT: §7)), so as to make manifest the largely implicit structures of intelligibility that inform that activity.

What does a phenomenology of everydayness reveal or make explicit? This question may best be answered by considering at length a single example. Working through the example will also bring into view some further Heideggerian concepts, along with some of his notoriously idiosyncratic terminology.

Allow me to describe an activity in which I frequently engage: working in my study. My study is a familiar space to me, and its familiarity is manifest in the way I enter and move around the room. I walk through the doorway without needing to make any special adjustments or pay special attention to the location of various items in my study. The lectern holding my dictionary is immediately to my right as I enter, the bookcases to the left. I walk past these items without usually needing to make any conscious effort to avoid them. At the same time, these various things are present to me, on hand for my use. On occasion, I will stop to turn the page of the dictionary to prevent fading or I will look up a word on my way to the desk; I may also stop to get a book off the shelf, if it is something I think I shall need during the stretch of writing I am planning to do. The bookcases and the lectern thus present themselves as there to be used for my various projects. Other entities in the study manifest themselves in similar fashion: desk, computer, chair, floor, lights, pens, pencils, paper and so on. I encounter all of these things not as discrete bits of matter or as "physical objects", but as "things of use" or equipment: what Heidegger calls the "ready-to-hand". That is, I identify these various things with reference to the ways in which they are caught up in my ongoing activity. I encounter my computer, variously, as something to write with, check my email on, or surf the Internet. I occasionally reach out for my coffee cup or for a book while writing, or I may simply stop to look around the room, resting my arms on the arms of my chair, my feet flat on the floor.

My activity in my study manifests what we might call "practical orientation". When I enter my study I more or less automatically orient myself to what the room contains, making use of and ignoring various things as my needs and interests dictate. I enter and move around the room with a readiness that is inflected by my various purposes, such as working on this book, finding an article I need to read, checking my email, getting a camera before heading outside and so on. I do not, for the most part, need to give much thought to the details of my activity, especially those basic activities such as walking, sitting, standing and reaching. When I spot the book I want on the shelf, my arm goes out to it without my needing first to gauge the distance or take further note of the exact location. When I sit down to type, my body adjusts to the contours of the chair and my fingers settle on the "home keys" without my needing to look. The general fluency of my activity indicates that my orientation embodies an understanding of the room and what it contains. My activity displays a general competence with respect to things such as computer keyboards, coffee cups, books, desks, chairs, floors and so on.

Attending to what I am here calling "practical orientation" gives Heidegger leverage in arguing against the claims of the Western philosophical tradition. Central to that tradition is a preoccupation with the notion of substance, with the fundamental building blocks of reality in terms of which everything else there is (or appears to be) can be explained. Descartes defined substance, famously, as "a thing which so exists that it needs no other thing in order to exist" (*Principles of Philosophy*, in Haldane & Ross 1984: 239). Without trying to cash out this definition (indeed, there are many ways of cashing it out, especially when it comes to the phrase "needs no other thing"), we can see that the basic idea is that substances enjoy a certain kind of independence or autonomy: a substance is the kind of thing that can exist in isolation, apart from anything else there might be. If something is a substance, then it is at least conceivable that such a thing exists as the only thing in reality: that there is a "possible world", as some philosophers are fond of saying, containing that one thing and nothing else.

Whether or not the notion of substance explored within the Western philosophical tradition is intelligible (and Heidegger is not the first philosopher to have his suspicions – witness Hume, for example), Heidegger's phenomenology of everydayness charges that substances are emphatically not what show themselves in our everyday, practical orientation. That is, we do not encounter things whose defining features can be sustained in isolation; rather, the ready-to-hand equipment we encounter is what it is only by standing in myriad "referential" relations to one another, as well as our various activities, projects and purposes. A hammer, for example, is something *with which to* hammer in nails *in order to* hold pieces of wood together *towards* the building of something *for the sake of* Dasein's self-understanding as (say) a carpenter. (All of the italicized terms are what Heidegger means by "referential relations": those relations in which items of equipment must stand in order to *be* the equipment that it is.) What we encounter in our everyday activity are not things that can be what they are regardless of the surrounding contexture. Although we might try to picture a "possible world" containing nothing but a hammer (a hammer floating in space springs to mind most readily), its being a hammer depends on things well beyond the confines of such a world: nails, timber, the activities of hammering and building, and projects such as building houses and furniture. Heidegger says in *Being and Time* that "taken strictly, there 'is' no such thing as *an* equipment" (BT: §15). Any particular item or kind of equipment is what it is only in so far as it belongs to a "totality" of equipment, which in turn is informed by our activity.

Given the relational nature of equipment, the ontology of free-standing substances with their own intrinsic properties is a far remove from the phenomenology of everydayness. If we carefully and honestly describe our everyday activity and what shows itself in that activity, substances as understood by the philosophical tradition will generally not appear as part of that description. Heidegger's argument against a substance-and-property ontology is not restricted, however, to this point about descriptive adequacy. His deeper point concerns the adequacy of a substance-and-property ontology, not just with respect to the phenomenological contours of our everyday activity and experience, but also with respect to its ability to explain those contours. That is, Heidegger argues in *Being and Time* that if one starts with a substance-and-property ontology, one will not be able to reach or recover the ontology revealed in everydayness; instead, he argues that an ontology of substances and properties (what he calls an ontology of the "present-at-hand") is an impoverished understanding of what there is, relative to the ontology of the ready-to-hand. We can understand the ontology of the present-at-hand by "dimming down" the ontology of the ready-to-hand, that is, by considering things stripped of their referential relations (Heidegger calls this way of considering things "decontextualization"), but not vice versa, at least not without distortion and falsification.

If we return to the referential relations in which items of equipment stand, it will be noticed that the terminus of these relations is always some particular self-understanding, related to all the other items and relations by "for the sake of". Such self-understandings are numerous and diverse, and what shows itself, and how, in everydayness will vary accordingly. Given my self-understanding as a professor of philosophy, my computer shows itself as something with which to write a draft of my book; given my self-understanding as a serious amateur photographer, my computer shows up as something with which to shop for equipment (on eBay, the classifieds of various photography websites, and so on) or as a tool for archiving and tinkering with my photographs; given my self-understanding as a father, the computer shows up as something with which to find websites on dinosaurs, visit Elmo and Cookie Monster or shop for a tricycle. These self-understandings do not flick on and off like light switches, but interpenetrate and interact, thereby conditioning what shows up. When engaged in the activity of writing, my computer's usefulness for things photographic shows up as a distraction; when shopping for a new lens, the computer's usefulness for such purposes will, given my ongoing project of writing a book, appear as something of a guilty pleasure; when my son Henry is around, the computer's capacities for transporting us to *Sesame Street* typically trump all others.

That the referential, significative relations constitutive of equipment ultimately trace back to, and are informed by, for-the-sake-of relations, or self-understandings, is apt to give rise to the following worry: is what shows itself in everyday activity inherently *subjective*, bound up as it seems to be with *my* purposes, interests, projects, and desires? This worry can be allayed by a number of observations. To begin with, even if we confine our attention to my own everyday experience of my own study, there are aspects of what shows up in that experience that cut against its being inherently or exhaustively subjective. If we consider all of those referential relations constituting the ready-to-hand, it will be noticed that there is a normative dimension to these relations: a pen is something for writing, a computer for typing or writing, a book for reading and so on. The "for" in all of these cases indicates a proper or standard use or purpose. Even if it is true that I can use a book to prop open the door or bonk an unwanted visitor on the head, use a pen to jab someone, or use my computer screen as a mirror to fix my hair, these uses are deviant ones, and strike us as such when they are put to these uses (being so struck may register, variously, as humour, shock or admiration at someone's ingenuity).

If we reflect further on the normative dimension of these referential relations, we may also come to appreciate the anonymous character of these normative relations. What I mean here is that the particular ways in which I (or anyone else, for that matter) encounter my everyday surroundings as normatively structured is not something that is up to me or that I decide. I do not imbue books with the significance of being for reading, pens for writing, and so on, but find them as having already been endowed with those meanings, but not by anyone in particular. Heidegger refers to this anonymous dimension of everyday existence as "*das Man*", sometimes translated as "the they", but more aptly rendered as "the one" or "the anyone" ("*Man*" in German just means "one", as in "*Man sagt auf Deutsch* ..." or "One says in German ..."). Heidegger says in *Being and Time* that *das Man* "articulates the referential totality of significance" (BT: §27), which means that everydayness is first and foremost structured by anonymous norms.

Heidegger's guiding claim throughout his phenomenological explication of Dasein in its everydayness is that Dasein's (our) way of being is "being-in-the-world", and these latest remarks concerning the anonymously articulated normative structure of our everyday experience indicate that the world I or we encounter is a *public* world, rather than something inherently private or subjective. While there is ample room in Heidegger's account for idiosyncratic appropriation and deviant uses, not to mention invention and innovation, all of these possibilities are themselves intelligible only against a background of taken-for-granted normative assignments (if nothing were for anything or had a proper use, then nothing would show up *as* deviant, idiosyncratic or innovative). In labelling our way of being "being-in-the-world", Heidegger is again emphasizing his departure from Husserlian phenomenology: the worldly character of our everyday existence tells against the performance of the reduction as an adequate method for delineating the structure of everyday experience. At the same time, we need to be careful not to understand Heidegger's terminology in an overly crude manner. The "in" in "being-in-the-world" does not, for example, mean simply spatial containment, in the way that water is in a glass. Rather, the "in" is meant to connote familiarity or involvement, along the lines of being in business or in the army. Moreover, we need to attend to the hyphenations in the label, which signal that being-in-the-world is what Heidegger calls a "unitary phenomenon". What this means is that the phenomenon of being-in-the-world cannot be understood piecemeal, as the combination of antecedently intelligible components.

There is another dimension to the public character of the world we encounter in everyday experience beyond the cataloguing of anonymous normative relations. Further attention to the character of everyday experience reveals both the direct and indirect presence of *others*. Even when I am working alone in my study, I am not ensconced in a kind of Cartesian solitude. On the contrary, the presence of others is intimated in numerous ways: I am surrounded by books written by others (and capable of being read by others); the significance of my activity of writing a book is bound up with the idea of an audience for the work; more personally, toys strewn in the corner indicate recent activities of my sons, Henry and Lowell, who like playing in my study; and when I check my email, I find myself addressed by colleagues, family and friends and likewise addressing them. Of course, I am not always alone, and so my experience takes in others more directly; in my daily activities, I encounter my wife, sons, neighbours, friends, students and colleagues, as well as cashiers, clerks, attendants, drivers, pedestrians and so on. All of these others show up in various ways, as friendly, aggressive, helpful, courteous, loving, affectionate, aloof and indifferent, among many others. One of Heidegger's principal claims is that others show themselves in everyday experience in a way that is radically different from the ways in which equipment is manifest. Perhaps confusingly, he labels our relation to equipment and the projects in which that equipment is bound up one of "concern" (although it must be remembered that indifference and inattention are among its possible modes), and our relation to others one of "solicitude" (where, again, this includes doing such things as ignoring

Husserl and the life-world

In his last published work, *The Crisis of European Sciences and Transcendental Phenomenology*, Husserl devotes considerable attention to the problem of the "life-world", his term for what "is pregiven to us all quite naturally, as persons within the horizon of our fellow men, i.e., in every actual connection with others, as 'the' world common to us all" (CES: §33). The life-world is "the constant ground of validity, an ever available source of what is taken for granted, to which we, whether as practical men or as scientists, lay claim as a matter of course" (*ibid.*). By "source" and "ground" Husserl means that the life-world serves as the basis for the possibility of the natural, "objective" sciences. All theorizing, as the activity of scientists, takes for granted this pre-theoretical, pre-scientific familiar world: "objective science has a constant reference of meaning to the world in which we always live" (CES: §34). The natural sciences can therefore neither discharge this presupposed life-world, nor make it the proper object of scientific investigation. Instead, Husserl thinks that a new kind of scientific investigation is called for, the "rigorous science" of phenomenology. The life-world is fully amenable to phenomenological investigation, via the technique of *epochē*, in this case applied doubly. The phenomenological investigator first performs the reduction with respect to the natural sciences, an abstaining from "all participation in the cognitions of the objective sciences" (CES: §35). Performing this first reduction more clearly delineates the pre-theoretical, pre-scientific dimensions of experience, which can themselves be subjected to a "total" or "transcendental" *epochē*, where the investigator "simply forbids himself – as a philosopher, in the uniqueness of his direction of interest – to continue the whole natural performance of his world-life" (CES: §41). The "correlation between world and world-consciousness" (ibid.) ensures the efficacy of this more complete reduction. Although the *general* shape of Husserl's interest in the life-world suggests a greater proximity to Heidegger's phenomenology, Husserl's appeals to the life-world as amenable to the performance of the reduction, as something correlated with "world-consciousness", as something "taken for granted" or "presupposed", make clear the continued divergence between their respective conceptions of phenomenology. Indeed, Heidegger's objections to Husserl's characterizations of the life-world precede those characterizations by several years: in *Being and Time*, Heidegger already criticizes "the doctrine that the subject must presuppose and indeed always does unconsciously presuppose the presence-at-hand of the 'external world'" (BT: §43). "With such presuppositions, Dasein always comes 'too late'", such that "the primordial phenomenon of being-in-the-world has been shattered" (*ibid.*).

someone or being patently unkind). The distinction between concern and solicitude is fundamental, according to Heidegger, and pervades the entirety of what shows itself in our everyday activity. A threatening glance is markedly different from a threatening precipice, and although I can ignore both my friend and my garden, I am not doing the same thing in both instances (try, for example, to insult or anger your garden by ignoring it!).

Just as our concernful understanding of the ready-to-hand is not something we piece together or derive from some more basic kind of experience (of material substance, for example), so too does Heidegger consider solicitude to be a fundamental aspect of our everyday being-in-the-world. That the others I both directly and indirectly experience in my everyday routines have the same way of being as I, that is, that we are all Dasein, is not something that I need to establish by inference or comparison. Heidegger thus has little patience for accounts of our relations to one another that appeal to "empathy" or "projection" as the means by which relations to others are established. He is equally impatient with the standard sceptical problem of "other minds", for which empathy and projection might be offered as solutions. The question of how I come to know or establish the presence of others is a bogus one. If one carefully explicates the way of being of the "I" mentioned in the question, an understanding of others will be revealed as more original than any question that might be asked about their presence or absence. Heidegger thus does not take himself to be offering a solution to the sceptical problem of other minds as much as dissolving the whole problematic: there is, ultimately, no intelligible sceptical question that stands in need of an answer.

Understanding and mattering

Heidegger's appeals to concern and solicitude as fundamental to our being-in-the-world indicate the overall structure of Dasein's way of being, which Heidegger labels "care" or the "care-structure". Care summarizes the idea that things show up as mattering to us in various ways, even when we find ourselves to be indifferent towards them. (It is misleading, according to Heidegger, to say that my desk, for example, is indifferent towards the coffee cup resting on it. Strictly speaking, my desk can be neither concerned nor indifferent, both of these being manifestations of an underlying care-structure that is absent from a desk's way of being.) Indeed, the ideas of things showing up or being manifest and their mattering are not two independent notions for Heidegger. When I attend to the way my study is manifest in my everyday routines, my projects and purposes are integral to the character of that manifestation: my desk shows up *as* the place where I write, check my email, surf the web, and so on; my bookcases show up *as* what hold my books, which in turn show up *as* to be read; my chair in the corner shows up *as* the place where I read; and so on. If I were to try to strip away these various significations, all of these ways in which the world I experience bears the stamp of my projects, purposes and interests, then it is not clear that anything would show up at all. It is tempting to say that I would encounter a bare array of objects, devoid of purpose or significance, but even delineating an array of objects, individuated and separated from one another, bespeaks some practical significance, however minimal, as, say, potential obstacles.

Heidegger summarizes the care-structure with the following formula: "The being of Dasein means ahead-of-itself-already-in (the-world) as being-alongside (entities encountered within-the-world)" (BT: §41). Unpacking this formula will take us further into Heidegger's analysis of Dasein's way of being, affording us a deeper insight into the connection between things being manifest and their mattering. In the process, we shall also get a glimpse (but only a glimpse) into the reasoning behind Heidegger's claim that being, both Dasein's and that of other entities as well, is ultimately to be understood in terms of time.

Heidegger's formula contains three moments or aspects, which can be described and analysed in relative independence, even if the three are ultimately inseparable from one another. The three aspects are:

1. ahead-of-itself;
2. already-in (the-world); and
3. being-alongside (entities encountered within-the-world).

The order in which Heidegger arranges these aspects, such that "ahead-of-itself" precedes "already-in", may initially seem rather odd, but the order is important as it serves to underline Dasein's distinctive way of being.

The first aspect, "ahead-of-itself", corresponds to what Heidegger labels "understanding" or "projection" (here, "understanding" is being used in a more specific, technical sense than it has been in our discussion until this point). Dasein is always ahead of itself in so far as it is always projecting itself in terms of some for-the-sake-of or other. Consider one such for-the-sake-of: my being a professor. Being a professor is not merely some standing fact or static property of me, the way my weight or hair colour might be, nor is being a professor some goal out there in the future that I might someday reach, so as then to make it a standing fact or static property. Being a professor is neither of these, but rather is something in terms of which I organize my activities (at least some of them) and direct those activities. To use Heidegger's terminology, being a professor, as a for-the-sake-of, is a "possibility", and to say that I am a professor is to say that I am always projecting myself onto, or in terms of, that possibility. Many of the things I do – preparing lectures, marking papers, meeting with students, conducting research, attending conferences – are subservient to my self-understanding as a professor, and if I were to stop doing all of these things, that is, stop projecting myself in terms of that self-understanding, I would no longer be a professor: being a professor would no longer be one of my possibilities. Notice that there is no one property or quality that singles me out as a professor, but a whole constellation of activities, projects and goals. Being a professor is not a property that I have, but a possibility in terms of which I understand myself and others understand me as well.

That I understand myself in terms of possibilities, rather than a set of actualities, expresses the idea that my being, as Heidegger puts it, "is an issue for me". What I am is at no point something fixed, settled or determined, but something I must continually project myself into or in terms of; as Heidegger puts it, Dasein "*is* existentially that which, in its potentiality-for-being, it is *not yet*" (BT: §31). Were it not the case that my existence involved a "not yet", then my existence would not in any way be an issue for me; I would confront my existence as something static and determined, if I could confront it at all. Heidegger is careful to distinguish possibility in the sense we have been considering from possibility in the sense of (mere) logical possibility, which means not yet actual, and neither necessary nor impossible. When I note that it might rain later today, I am simply noting something that is not currently happening but might happen in the near future; when that later time comes, that possibility will either be realized or not. At that point, it will be true either that it is raining or that it is not. Dasein's possibilities do not work that way. Dasein *is* its possibilities, not in the sense that they are already actualized, but because its way of being essentially involves this notion of projection.

The second aspect, "already-in (the world)", corresponds to what Heidegger calls "*Befindlichkeit*", translated rather poorly in the Macquarrie and Robinson edition as "state-of-mind". The term has no ready translation. It is constructed along the lines of the ordinary German question "*Wie befinden Sie sich?*", which means, clunkily, "How do you find yourself?" or, more smoothly, "How are you doing?" or "How's it going?". What *Befindlichkeit* names is our always finding ourselves in a situation (in a world), with a particular orientation to that situation, constituted by such things as mood, disposition, inclination, beliefs, past experience and so on. Indeed, mood, for Heidegger, is the principal manifestation of *Befindlichkeit*. We typically find ourselves *in* moods, that is, we do not choose them from some neutral, moodless standpoint or position. *Befindlichkeit* and mood are bound up with what Heidegger calls "thrownness", which underlines the idea that our being-in-the-world and many of its particular features in each case are not a matter of choice or decision. Put colloquially, we do not choose to be born, nor to be born into the particular circumstances in which we grow up. For each of us, our past – our upbringing, past experiences, dispositions, inclinations – conditions the way in which we confront any particular situation, and so conditions the ways in which situations are manifest to us. At the same time, our past is not something static and fixed in its givenness, but is itself dynamically affected by how we project ourselves onto our possibilities. The significance of what I have done or experienced in the past (or am currently doing and experiencing, for that matter) is greatly affected by what I go on to do. Something that I currently consider a misfortune, for example, or a terrible mistake, may later take on the significance of happy accident or prescient decision on my part. *Befindlichkeit* thus names the historical nature of Dasein. Each of us has a history, not just as an accumulation of facts concerning past events and experiences, but as something that pervades and conditions our self-understandings, which in turn pervade and condition that history.

The third, and final, aspect, "being-alongside (entities encountered within-the-world)", corresponds to what Heidegger calls "falling". "Falling" names my current absorption in whatever it is that I am doing. Dasein is always falling in so far as it is always caught up in some kind of ongoing activity, even when it is just idly musing or "killing time". Falling is conditioned by understanding and *Befindlichkeit*: my current activity is informed by the self-understanding in terms of which I am projecting myself, as well as by the mood and dispositions I bring, so to speak, to that current activity. When I sit down to write, for example, I do so in terms of my self-understanding as a philosophy professor, and I bring to the activity of writing the mood I find myself in. On any given day, I may confront the activity of writing with, variously, an eagerness to press on, dread at the prospect of having to work out sentence by sentence what *Befindlichkeit* means, reluctance because of a desire to be doing something else and so on.

Having sketched each of these three aspects, we can now return briefly to the issue of their being ordered as they are. The peculiarity of the ordering becomes apparent when we notice that each of the three aspects carries a temporal connotation: understanding, understood as projection, invokes the idea of futurity; *Befindlichkeit* refers to the past; and falling, as marking my current absorption, is bound up with the present. Thus, Heidegger's formula is ordered as future–past–present, which, from the standpoint of our ordinary understanding of time, might strike us as something of a jumble. After all, does the past not precede the present, which in turn precedes the future? Jumbled as it may appear from the perspective of our ordinary conception of time, Heidegger orders the aspects of the care-structure as he does so as to register the inadequacy of that conception for understanding Dasein's way of being. After all, the ordinary conception of time is hardly innocent, but owes some allegiance to the traditional kinds of ontology Heidegger attacks throughout *Being and Time* (the idea of substance, with its emphasis on actuality, involves a clear privileging of the present). Dasein, whose way of being is care, is not a substance in this traditional sense, and so is not something that can be properly understood in terms of actuality. As possibility, in Heidegger's special sense, Dasein is essentially futural. What I am is a function, so to speak, of what I am doing, and what I am doing is itself a function of some range of possibilities onto which I am projecting myself. Again, to take the example of being a professor, that is something that I am always "on the way" to being, something that I am perpetually becoming, in so far as I continue to understand myself that way. There is no point at which I can regard my being a professor as completed, since I am one only to the extent that I continue to engage in the kind of activities characteristic of, or required by, being a professor. My futurity thus conditions both my past (my understanding of where I have been) and my present, and so neither my past nor my present can be properly understood apart from my futurity.

Mattering, dying, authenticity

Being and Time is composed of two parts or divisions: Division One and Division Two. Thus far, we have devoted our attention almost exclusively to the first of these two divisions, wherein Heidegger concerns himself with explicating the structure of Dasein in its "everydayness". The analysis Heidegger provides in Division One is crucial, but it is also in important respects incomplete. Division Two extends the analysis of Division One in two ways: first, Division Two offers an account of Dasein's "authenticity", as opposed to its "undifferentiated" and "inauthentic" modes; secondly, Division Two begins the project of mapping being onto time or temporality. In this latter endeavour,

Being and Time is undeniably incomplete (Heidegger envisaged a third division, the three resulting divisions making up but Part One of a two-part work; Part Two was itself to consist of a further three divisions). We shall not consider this unfinished project here, but instead confine ourselves to some of the broader features of the first task of Division Two (although even this will allow for some further aspects of temporality to emerge).

Taken as a whole, Division One, and so Heidegger's account of Dasein in its everydayness, contains a rather puzzling tension. On the one hand, the structures revealed and analysed in Division One – the world as a "referential totality", *das Man* and the structural moments of the care-structure (understanding, *Befindlichkeit*, and falling) – are absolutely essential to the idea that Dasein is a being whose being is an issue for it. Minus those structures, Dasein would be reduced to a mere thing that does not in any way confront its own existence. On the other hand, Heidegger also claims that Dasein's absorption in its everyday existence tends to occlude the very idea that Dasein's being *is* an issue for it. This is especially evident in his account of *das Man*: the kind of anonymous normative authority that pervades everyday life. Everyday Dasein, according to Heidegger, is in thrall to this anonymous authority, acquiescing to it almost reflexively and so falling into line with all the others. Such conformity extends beyond such benign instances as gripping a hammer or tying one's shoes to the very core of one's sensibilities: everyday Dasein, Heidegger says, is a *Man*-self, an anyone, and so in a deep sense a nobody as well. Driven by an inordinate concern with how it "measures up" in relation to others (a phenomenon that Heidegger calls "distantiality"), Dasein tends in everydayness towards a kind of "averageness". Everything is held in common and commonly understood simply because everything has been "levelled down" to this average understanding. Although even in everydayness we are all *individuated* in a numerical sense, our immersion in, and identification with, this anonymous normative structure means that we lack any genuine sense of *individuality*. We have, in everydayness, surrendered our existence to the tyranny of *das Man*, allowing it to determine and evaluate the shape of our lives. By "toeing the line" and "going with the flow", we fail to give proper heed to our own capacities for self-determination.

We need to be clear here that the tension is not a contradiction, and we might see this by considering the particular case of speaking a language as illustrative of just these two dimensions. Speaking a language requires, among other things, a rather high degree of conformity of usage. The sounds that you make must be predictably similar to the sounds that I make, and these sounds must in turn be predictably related to the world we both find ourselves in, for you and I to be uttering words that we mutually recognize and understand. If sounds flowed from us haphazardly, with no rhyme or reason, it would not be the case that we all spoke different languages; on the contrary, we would, each of us, fail to speak at all. Similar considerations apply to writing as well. Writing must conform to regular patterns in order to be recognizable as writing, and so in order to be writing. Were I to continue this sentence with soxigldihsncidd%&%#kchigoet, the meaning of what I wrote would not be unclear; it would instead be clear that I had not written anything, at least not anything with a meaning. The vocabulary and grammatical rules of a language, although by no means fixed in stone, are sustained by our collective conformity. Even the most eccentric forms of self-expression and the furthest reaches of poetic creativity are intelligible only on the basis of this general agreement; even the poet for the most part uses recognizable words, rather than random noises or clusters of letter-shaped marks.

For there to be such a thing as language that we share among us we must all to a large extent speak and write in the same way. At the same time, when that conformity extends to what we say, as opposed simply to how we say it, then the darker side of collective normativity begins to emerge. Although words may flow from our individual mouths, when we only say what anyone says, or what anyone ought to say, then we in a deeper sense fail to speak for ourselves; our words do not in these instances belong to us. Heidegger labels this phenomenon "idle talk", by which he means the state where assertions and opinions are able to circulate without being owned, or owned up to, by the ones who utter them. Idle talk need not be sinister, since it is important to the proper functioning of language that utterances be repeatable without everyone possessing the proper authority to say them. If I, rummaging in the basement, tell my son Henry that we are nearly out of suet cakes for the birds, it is good and useful that he be able to tell his mother that very thing as she heads out to the supermarket, even though Henry did not himself ascertain that we were low on suet cakes and is only taking my word for it. It is less good and useful, however, when we repeat utterances simply on the basis of a kind of public pressure to do so, when our utterances are shaped by what we perceive, however unconsciously, to be received opinion. In these instances, our speech is reduced to a recitation of quotations, unconnected with the particulars of the situation, and so is pervaded by a kind of thoughtlessness and inattentiveness.

These observations about language make it clear that in trying to understand Heidegger's distinction between inauthenticity and authenticity, we need to be careful to avoid understanding the latter as the achievement of some kind of radical isolation or eccentricity, akin to the condition of a hermit who shuns society altogether. When we manage to speak for ourselves, to give voice to the particularities of our individual experience rather than parrot platitudes and received opinion, we do not speak a different language. Speaking for myself does not require that I give up English in exchange for a currently (for me) foreign tongue, nor that I deliberately and pervasively distort and violate the rules of English grammar. Heidegger notes late in *Being and Time* that with the achievement of authenticity, "the 'world' which is ready-to-hand does not become another one 'in its content,' nor does the circle of others get exchanged for a new one" (BT: §60). Whatever kind of "modification" authenticity is, it is not a wholesale repudiation of one's present social condition, nor just a matter of being "weird" or "unconventional".

Absorbed in familiar routines, a creature of habit, everyday Dasein is lost, "dispersed", as Heidegger puts it, into the world and into *das Man*. As lost, Dasein is "inauthentic", a translation of "*uneigentlich*", which more literally means "unowned". Dasein, as inauthentic, fails to own itself, and so fails to face up to its own existence as an issue for it. In so far as it considers them at all, everyday Dasein takes the patterns and routines in which it is immersed as given and final, as exhaustive of its existence. To make the transition to authenticity, to the state or condition of being "self-owned", something must occur that disrupts the patterns and routines that have everyday Dasein in their grip. Heidegger calls the moment of disruption "anxiety" (*Angst*), and, fittingly, the last chapter of Division One of *Being and Time* contains a lengthy phenomenological explication of this pivotal notion.

Anxiety is qualitatively akin to fear (indeed, in German *Angst* can just mean "fear"), although it differs from fear in the following, crucial respect: fear always has an object (when I am afraid, I am afraid of something, someone, some event or eventuality), but anxiety lacks one. The experience of anxiety is in part unsettling precisely because of the absence of any specifiable object to which the experience can be traced. More dramatically, in anxiety the world and all that it contains fall away as irrelevant, as no longer making a claim on one's attention or concern. This is not a matter of "blacking out", so that in anxiety one simply ceases to see one's surroundings, but more a matter of detachment and disaffection; the world and what it has to offer registers as entirely without import or appeal. Heidegger says in *Being and Time*,

"That in the face of which one has anxiety is being-in-the-world as such" (BT: §40), which registers the idea that in anxiety Dasein confronts the fact of its own particular existence, as well as the particular manner of existence, precisely as being-in-the-world and as possibility: "Anxiety individualizes Dasein for its ownmost being-in-the-world, which as something that understands, projects itself essentially upon possibilities" (*ibid.*). By lifting Dasein out of its absorption in its usual patterns and routines, anxiety makes manifest Dasein's own complicity in that absorption, as a being that, however unwittingly, projects itself onto possibilities. Anxiety thus serves as a kind of "wake-up call" to Dasein to confront its own existence, to acknowledge its inherent capacity to choose, and so take responsibility for, the shape of its own existence.

For Heidegger, the experience of anxiety is fundamentally threatening. This is due partly to the experience of separation from one's everyday concerns; as the world "falls away", leaving Dasein with only a sense of its own existence, the experience of anxiety becomes ever more unsettling. But there is a further dimension to the sense of threat or violence, since what anxiety ultimately makes manifest to me about my own existence is its finitude. That is, in anxiety, I am brought face to face with my own *death*. This last formulation is incautious, but seeing why this is so will take some doing. To start, consider (and try saying to yourself) the statement, "I am dead". There is something peculiar about the statement when one tries to utter it or think it to oneself, in the sense that neither of these can be done truthfully (apart, of course, from more slangy or metaphorical uses of the "Dude, I am so dead" variety). "I am dead" is something like the inverse of Descartes's famous dictum that "I am, I exist" is necessarily true whenever uttered or entertained in thought. As one can always, no matter what, affirm the bare fact of one's existence, at the same time one can never succeed in negating it: "I am dead" and "I do not exist" are necessarily false whenever uttered or entertained in thought. (Just try it.) What these observations indicate is that death marks a kind of limit on our experience: that we cannot truthfully entertain the statement "I am dead" shows that the state of being dead is beyond the reach of our experience.

Heidegger says that "death is the possibility of the absolute impossibility of Dasein" (BT: §50). His appeal to "absolute impossibility" tallies with the observations above that death does not mark out a way for Dasein to be, but instead imposes a limit on its being. At the same time, Heidegger refers to death as a "possibility", which would suggest that death is a way to be after all (recall our examination above of the sense in which Dasein is its possibilities). How can we make sense of this ostensibly impossible formulation? To answer this question, consider first the following remark from Heidegger's discussion of death in *Being and Time*: "In accordance with its essence, this possibility [death] offers no support for becoming intent on something, 'picturing' to oneself the actuality which is possible, and so forgetting its possibility" (BT: §53). What this remark indicates is that in our thinking about death we conceive of it as a kind of distant actuality: something that will occur some time in the future. In other words, we tend to think of death as a possibility in the sense in which it is possible that it will rain tomorrow, but since, unlike the case of tomorrow's possible rain, we find nothing to picture or imagine (again, "I am dead" contains nothing genuinely thinkable), we lapse into a kind of forgetfulness about death. As only a distant actuality, death has nothing to do with my existence now.

We have seen already that the sense of "possibility" in play when Heidegger talks of Dasein's being its possibilities does not follow the standard logic of possibility and actuality, that is, Dasein's possibilities are not merely states or events that are not-yet-actual. Dasein *is* its possibilities, which is to say that Dasein is projecting itself onto, and in accordance with, particular understandings of what it is to be. But what does it mean to speak of death as a possibility in this sense? How can death be a way to be? And what is gained with respect to authenticity by thinking of death in these terms? To say that death is a possibility in Heidegger's sense is to say that death is a kind of self-understanding in terms of which Dasein can project itself. But what kind of self-understanding is it? After all, Heidegger is not recommending suicide as the key to authenticity; nor is he saying that Dasein becomes authentic when it *is* dead. Instead of death, which leads us to think of a not-yet-actual event in the future, Heidegger sometimes writes of "being-toward-death" as the name for the possibility in terms of which Dasein may, or may fail to, project itself. Being-toward-death is not entirely divorced from death understood as a not-yet-actual event (what Heidegger calls "demise"), but involves a more enlightened acknowledgment and understanding of it. When we think of death only as something not-yet-actual, an eventuality in the indefinite future, we hold death at arm's length, treating it as something that does not bear on us now. Being-toward-death brings death closer, not by hastening my demise, nor by exciting a longing for it or any such thing, but by impressing on us our condition of *always* being *mortal*.

Heidegger says that death, understood as being-toward-death, is Dasein's "ownmost, non-relational possibility", which "is *not to be out-stripped*" (BT: §53). Taken together, these three aspects – being ownmost, non-relational and not to be outstripped – of being-toward-death help to explain death's distinctive role in Dasein's attainment of authenticity or self-ownership. The first and third of the three aspects are closely connected; indeed, the third aspect can be understood as explanatory with respect to the first: death is Dasein's ownmost possibility precisely because it cannot be outstripped. What this means is that although I might "escape death" on some particular occasion (or even on numerous occasions), thereby making it the case that some particular eventuality did not in fact occur, such evasions in no way diminish my mortality. I might stop smoking, exercise harder and more frequently, obey the speed limit, avoid "trouble spots" around the globe and so on, but nothing I can do makes me any less mortal. In this respect I am absolutely vulnerable, no matter what steps I might take to protect myself. Even if steps can be taken to avoid dying on some particular occasion, nothing can take my dying away from me in an absolute sense.

My mortality is my "ownmost" possibility because I cannot give it up, hand it off, or let it go, in the way I might with other possibilities I might project myself in terms of. Tomorrow, I might give up being a professor or a husband or an amateur photographer, but throughout any of these transformations my mortality remains. Moreover, my mortality is not something I can "delegate" to someone else. Although someone else might go to his or her death for me on a particular occasion (the lifeboat can only hold so many, and one of my fellow passengers nobly volunteers or unluckily draws the shortest straw; our captors insist on killing one of us, and one of the others is chosen instead of me), this does not make it the case that the other has died my death and now I do not have to do it. The other's dying his or her own death leaves my death, that is, my own mortality, entirely unaffected. The middle term, that death is "non-relational", is connected with the idea of death as one's ownmost possibility that cannot be outstripped. That death cannot be outstripped helps to explain why death is a non-relational possibility. Other possibilities I might take up or project myself in terms of are clearly relational. I can only project myself as a professor by being immersed in a world constituted in very particular ways: as including universities, academic departments, students, the discipline of philosophy and so on. My mortality does not work that way. Being-toward-death is my possibility regardless of the particular features of my surrounding world and regardless of how those features might change over time (if universities were for some reason abolished tomorrow, the particular self-understanding of being a professor would thereby collapse, but no such eventuality could remove my mortality).

By realizing that there is a possibility that is indelibly its own, Dasein is lifted out of the everyday world constituted in terms of *das Man* and in two respects. First, in everydayness, Dasein projects itself in terms of publicly available possibilities (professor, teacher, father, friend) that are all, as we have seen, relational in nature. All of these everyday possibilities are optional, in the sense that they can be given up, traded in, or taken away. By acknowledging its mortality, Dasein for the first time recognizes something as genuinely its own and so is able to see itself in terms other than those dictated by the average understanding of *das Man*. To borrow from the title of an American soap opera, by facing up to the idea that it has one death to die, Dasein is able thereby to comprehend that it has "one life to live". More than that, it is because of being-toward-death that Dasein is able to conceive of itself as having a life. But why does Dasein in everydayness fail to achieve this level of comprehension? Although Dasein's absorption in its various projects and pursuits is no doubt part of the answer, Heidegger ascribes to *das Man* and so everydayness a more pernicious effect with respect to acknowledging being-toward-death; this is the second respect in which being-toward-death lifts Dasein out of the everyday understanding articulated by *das Man*. Heidegger refers to everyday existence as "tranquillizing", and the particular way in which it is so is by shielding us from our mortality. The "idle talk" that Heidegger disparages most encodes and circulates a way of thinking about death as only a distant actuality. We tend, in everyday life, not to think much about death at all, but even when we do, we think of it as something that happens to other people, mostly to people we do not know, but occasionally to friends or family members. With respect to others, we rarely acknowledge one another's mortality as standing features of our existence. When someone is ill, for example, and then recovers, we tend to view that person as having evaded death and so as no longer being related to death in any way. And even when we overcome this tendency in the case of another person (when a person is, as we say, "terminally ill"), we rarely make the reflexive move of applying this realization to ourselves. Heidegger says that *das Man* "*does not permit us the courage for anxiety in the face of death*" (BT: §51), which means that in everyday life death is regarded as an exceptional condition, to be dealt with only occasionally; any further thoughts of, or concerns with, death are often dismissed as being excessively morbid.

Heidegger calls the stance fostered by an acknowledgment of one's being-toward-death (as one's ownmost possibility, which is non-relational and not to be outstripped) "anticipation". Anticipation is not a matter of brooding about one's eventual demise, of wondering when and how it might happen, but instead involves accepting one's mortality, and so one's finitude, as an ever-present structural feature of one's existence. A proper acknowledgment of this structural feature (as opposed, say, to denial, forgetfulness or oblivion) reverberates throughout the entirety of Dasein's existence, changing the weight and importance attached to all of its choices, plans and projects. When I project myself in light of my mortality, I see my choices as mattering, as indelibly and irrevocably shaping my finite allotment of time. Indeed, by acknowledging my mortality, I see myself in a more profound way as having time to use poorly or wisely, squander or value. (It is not clear to me that an animal, such as a squirrel, can waste time or use its time poorly rather than wisely. At the very least, an inanimate object, such as a cup or a table, has no such stance with respect to time; the table stored in the attic is not wasting *its* time by failing to be used daily in the dining room.) Being-toward-death delineates fully Dasein's structure as a futural being, a being that has time as opposed to an entity that merely exists *in* time. Being-toward-death imposes a limit on Dasein's "not-yet", making vivid the idea that plans or projects indefinitely postponed incur the risk of never being realized. Heidegger is not recommending an attitude of "*carpe diem*" or "live each day as though it were your last", but an acknowledgment of one's finitude is meant to give Dasein a more sober and serious outlook on its existence.

By acknowledging its being-toward-death, Dasein is thereby in a position to be authentic. Authenticity, for Heidegger, is a matter of what he calls "resoluteness", which is a matter of taking up wholeheartedly the task of projecting oneself onto possibilities. A resolute, authentic Dasein "chooses to choose", rather than let itself drift along and be chosen by the anonymous pressures of *das Man*. By connecting authenticity with the idea of "choosing to choose", we can see more clearly the force of the literal translation of *Eigentlichkeit* as "self-ownership". A being that chooses itself, that takes responsibility for the ways in which it projects itself onto possibilities, is a being that has full possession of itself; self-ownership and self-determination go hand in hand. But what does authentic Dasein choose? What possibilities present themselves as appropriate for Dasein to project itself in terms of authentically? Heidegger does not say. Indeed, he emphasizes that he *cannot* say; to delimit a range of possibilities in advance would be to undermine authentic Dasein's freedom. As Heidegger makes clear, the specific choice authentic Dasein is to make becomes apparent only to the one who has on that occasion chosen to choose:

> But on what basis does Dasein disclose itself in resoluteness? On what is it to resolve? *Only* the resolution itself can give

the answer. One would completely misunderstand the phenomenon of resoluteness if one should want to suppose that this consists simply in taking up possibilities which have been proposed and recommended, and seizing hold of them.

(BT: §60)

In other words, if you are still looking for someone or something else to tell you what to do, you have not yet reached the point of resoluteness.

Reflections and projections

It should be evident by this point that in Heidegger's hands, phenomenology undergoes a dramatic transformation from the "pure" form bequeathed by Husserl. Procedurally, Heideggerian phenomenology no longer seeks to describe, to the exclusion of all else, a sphere of conscious awareness apprehensible only from the first-person point of view. The phenomena of phenomenology, from Heidegger's perspective, are available from numerous points of view, and his methods throughout *Being and Time* reflect this multiplicity. Much of the description in Division One of Dasein in its everydayness proceeds in the third-person, in keeping with the manner of Dasein's existence in that domain. The "referential totality" of the everyday world offers no special privilege to one perspective over another; what a hammer is for is as intelligible from the third-person point of view as it is from the first-person standpoint. Indeed, Dasein's conformity to the anonymous norms of *das Man* are such that we hardly notice their pervasiveness in our day-to-day lives, and so it is often only from the outside, so to speak, that we can be struck by them.

Even when we restrict our attention to the phenomenology of everydayness in Division One, with its emphasis on third-person description, the guiding idea of describing the way in which things are manifest relies, however implicitly, on the availability of a first-person point of view. That Dasein's way of being is "an issue" for it underwrites the very idea of things being manifest or showing up, and it is only when we get to the very end of Division One, with its discussion of anxiety, and into Division Two, with its discussions of death, resoluteness and authenticity, that the specific contours of Dasein's self-concern come fully into view. All of these latter phenomena *do* privilege the first-person point of view; indeed, it is not clear to me that the experience of anxiety can be made fully intelligible from the outside (this has become abundantly clear to me from my efforts over the years to convey the nature and import of the experience to those of my students who enjoy a great deal in the way of existential complacency). But even when this shift occurs in *Being and Time*, such that the individual's concern with his or her own existence becomes the explicit theme, we are still miles away from the kind of first-person perspective of Husserlian phenomenology. That is, the kind of reflective self-awareness championed by *Being and Time* is structurally different from the "pure ego" constituted in the flow of conscious experience. In keeping with the reduction, the pure ego is something that is available from the standpoint of consciousness alone, as one "pole" of the ego–noesis–noema triad. Although there is ample room in Husserl's account for the idea that the pure ego is active (in forming beliefs, making judgements, reviewing past experience and so on), Husserl's ego still lacks the kind of projective structure inherent to Dasein's way of being. Dasein's achievement of selfhood is not a matter of its recognizing its own accumulated content, built up from the ongoing flow of experience, but is instead a matter of how it projects itself into a future. The nature and quality of Dasein's "futurity" is not a matter of what it has in mind, but a function of how it takes action in the situation in which it finds itself: "As resolute, Dasein is already *taking action*" (BT: §60). Thus, even when Heidegger attends to Dasein in its authenticity, its becoming an authentic self, the idea that Dasein is being-in-the-world (and so not a pure ego) never recedes from view.

We shall see in later chapters that the structure of the self, of the one to whom things are manifest, is an ongoing concern of phenomenology, analysed and reconceived by all of the major figures we shall consider in this book. With the exception of Husserl, these figures are part of the tradition of existential phenomenology, and so all of their respective conceptions of the self and self-consciousness build on criticisms of Husserl's initial views. This has, I think, been made abundantly clear in our examination of Heidegger, and it will continue to be the case when we turn to Sartre.

Summary of key points

- *Being and Time* begins with the "question of being": the question of what it means for anything to be.
- Human beings or Dasein have an understanding of being, and so the way to begin to answer the question of being is to "interrogate" Dasein in its way of being.

- The most basic descriptions of the way things are manifest to Dasein involve Dasein's being situated within, or oriented towards, a world.
- In everydayness, Dasein understands both itself and what it encounters largely in terms of anonymous norms articulated by what Heidegger calls *das Man* or the "they".
- Dasein is a being whose "being is an issue for it", and so its way of being is care, whose three constitutive aspects are understanding, *Befindlichkeit* and falling.
- Anxiety reveals to Dasein that death is its "ownmost possibility".
- Dasein can either choose its possibilities in light of its own mortality and so be authentic, or it can flee from its mortality and remain inauthentic.

three

Sartre and subjectivity

Sartre: life and works

The third of our major figures in phenomenology, Jean-Paul Sartre, was born in Paris in 1905. Unlike Husserl and Heidegger, Sartre did not lead the life of an academic philosopher. Although he did teach philosophy at certain points in his life, he did not occupy a professorship. Instead, he led the life of an author, playwright and public intellectual.

In this chapter, our interest will be restricted to Sartre's work during ten to fifteen years of his life, beginning in roughly 1933, when he

---

Sartre meets phenomenology

In *The Prime of Life*, Simone de Beauvoir recounts Sartre's first encounter with phenomenology. As she recalls the episode, she and Sartre were spending an evening with their friend Raymond Aron, who was at the time studying Husserl at the French Institute in Berlin. Pointing to an apricot cocktail, Aron demonstrated the importance of phenomenological method to Sartre: "You see, my dear fellow, if you are a phenomenologist, you can talk about this cocktail and make philosophy out of it!" At these words, Sartre is reported to have "turned pale with emotion". The change in pallor was due to the realization that he could, using phenomenological methods, "describe objects just as he saw and touched them, and extract philosophy from them". Phenomenology thus appeared to "affirm simultaneously both the supremacy of reason and the reality of the visible world as it appears to our senses". Immediately after this episode, Sartre purchased a copy of Levinas's early study of Husserl. According to de Beauvoir, when Sartre first read it his "heart missed a beat" (all quotations from de Beauvoir 1962: 112).

---

received a grant to study at the French Institute in Berlin. Here, Sartre immersed himself in phenomenology and the works of Husserl. This immersion led quickly to the publication of *The Transcendence of the Ego*, a slim volume that sharply criticizes Husserl's conception of the ego and its role in phenomenology. The ensuing years were productive for Sartre. He published his novel *Nausea* (1938), as well as works in philosophical psychology: *Imagination, a Psychological Critique* (1936), *Sketch for a Theory of the Emotions* (1939) and *The Imaginary* (1940). At the outbreak of the Second World War, Sartre served as an officer in the French army, and was taken prisoner by occupying German forces (he used this time to teach Heidegger to his fellow prisoners). After his release, Sartre resumed teaching philosophy and writing works in both philosophy and literature. In 1943, he published both his play *The Flies* and his major work in philosophy, *Being and Nothingness*, subtitled "A Phenomenological Essay in Ontology". These works were quickly followed by the play *No Exit* and the novel *The Age of Reason*, the first of an eventual trilogy that Sartre collectively titled *The Roads to Freedom*. He also founded the journal *Les Temps modernes*, which published works by such figures as Albert Camus and Merleau-Ponty. In 1946, Sartre published a shorter philosophical essay, *The Humanism of Existentialism*, which began as a public lecture given in 1945. In this work, Sartre for the first time characterized his philosophy as existentialism (the term was first coined by Sartre's friend, Gabriel Marcel, but Sartre initially resisted the label), which quickly developed into a widespread intellectual movement, finding devotees not just in philosophy, but also in psychology, literature, drama and film.

Sartre continued to write in the ensuing decades, including a study of the writer Jean Genet, as well as works on Mallarmé, Flaubert and Freud. In 1960, he published *Critique of Dialectical Reason*, which brought together the existentialist and Marxist strands of his thinking. During these years, Sartre was outspokenly political, taking stands against French colonialism and the Vietnam War, and first for, then against, the Soviet Union and Cuba. He was awarded the Nobel Prize for Literature in 1964, but he declined the award on political grounds. He died in 1980.

From Hume to Descartes: Husserl on the ego

The phenomenological tradition is, of course, but a part of the modern philosophical tradition that begins with Descartes. A cornerstone of

Descartes's philosophy is the discovery of the "I" or "self" as the epistemological foundation for any knowledge whatsoever. In the second of his *Meditations on First Philosophy*, Descartes puts an end to his "radical doubt" by announcing that his own existence ("I am, I exist") admits of complete certainty. Vouchsafed as well is Descartes's thinking; even his doubting, as a species of thought, attests to the reality of his thinking, and so "I think" has credentials equally strong as "I exist". In the Second Meditation, Descartes notes further how any of his experiences, regardless of their focus (the example he fastens on is looking at a piece of wax), serve to testify to his own existence as a thinking thing: the existence of the "I" or the "self" is confirmed at every moment of one's awareness.

Modern philosophy begins with Descartes, but by no means ends there. Not every subsequent philosopher has shared his confidence concerning the discovery of a self or "I", a thinking thing at the heart of all thought or experience. A particularly vivid example of this lack of sympathy is that of Hume, who, in a famous passage, announces with equal confidence that no such self is to be found:

> For my part, when I enter most intimately into what I call *myself*, I always stumble on some particular perception or other, of heat or cold, light or shade, love or hatred, pain or pleasure. I never can catch *myself* at any time without a perception, and never can observe anything but the perception …. If any one upon serious and unprejudic'd reflexion, thinks he has a different notion of *himself*, I must confess I can no longer reason with him. All I can allow him is, that he may be in the right as well as I, and that we are essentially different in this particular. He may, perhaps, perceive something simple and continu'd, which he calls *himself*; tho' I am certain there is no such principle in me.   ([1739/40] 1978: I, IV, §VI)

I rehearse these perhaps familiar moments from early modern philosophy because the disagreements they record can be discerned within the phenomenological tradition. Indeed, each of these two positions can be located within Husserl's philosophy alone. In Chapter 1, our discussion was confined primarily to Husserl's conception of phenomenology after his "transcendental turn", which occurred around 1905. However, in his "breakthrough" work, *Logical Investigations*, Husserl's views concerning the ego or self have a distinctly Humean ring to them, as can be seen in the following passage, wherein he, like Hume before him, "confesses" his inability to find an ever-present ego at the centre of experience:

> I must frankly confess, however, that I am quite unable to find this ego, this primitive, necessary centre of relations.* The only thing I can take note of, and therefore perceive, are the empirical ego and its empirical relations to its own experiences, or to such external objects as are receiving special attention at the moment, while much remains, whether "without" or "within", which has no such relation to the ego. (LI: 549–50)

The asterisk at the end of the first sentence signals a footnote that Husserl added in the second edition of *Logical Investigations*, which appeared after the publication of the first volume of *Ideas*. Although Husserl did not undertake a complete revision of *Logical Investigations* so as to align it with his then current conception of phenomenology, he did add qualifications and corrections by way of notes and appendices (as well as the occasional deletion of whole sections). This particular note is especially striking as it constitutes a complete reversal in his position. In the note, Husserl announces the discovery of what had previously eluded his every effort at detection. The note reads: "I have since managed to find it, i.e. have learnt not to be led astray from a pure grasp of the given through corrupt forms of ego-metaphysic" (LI: 549).

As Husserl's conception of phenomenology develops, his view concerning the place of the ego within phenomenology works its way back, in terms of historical precedent, from a more or less Humean position to one more closely aligned with that of Descartes. The "pure grasp of the given" achieved through the phenomenological reduction includes a grasp of the pure or transcendental ego as an essential element of the given. Three passages from the aptly titled *Cartesian Meditations* may be illustrative here:

> If I keep purely what comes into view – for me, the one who is meditating – by virtue of the free epoché with respect to the being of the experienced world, the momentous fact is that I, with my life, remain untouched in my existential status, regardless of whether or not the world exists and regardless of what my eventual decision concerning its being or non-being might be. This Ego, with his Ego-life, who necessarily remains for me, by virtue of such epoché, is not a piece of the world; and if he

says, "I exist, *ego cogito*", that no longer signifies, "I, this man, exist".   (CM: §11)

The truly first utterance, however, is the Cartesian utterance of the *ego cogito* – for example: "I perceive – this house" or "I remember – a certain commotion in the street".   (CM: §16)

I exist for myself and am continually given to myself, by experiential evidence, as "*I myself*". This is true of the transcendental ego, and, correspondingly, of the psychologically pure ego; it is true, moreover, with respect to any sense of the word ego.
                                                                                  (CM: §33)

Notice how in each of these passages Husserl appeals to the presence or givenness of the ego as pervasive: the ego remains after the performance of the reduction as an essential feature of consciousness, is involved in the "truly first utterance" and is "continually given".

The claim that an "I" is persistently given in experience is Sartre's principal target in *The Transcendence of the Ego*. As Sartre says on the opening page: "We should like to show here that the ego is neither formally nor materially *in* consciousness: it is outside, *in the world*. It is a being of the world, like the ego of another" (TE: 31). Sartre's claim, if borne out, constitutes an especially acute criticism of Husserlian phenomenology, since it carries critical weight even if one accepts the basic framework of the phenomenological reduction. As a "being of the world", the ego cannot survive the phenomenological reduction as a constitutive element of "pure consciousness", any more than can my desk or coffee cup, understood as entities existing in the world.

Phenomenological revisions

We saw in the passages from *Cartesian Meditations* that the phenomenological reduction affirms that "I exist for myself and am continually given to myself". The affirmation of a "continually given 'I' or ego" is integral to Husserl's broader claims about the essential tripartite structure of all intentional experience:

Ego --------- Cogito -------- Cogitatum

[I ----------- Noesis ----------- Noema]

Every experience, Husserl claims, has this structure, where the I and the "cogitatum", that is, the ego and the object-as-intended, form the two "poles" of the experience. The middle term, the cogito or noesis, designates the kind or mode of the experience, for example perception, recollection, desire, hope, fear and so on.

Does all conscious experience really have this tripartite structure? If we recall a slogan introduced early on in our discussion that "all consciousness is consciousness of something", that is, that intentionality is the defining feature of consciousness, then the middle and rightmost elements of this three-part formula do indeed appear essential. Every (intentional) experience requires an object (cogitatum/noema) and that object must be experienced in some way or other, for example, perceived, desired, feared, recollected and so on (cogito/noesis). Whereas Husserl argues that the left-most element is equally essential, Sartre claims that careful attention to experience shows this not to be so. That is, Sartre argues that when we restrict our attention to the flow of experience strictly *as* experienced, which, after all, is what the phenomenological reduction purports to facilitate, no "I", "self" or "ego" is manifest as part of that flow. This, at least, is true of what Sartre calls "first-degree consciousness".

Consider the following example. I am in my kitchen making bread. My large green ceramic bowl stands before me on the counter. I have already added warm water and yeast to the bowl, and I am now stirring in flour to make the dough. The interior of the bowl nearly exhausts my visual field as I intently watch the slowly forming dough (too much flour yields a solid cannonball, unworthy of baking, let alone eating; too little makes for a sticky mess), but I am peripherally aware of the surrounding countertop, the measuring cup and bag of flour just to the right, the corner of the cookbook just to the left, the toaster sitting unused behind the bowl. At the same time, I smell the familiar, yeasty odours that are integral to making bread, along with the lingering, although fainter, aroma of the morning's coffee. I hear the spoon as it knocks against the side of the bowl, but I have the radio on and intermittently attend to the music being played or the words of the programme's host. My left hand grips the side of the bowl, which is cool and smooth, and my right hand holds the rougher wooden spoon. I quickly feel a dull ache in my right bicep as the added flour increases the resistance of the mixture.

If we reflect on this sketch of a description, it would all seem to be just so much grist for Husserl's mill. After all, every sentence of the description contains at least one occurrence of "I" or "my" (or both), and so each sentence refers explicitly to an ego or self: *I* am in the kitchen, *I* smell the yeast, *my* left hand grips the bowl and so on. Thus, it is hard, on the face of it, to make out Sartre's claim that the I or ego is not a manifest part of first-degree consciousness. However, we should not be so hasty in drawing such a conclusion, since the proffered description of my activity is not purely phenomenological. Consider, for example, the third sentence, which begins "I have already added …". This sentence may be part of a narrative account of my making bread, something that I might recite while doing so if I were, say, teaching someone else how to make bread or perhaps demonstrating the bread-making process as a talk-show guest ("Ok, Rosie, I'm now going to begin kneading the dough …"), but it is unlikely that anything corresponding to this sentence figures in my experience while I am alone in the kitchen. A narrative account is something of a mixed description, containing both objective and subjective elements, recounting both what I am doing and my experience of what I am doing. A phenomenological description, by contrast, confines itself entirely to how things are manifest in experience, the activity *as* experienced, and here, Sartre would claim, the many occurrences of "I" and "my" that populate the narrative account are out of place. As I dissolve the yeast, stir in the flour and so on, the content of my experience is simply the dissolving yeast smelled in the bowl, the bowl and flour seen on the countertop, the music heard on the radio, the ache felt in the arm and so on, but there need not be, and usually is not, any experience of an I that is doing all this smelling, seeing, hearing and feeling. My absorption may, of course, be disrupted at any point, such that I might then reflectively apprehend what I have been up to, perhaps even to the point of explicitly thinking to myself such thoughts as, "Here I am making bread", or "I really love the smell of yeast", or "Now I have nearly finished stirring in the flour", but it would be a mistake, Sartre contends, to impose the structure of this reflective apprehension onto non-reflective experience. (We also need to be careful, Sartre thinks, in how we describe the structure of this reflective apprehension, but more on that later.) Although Sartre accepts the Kantian idea that it must always be possible to attach an "I think" (or, better, "I experience") to each of my experiences, we should not inflate that possibility into an actuality.

At this juncture, we might imagine the following Husserlian objection: why think of the structure of reflective apprehension as an imposition; why not instead a revelation? The reflective apprehension of my experience reveals the ego or I as an essential element of that experience. Does not the fact that I can label all of these experiences as *mine* show this to be the case? For Sartre, these questions provide little in the way of argumentative leverage. To begin with the most basic issue, nothing is gained by substituting "revelation" for "imposition", since to speak of reflection as revealing an ego implies that such an ego was hidden prior to reflection and so not manifest in non-reflective experience, which is precisely Sartre's point. Anything that requires reflection to bring it to the level of manifestation could not be part of the content of first-degree consciousness; the very idea of an unexperienced content of experience displays its own absurdity.

This initial response to our imagined objection can be further developed so as to reveal an even deeper problem with an appeal to an I or ego as an essential element in all experience. If we allow that reflection reveals the I or ego, and so concede that the I or ego is not manifest in first-degree consciousness before the act of reflection, then to posit that the ego is always a structural feature of consciousness is to violate the most fundamental principle of phenomenology. That is, phenomenology casts itself as a non-speculative, non-hypothetical enterprise. The whole point of the phenomenological reduction, as Husserl develops it, is to work in accordance with his "principle of all principles", which, it will be recalled, demands "that *everything originarily* (so to speak, in its 'personal' actuality) *offered* to us *in 'intuition' is to be accepted simply as what it is presented as being*, but also *only within the limits in which it is presented there*" (*Ideas* I: §24). The final clause is what is most important for our purposes, since the postulation of an ever-present ego amounts to an inference that goes beyond the "limits" of what is presented in experience. The content of experience is nothing other than what is experienced: there are no non-experienced elements of experience. Careful phenomenological description shows that Husserl's transcendental ego is just such a non-experienced element. To posit an ego at the level of first-degree consciousness is to introduce an "opaque" element into consciousness, thereby occluding what Sartre calls its "translucency", and so, as Sartre rather colourfully puts it, the transcendental ego is "the death of consciousness" (TE: 40).

We are now in the vicinity of Sartre's second main objection to Husserl's conception of the transcendental ego, namely, that the I or ego does not serve to unite consciousness. More strongly put, Sartre's claim is that such an I or ego could not play this role, since, as we have seen, the introduction of a non-experienced element marks "the death of consciousness", rather than establishing its unity. According to Sartre, consciousness needs nothing beyond itself for its unity; the intentionality of consciousness, its synthetic–horizontal structure, confers all the unity it requires. To return to the example of my experience of making bread, the moments and modalities of that stretch of experience all form an interconnected, united flow – the adumbrational presentations of the bowl as it turns, the unseen sides predictably becoming seen, the simultaneity of the smells of yeast and the hearing of the radio – without any further synthesizing agent lying behind or beneath them, that is, without any subject. For Sartre, then, the ego is not a source of unity, but instead is founded on a prior unity that it did not create.

Sartre certainly does not want to deny that an I or ego is ever manifest in or to consciousness; reflective, or second-degree, consciousness is a genuine phenomenon, and here an I or ego does indeed make an appearance. However, Sartre contends that careful attention to reflective consciousness further illustrates the flaws in Husserl's conception of the ego and its place in phenomenology. Rather than a transcendental, structurally essential feature of consciousness, the ego is a transcendent object *for* consciousness, no different in this respect than any other worldly entity. What this means is that even acts of reflection, of second-degree consciousness, are still in an important sense subjectless; the I appears as an object, as part of the intentional content of the experience, and not as its subject. This transcendent, objective character of the I dictates, by Husserl's own criteria, that it must "fall before the stroke of the phenomenological reduction" (TE: 53). Here we can see the way in which Sartre intends his critique of Husserlian phenomenology to constitute a series of internal criticisms, amounting to a more careful observance of Husserl's own strictures and methods. In *The Transcendence of the Ego*, at least, Sartre does not reject the phenomenological reduction (as Heidegger does in *Being and Time*, for example), as much as reconsider the results of that procedure.

Despite the desire to maintain a certain fidelity to Husserl's mature conception of phenomenology (minus, of course, what Sartre views as the mistaken inclusion of a transcendental ego), Sartre's actual practice of phenomenology, and so his conception of phenomenological method, in effect constitutes a significant departure. What I mean here is that Husserl regards reflection as integral to phenomenological method. As we have seen, "acts of the second degree", that is, reflective acts, constitute "the fundamental *field of phenomenology*" (*Ideas* I: §50). Now, Husserl recognizes that reflection does constitute a "modification" of first-degree experience. Reflection, Husserl acknowledges, "*alters* the original subjective process", so that it "loses its original mode, 'straightforward', by the very fact that reflection makes an object out of what was previously a subjective process but not objective" (CM: §15).

At the same time, Husserl is unworried by these alterations, since the "task of reflection … is not to repeat the original process"; instead, the goal of reflection is to "consider … and explicate what can be found" in the original process (*ibid.*). In *The Transcendence of the Ego*, Sartre writes:

> Husserl would be the first to acknowledge that an unreflected thought undergoes a radical modification in becoming reflected. But need one confine this modification to the loss of "naiveté"? Would not the appearance of the *I* be what is essential in this change? (TE: 45–6)

The critical weight of Sartre's second question should not be underestimated, since if he is right, the modifications effected by reflection reach into the *content*, as opposed to just the "mode", of first-degree consciousness, radically and misleadingly altering it. But if this is so, reflection cannot be the proper method for "considering and explicating" acts of first-degree consciousness, since it will inevitably claim as essential features what are in fact artifacts of its own operation, the claimed presence of the I or ego being a principal case in point.

Sartre's criticisms force not just a re-evaluation of the results of phenomenological procedures, but reconsideration of those procedures themselves. Proper phenomenological description of first-degree consciousness cannot be via reflection, since reflection fails to preserve the subjectless character of non-reflective experience. But how then should phenomenology proceed? How does one establish that first-degree consciousness lacks an I or ego if reflection leads us astray by introducing one? After all, does Sartre himself not claim to be carefully attending to first-degree consciousness, describing and explicating it, and is not such careful attention just the kind of reflective apprehension Husserl recommends? How could there be phenomenology without reflection? Rather than reflecting on his non-reflective experience, Sartre instead characterizes himself as "conspiring" with that experience, where that means reviving the experience while following alongside it. As Sartre puts it: "I must direct my attention to the revived objects, but *without losing sight of the unreflected consciousness*, by joining in a sort of conspiracy with it and by drawing up an inventory of its content in a non-positional manner" (TE: 46). This conspiratorial phenomenological practice of observing experience as it is re-enacted in memory rather than interrupting it as it occurs is inherently retrospective for Sartre. If, while making bread, I were to stop and reflect, my absorption in my activity would be broken and I would have the experience of *myself* seeing, hearing, smelling and feeling, and I would go wrong, phenomenologically, were I to read that appearing self back into my experience up until that moment of reflection. Instead, I apprehend that my experience while making bread lacked an I or ego by reliving it after it has transpired. By calling it to mind *as* it was lived initially, I can now apprehend that no I or ego figured in that episode of awareness.

Consider as a further example those times where we, as it is commonly put, "lose ourselves" in thought. During any such time where I am so "lost", I do not apprehend that an I is absent from my experience. Were I to be struck by such a thought, I would no longer be lost, but instead would thereby be reflectively aware of myself. In other words, I cannot have the thought, "Here I am having I-less experiences", since the very occurrence of that kind of thought introduces precisely what was until then missing. Nonetheless, when I am roused from my musings, I can at that time acknowledge that I was indeed lost in thought and I can also rehearse the episode in considerable detail: what I was thinking; the order of my thoughts; the feelings attendant on such thoughts, including the character of the episode as marked by my *being lost*. As long as such retrospective, rather than reflective, appraisals are possible (and Sartre claims that it "by definition is always possible" to "reconstitute the complete moment" (TE: 46) of unreflected consciousness), then there is ample material for phenomenological description.

The qualification with which this final claim is entered may turn out to be considerably more severe than Sartre's confidence would suggest. Lacking in Sartre is any argument to the effect that it is "by definition always possible" to reconstitute first-degree consciousness, and certainly nothing that tells us how to ensure that any such "reconstitution" faithfully reproduces the original experience. That is, Sartre does not answer the question of how we separate accurate from inaccurate revivals of previously enjoyed experiences, so as to determine, for example, that one re-enactment is a more faithful reproduction than another; nor does he tell us how to guard against the introduction of features that were not present the first time around. Leaving such worries unaddressed at the very least threatens to place Sartre's "retrospective conspiring" in the same boat as reflection, namely, as a source of distortion and corruption rather than guarantor of descriptive fidelity. As we shall see in Chapter 5, these worries run even deeper, such that ignoring them is no minor oversight or omission on Sartre's part; on the contrary, some have argued that these worries, sufficiently developed, undermine the very possibility of phenomenology.

The constitution of the ego revisited

If the ego is an object transcendent to consciousness, appearing to it in second-degree, reflective acts, what kind of an object is it? This question is intended as a purely phenomenological one, that is, as asking after the ways in which the ego appears in and to consciousness; the question is thus one concerning the constitution of the ego in precisely the same manner as phenomenology asks after the constitution of other transcendent entities, such as the rock and the melody explored in Chapter 1. That for Sartre the ego is transcendent to consciousness, a "being of the world", as he puts it, provides a clue as to how an account of its constitution should go. That is, in Husserl's phenomenology a defining feature of transcendent entities is that they are given adumbrationally, by partial, perspectival presentations: I always hear the melody note by note; I always see the rock from one side or another; and so on. On Sartre's account, this is the case with the ego as well: its appearance in second-degree consciousness is always partial, a matter of presentations that afford only incomplete perspectives on it. Consider one of Sartre's own examples: the transition from a momentary feeling of revulsion in the presence of Peter to the more reflective conclusion that I hate Peter. The momentary feeling, as an episode of first-degree consciousness, is unowned and so ego-less; moreover, the feeling is entirely present in the episode. There is no distinction to be made here between seeming to feel revulsion in the presence of Peter and really feeling revulsion, which indicates the non-adumbrational character of the feeling's manifestation to consciousness. The case of hatred, however, is markedly different, extending well beyond any momentary episode of consciousness. Hatred is an enduring state, attaching to the I, and so to conclude that I hate Peter is to stake myself to a future pattern of feelings and attitudes. To say that I hate Peter is to say more than that present to consciousness right now is a rush of revulsion, even an intense one. Actually hating Peter means, for example, that when I wake up tomorrow, it will still be the case that I hate him; that thinking of him will occasion similar feelings; that I shall be inclined to say, or at least think to myself, that I hate him; that I shall not go out of my way to be nice to him, except hypocritically, and so on. As Sartre artfully puts it, the reflective postulation of hatred involves a "passage to infinity" (TE: 63). (The case is precisely analogous to concluding "I see a chair" on the basis of one, perspectival presentation, since that presentation's being of a (real) chair means, among other things, that I can see it from other sides, that if I reach out to touch it my hand will not pass through it, that I can sit down on it, that it will not disappear and reappear several times in the next five minutes and so on.) And of course I can be wrong about such things: the feeling may subside; Peter and I may "make nice"; the many envisaged episodes of unpleasantness may not come to pass. Thus, unlike in the case of the feeling of revulsion, a distinction between seeming to hate and really hating *can* be drawn; I might only seem to hate Peter. That I hate him is a hasty conclusion, drawn from what turns out to be merely a fleeting episode of bad feelings.

The example of hatred can be both generalized and extended, since for Sartre the ego that appears in reflective consciousness is ultimately the *unity* of *states* such as hatred, as well as *actions* (although Sartre also includes a third category, *qualities*, as a kind of optional intermediary between states and actions: for example, as a *spiteful* (quality) person, I am inclined to *hate* (state) Peter and *wish* (action) him dead). By "actions" here, Sartre does not mean bodily actions (those occupy a separate category, discussed briefly below), but rather "psychic" ones, such as the actions of doubting, believing, wishing and the like. The I appears in these reflective states and actions as one and the same, such that, for example, the I who hates Peter is the same I who doubts that Paul will be on time. There is, however, a peculiarity Sartre notes in the constitution of the I or ego. On the one hand, whatever content the I has is given via the reflective states and actions of second-degree consciousness, that is, there appears to be nothing more to the I than the role it plays in uniting these various states and actions (here is a place where, despite their overarching disagreement, Sartre's ideas are akin to Husserl's concerning the constitution of the pure ego). Sartre says, variously, that the ego is "the infinite totality of states and of actions which is never reducible to *an* action or *a* state" (TE: 74), and that "it does not seem that we could find a skeletal pole if we took away, one after the other, all the qualities ... at the end of this plundering nothing would remain; the ego would have vanished" (TE: 78). On the other hand, the I appears in reflection as something like the source or substrate of these very states, actions and qualities and so as having a kind of priority relative to them. Paradoxically, "reflection intends a relation which traverses time backwards and which gives the *me* as the source of the state" (TE: 77).

The ego whose constitution we have been considering is an object exclusively available to and for second-degree consciousness, that is, for reflective acts. There is, however, another sense of "I" that Sartre considers that does not involve reflection. This non-reflective I appears when, while making bread for example, I am asked what I am doing and

I reply, without interrupting my activity, "I am making bread". The "I" here, Sartre maintains, is "empty", as nothing determinate is presented in connection with it; an I does not show itself here, however adumbratively, as the "source" of the doing, as the owner of the action, and so as the referent of the report. When I use "I" in this way, I am almost using it in a third-person manner, as another way to pick out something going on in the objective world, rather than revealing or reporting my interior existence. In so far as anything is picked out by this use of "I", it would be my body as the locus or centre of these activities. Sartre refers to the body here as constituting an "illusory fulfillment" (TE: 90), by which I take him to mean that my body is not in any particular way manifest to consciousness on the occasion of these sorts of reports. Think here of the peculiarity of replacing "I" with "my body": "My body is making bread", instead of "I am making bread". The artificiality of the substitution indicates that my body does not really serve to fulfil the sense of "I" when used in a non-reflective way.

Selfhood and self-knowledge

One consequence of Sartre's commitment to the transcendence of the ego is a sharp distinction between consciousness and the psychic. As Sartre puts it, "The psychic is the transcendent object of reflective consciousness", and is also "the object of the science called 'psychology'" (TE: 71). Whereas consciousness is "translucent", immediately and exhaustively manifest (indeed, consciousness is nothing but manifestation), the psychic in general, as a transcendent object, enjoys no special epistemological status in comparison with any other category of transcendent entities; knowledge in all of these categories is equally partial, incomplete, fallible and revisable. More radically, perhaps, Sartre draws this conclusion even when it comes to self-knowledge: to knowledge, so to speak, of my own I or ego. I occupy no special position, have no special access, when it comes to acquiring knowledge of my own ego: I am manifest to myself no less adumbrationally than I am to you; my conclusions about my own states and actions are as fallible and open to revision as my conclusions about yours; and so on. There still is, for Sartre, a kind of asymmetry between the first-person and third-person perspective with respect to any particular ego, but this is only a matter of what Sartre calls "intimacy", by which he means that my ego constitutes, for me, a kind of interiority, a psychic life of which I partake. As such, my ego is manifest to me from within this ongoing life. The ego who hates Peter is manifest to me via feelings of revulsion that ego has, when I am that ego, whereas someone else would have to draw that conclusion about me by other means (and certainly not by feeling *my* feelings). But although I am more intimately connected with my feelings of revulsion, that is, by having or undergoing them, I can still be wrong about my conclusion that I hate Peter, that such a state actually attaches to my ego. Someone else, only watching my fit of rage rather than living it, may nonetheless be more correct in concluding that I do not really hate Peter, that my anger will pass and that tomorrow it will be as though nothing happened. Intimacy, then, is not to be conflated with authority.

Sartre's worries about self-knowledge run even deeper, and these worries arise ultimately from his conclusions concerning the peculiar status of the ego relative to other transcendent entities. What I mean here is that even if we, as Sartre does, deny any kind of first-person authority when it comes to self-knowledge, so that I have no "privileged access" to myself, that on its own does not totally foreclose the possibility of self-knowledge. Such a denial only means that self-knowledge is not as special as philosophers have often made it out to be: that it is fallible, open to revision, liable to correction even from a third-person perspective and so on. That, as I have suggested, is already a radical conclusion, relative to many philosophical points of view, but Sartre appears to go further even than this. At some points, he suggests not just that self-knowledge is no more authoritative than knowledge of another, but rather that it is invariably less so. The very intimacy with which the ego is given in my own case stands in the way of my coming to know it. All of what Sartre regards as the standard procedures for knowing a transcendent entity (Sartre lists observation, approximation and anticipation as examples of such procedures – see TE: 86) involve taking up an external point of view on the entity to be known, and so, owing to the internality of my perspective on the ego, these procedures are ill-suited to the project of my gathering knowledge about myself. Although I may try to achieve some detachment with respect to my own ego, gathering information in the same manner as I would in the task of learning about someone else, in doing so I lose sight of the very thing I want to know. The quest for detachment negates the very intimacy with which the ego is given, thereby effacing the object of my investigation. As Sartre concludes, "Thus, 'really to know oneself' is inevitably to take toward oneself the point of view of others, that is to say, a point of view which is necessarily false" (TE: 87).

Recall the passage from Hume quoted near the start of this chapter. There Hume suggests that any attempt through introspection to locate his self – that is, that which has his various perceptions – comes up empty; all Hume reports being able to find are just more perceptions, various thoughts and feelings. Hume concludes that nothing corresponds to the notion of a self: the notion fails to pick anything out above and beyond the various perceptions detected through introspection. The self is thus a kind of fiction, according to Hume, and so in that sense self-knowledge is impossible, not through any difficulties with respect to access or perspective, but because there is no self to know. Sartre's position on the ego may at first appear to be wholly contrary to Hume's. For example, while the ego is only given adumbrationally, and so possesses the kind of "opacity" common to all transcendent entities, Sartre insists that the ego is not given only hypothetically. Even though, for any given state or action that I judge my ego to have or perform, I can always entertain the possibility that such a judgement is mistaken ("Perhaps I do not hate Peter", "Perhaps I do not doubt Paul's friendship" and so on), it makes no sense, Sartre thinks, to reason in this fashion about the ego itself. "Perhaps I have no ego" is patently absurd, as is the conjecture "Perhaps I have an ego". Although Sartre's rejection of the idea that the ego's existence is hypothetical may appear to confer a kind of certainty on its existence, this is not the case. Instead, the absurdity of these two hypothetical statements stems, according to Sartre, from the idea that ascribing states and actions to an ego adds nothing to them and so I do not incur a further commitment through such an ascription. Indeed, Sartre likens the relation between the ego and its states to one of "poetic production" (TE: 77), in keeping with his depiction of the ego's manifestation as involving a backwards traversal of time that lends to the ego a rather magical aura. Indeed, Sartre claims that "it is exclusively in magical terms that we should speak of the relations of the *me* to consciousness" (TE: 68), and that "we are sorcerers of ourselves each time we view our *me*" (TE: 82). Sartre thus appears here rather closer to Hume than one may have initially thought. The "poetic", even "magical", manifestation of the ego recalls Hume's general strategy of explaining the origin of ideas for which there is no corresponding impression by appealing to the workings of the imagination.

Equally magical is Sartre's talk of the "vanishing" of the ego on the removal of all the states, actions and qualities it shows itself as uniting. Now this idea need not be construed as undermining the reality of the ego. After all, for any transcendent entity, we might well wonder what remains when all of its various properties or qualities are imagined away. To maintain that a transcendent entity is real, we need not be committed to the idea that it exists as some sort of bare substratum, independent of any and every quality it may possess. However, what Sartre has in mind here goes further, suggesting something disanalogous to what holds for other transcendent objects. The point may be put like this. Even if we maintain that a chair, for example, is nothing over and above its various properties or qualities, still we by and large think that when we apprehend those qualities, we thereby apprehend the chair. The chair is open to view when its qualities are manifest, even if we concede that the view is partial, incomplete, open to revision and so on. According to Sartre, things are otherwise in the case of the ego: "The ego never appears, in fact, except when one is not looking at it" (TE: 88). (Try saying this about a chair!) To understand why Sartre holds this view, recall his central idea, namely, that the ego is manifest in reflective consciousness as the unity of states and actions. The ego is apprehended in these moments of consciousness via the states and actions; the ego appears "behind the state, at the horizon" (TE: 88). To try to apprehend the ego directly, to make it alone the object of consciousness, breaks the hold of reflection: "I fall back onto the unreflected level, and the ego disappears along with the reflected act" (TE: 88–9). The disappearance noted here again signals a sharp disanalogy between the ego and other transcendent entities. "The ego", Sartre writes, "is an object which appears only to reflection, and which is thereby radically cut off from the World [*sic.*]" (TE: 83). (I should note here that there is a rather obvious tension between this last claim and the opening claim of *The Transcendence of the Ego*, namely, that the ego "is outside, *in the world* … a being of the world, like the ego of another". For his part, Sartre does not address this apparent contradiction.) The futility of trying to get a direct "look" at the ego, front and centre in one's conscious awareness rather than lurking at the horizon, leads Sartre to conclude that "the ego is *by nature* fugitive" (TE: 89). Although not exactly Hume's position, Sartre's is perhaps an explanation of it; that is, if Sartre is correct, then we can understand why Hume's search was doomed from the start.

Consciousness, nothingness and bad faith

As mentioned at the start of the chapter, *The Transcendence of the Ego* is an early work of Sartre's, written shortly after his introduction to phenomenology, over a decade before his own self-description as an "existentialist", and nearly a decade before the publication of his massive *Being and Nothingness* in 1943. Despite this lapse in time, and despite the roughly tenfold increase in size from the first work to the second, many central themes of *Being and Nothingness* are foreshadowed by *The Transcendence of the Ego*. In the remainder of this chapter, rather than attempt anything like a comprehensive summary of *Being and Nothingness*, I shall try to sketch some of those lines of continuity, in order to show how Sartre's early criticisms of Husserl initiated the development of an elaborate, richly textured philosophical view.

As we have seen, in *The Transcendence of the Ego* Sartre still conceives of phenomenology as operating within a largely Husserlian framework: his dispute with Husserl concerning the question of the transcendental ego is, we might say, an intramural one. Sartre thus conceives of consciousness, at least as studied by phenomenology, in terms of purity and translucency, and so in terms of the phenomenological reduction. Indeed, Sartre sees his practice of the reduction as more rigorous than Husserl's, purging the field of conscious awareness of *all* transcendent entities, including the I or ego. The resultant field is entirely devoid of objects, and so, odd as this may sound, is not really a something at all. As Sartre puts it towards the end of *The Transcendence of the Ego*:

> The Transcendental Field, purified of all egological structure, recovers its primary transparency. In a sense, it is a *nothing*, since all physical, psycho-physical, and psychic objects, all truths, all values are outside of it; since my *me* has itself ceased to be any part of it. (TE: 93)

Sartre's equating of consciousness with nothingness anticipates the opening sections of *Being and Nothingness*, wherein he argues that human existence, an essential aspect of which is consciousness or what Sartre comes to call "being-for-itself" (where the "for" indicates self-presence or self-awareness, rather than selfishness, as when we say that someone is only out for himself) is the source of non-being. That is, Sartre argues that if we try to conceive of reality in and of itself, what he calls the "in-itself", then we find "pure positivity", that is, what is real or purely actual includes nothing unreal or non-existent. Nonetheless, when we describe the world as we experience it, we characterize it in both positive and negative terms. I say, for example, that my coffee cup is on my desk, but also that it is not downstairs; that my keys are missing from the key-hooks by the door; that I no longer have a favourite sweater because it was destroyed by moths. All of these descriptions incorporate some kind of negativity, depicting the world both in terms of how it is and how it is not.

If we reflect on these examples, we may come to notice the ubiquity of these modes of description, so much so that it may begin to appear difficult to describe the world without availing oneself of negatively charged terms. Indeed, the difficulty here is not just one concerning how we might describe the world, but concerns, more basically, all of our ways of encountering and acting in the world. Hence my saying above that "if we try to conceive of reality in and of itself", since Sartre thinks that in so far as we perceive and describe the world in determinate ways, those perceptions and descriptions incorporate some kind of negativity. Indeed, the very idea of determination presupposes this: when something is determinate, then it exists in some particular way and not another (my dog is, in being a dog, not a cat; my coffee cup, in being a coffee cup, is not a dog; and so on). The most sense we can make of reality in and of itself is an undifferentiated fullness of existence, something that Sartre thinks is just barely manifest in moments of what he calls "nausea", when we experience reality as just a bare, sickening that-it-is.

Although his account of the origin of nothingness holds that consciousness or subjectivity is somehow the source of it, Sartre argues against the idea that nothingness is to be accounted for by deriving it from the subjective act of negation, through the making of negative judgements. Negativity is, Sartre insists, "pre-judicative", which means that negative judgements are founded on nothingness, and not vice versa. To use Sartre's example (see BN: 40–44), when I am looking for Pierre in the cafe and find him to be missing, his absence is as much a part of my perceptual experience of the cafe as the tables and chairs that are there. That is, I do not merely judge that Pierre is absent on the basis of what I perceive; rather, I perceive his absence along with the tables and chairs (indeed, he argues that Pierre's absence is the more prominent object of my perceptual experience, the other, actually present items in the cafe forming only the background). The palpable absence of Pierre is markedly different from absences that I might note in a more purely intellectual way, for example, if I were to judge that Abraham Lincoln was also not in the cafe, along with Socrates, Napoleon and a whole host of others. These latter cases are exclusively creatures of judgement, superadded to the cafe as I experience it. Pierre's absence, by contrast, is an example of what Sartre calls "*negatités*": negatively charged features of the world; "pools of nothingness" populating reality as we perceive and conceive it. Although nothingness cannot be conceived as a subjective imposition via the act of judgement, nonetheless I am inextricably involved in Pierre's absence being a perceptual feature of the situation. It is only because I am looking for Pierre, only because I expect to find him at the cafe, and so on, that Pierre is absent from the cafe. Minus those expectations, Pierre's absence is no more a feature of the cafe than Napoleon's. This point can be generalized: the negative features of the world, all of the *negatités*, cannot be accounted for except in relation to human attitudes towards the world. "Man is the being through whom nothingness comes to the world" (BN: 59).

This appeal to human attitudes places us squarely in the domain of intentionality, in the domain of consciousness, and this provides deeper insight into the origins of nothingness. As we saw in the passage cited from *The Transcendence of the Ego*, the very idea of consciousness involves the idea of nothingness. Consciousness "is a nothing", and this can be discerned in the notion of intentionality itself. Conscious states are of objects but are not those objects. Intentionality thus involves a kind of slippage or gap, presenting and representing objects without literally having or being those objects. Consciousness is of something that it is not, and so in that sense is what it is not. Sartre thus thinks that a defining feature of the for-itself, of human existence understood in terms of consciousness, is the failure of the principle of identity (Bishop Butler's maxim that "everything is what it is and not another thing" fails to hold true in the domain of the for-itself). Again, this idea is foreshadowed in *The Transcendence of the Ego*, where Sartre concludes that conscious states, as a kind of nothing, cannot be accounted for by any preceding actualities:

> Thus each instant of our conscious life reveals to us a creation *ex nihilo*. Not a new *arrangement*, but a new existence. There is something distressing for each of us, to catch in the act this tireless creation of existence of which *we* are not the creators. At this level man has the impression of ceaselessly escaping from himself, of overflowing himself, of being surprised by riches which are always unexpected. (TE: 98–9)

I want to emphasize especially the conclusion of this passage, with its imagery of escape and overflow. These images anticipate the later rejection of the principle of identity in defining the for-itself. As non-self-coinciding, human existence is inherently paradoxical, as can be seen in many of Sartre's formulations, for example when he says that a human being is "a being which is what it is not and which is not what it is" (BN: 107), and, writing in the first-person, "I am the self which I will be, in the mode of not being it" (BN: 68). These formulations, built on ideas in *The Transcendence of the Ego*, but not fully formed until *Being and Nothingness*, in turn underwrite Sartre's claim that in the case of human beings, "existence precedes essence" (see BN: 438, 439, 480), which would become the defining slogan of Sartre's existentialism (see HE: 34).

There is a further anticipatory element of the above passage, along with the imagery of escape and overflow, and that is Sartre's suggestion that these images are "distressing". The inherent paradoxicality of human existence means that human beings are ineliminably prone to anguish. Because human existence is unsettled, it is therefore also unsettling. Here we see an echo of Heidegger's earlier ideas about Dasein; as a being whose "being is an issue", and so a being whose being always involves a "not-yet", anxiety is a standing possibility. There is a further echo of Heidegger in Sartre's view. Just as Dasein devises strategies to evade the threat of anxiety and its revelation of the ineliminable "not-yet", so too do human beings on Sartre's account often strive to cover over this unhappy fact about our manner of existence. Rather than inauthenticity, Sartre writes instead of "bad faith". The idea of bad faith is again foreshadowed by Sartre's earlier account of the ego, which manifests

---

Existentialism

The term "existentialism" (actually its French equivalent) was coined by Marcel, who applied it to the thought of Sartre and de Beauvoir. Sartre at first rejected the label, claiming not to know what it meant. Shortly thereafter, in his *The Humanism of Existentialism*, Sartre happily applied the term both to his own view and to those of others before him, including Heidegger, despite the roughly two-decade lag between the appearance of *Being and Time* and Marcel's neologism. The term has come to be associated not just with Heidegger, but also other earlier twentieth-century figures such as Karl Jaspers (whose "*Existenzphilosophie*" was no doubt a source of inspiration for Marcel's coinage) and Martin Buber, and nineteenth-century figures such as Friedrich Nietzsche and Søren Kierkegaard. Various of Sartre's contemporaries were also labelled as existentialist thinkers, including Merleau-Ponty and Albert Camus. For Sartre, the defining commitments of existentialism are first that, in the case of human beings, "existence precedes essence", and secondly, that "subjectivity must be the starting point". What these two statements indicate is existentialism's concern with the special character of human existence, as something irreducibly subjective and so incapable of being fully appreciated or explained from an objective point of view. For the existentialist, this concern is not merely of theoretical importance, but carries practical significance as well. A genuinely human life can only be lived in the recognition of this insight about human existence; at the same time, the existentialist worries that we all too often lose or efface our freedom, and live out our lives afflicted instead with "despair" (Kierkegaard), as members of "the herd" (Nietzsche), as mired in "inauthenticity" (Heidegger), or in "bad faith" (Sartre).

---

itself to consciousness both as a transcendent object and as the source of consciousness. Consciousness is thus lured to identify with this ego, and the various, futile quests to experience and know this self indicate consciousness's struggle to achieve a kind of fixity or stasis. Writing in the Conclusion of *The Transcendence of the Ego*, Sartre characterizes a possible relation between consciousness and the ego that anticipates one of the patterns characteristic of bad faith:

> Everything happens, therefore, as if consciousness constituted the ego as a false representation of itself, as if consciousness hypnotized itself before this ego which it has constituted, absorbing itself in the ego as if to make the ego its guardian and its law. (TE: 101)

Sartre's appeals in this passage to false representation, hypnosis and absorption indicate attempts by consciousness to evade its own nothingness: to quell the anguish inherent to it. Bad faith, as Sartre comes to conceive of these attempts in *Being and Nothingness*, shares in this imagery, but the structure of bad faith is more complex than his earlier formulations, owing to his more comprehensive departure from Husserlian phenomenology. In particular, at the start of Part I of *Being and Nothingness*, Sartre disavows the phenomenological reduction as the appropriate starting-point for a phenomenological ontology. Any attempt to purify or isolate consciousness, or being-for-itself, rigorously quarantined from being-in-itself, is a species of abstraction, and Sartre suggests that one will be unable to bring the for-itself and the in-itself back together again once abstracted; like Humpty Dumpty after his fall, these two regions of being will be irreparably broken apart. (If Sartre is correct here, the conclusion is devastating for Husserl's transcendental project, which seeks to answer the question of how it is possible for consciousness to "reach" or "contact" an object. Sartre likens a Husserlian conception of conscious states to "flies bumping their noses on the window without being able to clear the glass" (BN: 153).) Instead, phenomenology must proceed "concretely", by investigating human existence as it plays out in the world. Sartre's account of the origins of nothingness illustrates this concrete method, as he moves seamlessly between aspects of objective reality and various, more subjective ways of apprehending reality, showing how the two are ultimately intertwined (no *negatités* without human existence, but no human existence without a world as a locus for its "conducts"). Human existence is not purely a matter of being-for-itself, but nor can it be reduced to being-in-itself (as, for example, various scientifically informed versions of materialism might have it). Human existence is a blend of the two, a combination of what Sartre calls "facticity" and "transcendence". Facticity refers to the ways in which human existence always has some measure of objective determination and accumulated history, and "transcendence" registers the ways in which human existence is always not fully determined, and so "ahead of itself". (The terminology, read in close proximity to our discussion of Sartre's earlier work, is apt to be confusing, since the sense of "transcendence" here must not be conflated with his prior talk of the ego's transcendence. Whereas it formerly marked the ego's being transcendent to consciousness, an object appearing in it, but as outside of it, "transcendence" now registers the idea that consciousness is always outside itself, surpassing any momentary determination.) That human existence has this combinatorial structure again signals its paradoxical nature. Bad faith, as a strategy to quell this sense of paradox and its attending feeling of anguish, can move in either direction. Whereas in *The Transcendence of the Ego*, the forerunner of bad faith was a matter of consciousness striving for the fixity and determination tantalizingly offered by the manifestation of the ego, in *Being and Nothingness*, human existence can, through bad faith, strive either to be more object-like or to deny its objectivity altogether, that is, I can be in bad faith by regarding myself as pure facticity or as pure transcendence. As we shall see shortly, this last formulation is misleading, since talk of "regarding myself" in one way or another sounds too active, as though I explicitly think of myself in one way or another. Bad faith cannot be a matter of explicit thoughts, but rather patterns of activity that manifest this self-understanding.

The combinatorial structure of human existence not only provides the motivation for bad faith, but also serves to explain its possibility. That bad faith requires a special explanation can be seen in Sartre's discussion of self-deception, since "bad faith is a lie to oneself" (BN: 87). Such lies, Sartre cautions, must be carefully distinguished from the kinds of lies we tell to one another. Consider first ordinary deception, or what Sartre calls "cynical consciousness" (*ibid.*). There is nothing particularly mysterious or puzzling about ordinary deception. When I deceive someone else, I keep hidden away from him what I know to be true, usually while endeavouring to get him to believe, or at least maintain his believing, the opposite. As a relation between two or more consciousnesses, it is easy to understand how the truth can remain hidden; that my consciousness and the consciousness of the one I wish to deceive are separate from one another ensures that I shall be able to keep what

I know to be true secreted away, unavailable to the one I wish to deceive (provided, of course, that I am careful and clever, so as not to give myself away or let the truth be discovered).

Self-deception, by contrast, cannot partake of this straightforward model: "Bad faith ... has in appearance the structure of falsehood. Only what changes everything is the fact that in bad faith it is from myself that I am hiding the truth" (BN: 89). Since the deceiver and the one deceived are one and the same consciousness, it is far from clear how anything can both be known by me to be true (which is necessary for me to play the role of the deceiver) and at the same time be kept hidden from me (which is necessary for me to play the role of the deceived). If I know something to be true, then I cannot hide that fact from myself, and if something is hidden from me, then I cannot know it to be true. The very idea of self-deception appears to pull itself apart by involving requirements that cannot be simultaneously met. If self-deception is indeed possible, then we need an account of consciousness and human existence that makes that possibility intelligible.

One way we might try to understand the possibility of self-deception (and so the possibility of bad faith) is by introducing a split or division within consciousness, so as to replicate the structure of ordinary deception; the truth is kept hidden away in one part of the mind, while the opposite is held to be true in the other. In *Being and Nothingness*, Sartre devotes considerable attention to one extremely influential conception of such a split or division, namely, Freud's conception of the mind as involving both consciousness and a more subterranean region, the "unconscious" (see BN: 90–96). Freud's bifurcated model of the mind, together with the mechanism of "repression", would appear to solve the puzzle of self-deception. The deep, dark truth is kept repressed in the region of the unconscious, while consciousness blithely carries on in blissful ignorance of that truth. Despite its allure, however, Sartre finds Freud's model highly unsatisfactory. I will not rehearse the entirety of Sartre's argument here, but the basic idea is that Freud's model, to serve as an explanation of self-deception, ultimately presupposes the idea of bad faith, and so is no explanation at all. That is, Freud's division in the mind runs the danger of treating the mind in terms of the in-itself, as two repositories, one marked "conscious", the other "unconscious", filled with various items (beliefs, wishes, desires, etc.). So conceived, the mind is purely passive, and so cannot be conceived of as doing anything with respect to itself. To avoid this passivity, Freud can, of course, appeal to the activity of repression, and so postulate a censor that stands between the unconscious and consciousness, not allowing the problematic items to leave the unconscious and enter consciousness. But how does the censor "know" which items are problematic? To be problematic, they must be ones that the person whose consciousness it is would find disturbing or disruptive, and so these various, repressed items must be both known to be problematic in order to be repressed and they must, as repressed, remain unknown. As both known and unknown, we find ourselves simply duplicating the paradox of self-deception rather than accounting for it, and that, Sartre thinks, is no explanation at all. In order for someone to succeed in repressing unwanted truths, that person must be in bad faith with respect to himself. Repression thus presupposes, rather than makes intelligible, the possibility of bad faith.

Ultimately, Sartre thinks that what makes bad faith possible is precisely the combinatorial structure of human existence: that human beings are a combination of facticity and transcendence. Because this combination is inherently unstable, human beings are in danger of accentuating one rather than the other combinatorial aspect. Human beings can live, and likewise regard themselves, in predominantly objective terms (e.g. when I become "set in my ways" and think of my patterns and routines as fully determined) or in predominantly transcendent terms (e.g. when I disavow my past entirely, claiming that it has nothing whatsoever to do with me or who I am). In other words, human beings lapse into bad faith whenever they are tempted to assert identity claims with any finality (this is who I am or what I am all about) or to deny that anything serves to identify them. Sartre refers to bad faith as "metastable", by which he means that it is an inherently unstable, effervescent phenomenon, something we slip into and out of at various times and in various moods.

Consider Sartre's most famous example of bad faith: the cafe waiter (see BN: 101–3). Sartre imagines himself sitting at a table, watching the waiter ply his trade. The waiter, Sartre notes, is precise and dutiful in his actions. His gait as he moves from one table to another, the manner in which he carries the tray so as to appear both precarious and secure, the angle of his head as he inclines towards a customer to take an order: all of these would appear to exemplify perfectly the defining patterns of a cafe waiter. They exemplify them, Sartre notes, almost too perfectly, which leads him to conclude that the waiter is playing at being a waiter: treating his occupation as a role that he inhabits rather than something with which he identifies. Now, given the lack of self-coincidence in human existence, there would not appear to be anything especially problematic about the waiter, but Sartre declares that he is in bad faith. The tension in the cafe waiter can be discerned in the oscillation between different senses in which he might assert identity claims with respect to himself. That is, there are various ways in which he might assert, "I am not a cafe waiter", and his manner of comporting himself betrays a conflation of these different senses. In one sense, "I am not a cafe waiter", asserted of himself by the waiter, is perfectly in order, since he is not a waiter in the way that, for example, my coffee cup is a coffee cup; since human beings lack fixed identities, no identity statement is fully true of them. Still, there is something misleading in the waiter's assertion, in the sense that it is less true when asserted by him than by, for example, the grocer down the street: the cafe waiter is a cafe waiter in a way that the grocer is not, in the sense that being a waiter does pick out one of his patterns of activity, and not one of the grocer's. The waiter, by only playing at being a waiter, thus exemplifies this latter sense of "I am not a cafe waiter", thereby denying that being a waiter has anything to do with who he is. He thus denies his facticity, identifying exclusively with his transcendence, and so is in bad faith.

Given the instability and paradoxicality of human existence, one might well wonder how bad faith can be avoided: we are always, it appears, in danger of overemphasizing one rather than the other of our constitutive dimensions. This may be so, but Sartre also claims that "these two aspects of human reality are and ought to be capable of valid coordination" (BN: 98). Whatever this "valid coordination" ultimately looks like, Sartre is clear that the antidote to the deceiving patterns of bad faith is not to be found in notions such as sincerity, honesty and good faith. Indeed, Sartre argues that sincerity is itself a pattern of bad faith, since the admonition to "be who you really are" affirms of human existence precisely the kind of fixity and determination that it lacks. But if good faith is no better than bad, what further possibilities are there?

To answer this last question, we need to consider a further idea that I have until this point omitted from our discussion. Sartre holds that since human beings, as conscious beings, are non-self-coinciding, they are also beings whose mode of existence is freedom. We are, as Sartre famously puts it, "condemned to be free" (HE: 41), precisely because we are not fully determined, and so incapable of being summarized by a standing body of facts. Our anguish and our freedom are bound up with one another (hence the idea that we are *condemned* to freedom). Our existence is something we have to confront and determine through existing, through the choices and decisions that we make. Human beings, Sartre thinks, can always confront their existence in terms of choice, as patterns of activity they can either continue or discontinue projecting into the future.

The idea that human beings are free beings means too that human beings, through their capacity for choice, are always and fully responsible for the shape of their existence, and this idea of responsibility, I would suggest, provides the antidote to bad faith. That is, I avoid bad faith when I actively and openly affirm my full responsibility for everything about my existence (and live accordingly). At first blush this may just sound like another pattern of bad faith, since the notion of "full responsibility" is apt to sound like a variation on "pure transcendence", equally shot through with fantasy and distortion. When I regard myself as fully responsible, however, I do not disown or disavow my facticity; being fully responsible requires recognition of, and responsiveness to, the patterns of activity that have served to define me up until the present. Rather than simply denying those patterns, declaring their irrelevance to who I currently am, in taking responsibility for them, I acknowledge that their continuation is up to me: that I can either project those patterns into the future or choose not to. Doing the latter may not always be easy, and certainly requires more than just deciding not to project them or live in the manner that I have until now. To view such life changes as turning on a momentary decision or declaration would mean lapsing once again into bad faith.

That Sartre's phenomenology ultimately implies the human subject's full responsibility for his or her own existence reveals the overarching ethical dimension of his philosophy. Condemned to be free, conscious beings confront the world in terms of choices and decisions, and so they must evaluate their actions in the light of that freedom. To opt out of the task of evaluation is once more a kind of bad faith, since doing so involves a refusal to own up to the distinctive character of human existence. The task of phenomenology, by contrast, is precisely to combat this refusal: to awaken the for-itself to its own self-responsibility. Although we have not given it much attention, the idea that phenomenology has an ethical dimension is not new with Sartre's conception. *Being and Time* is likewise concerned to awaken Dasein to the possibility of its "authenticity", and even Husserl, despite his often cooler theoretical approach, sees phenomenology as bound up with the attainment of a kind of cognitive and ethical autonomy. Although phenomenology often, if not always, characterizes itself as a purely descriptive enterprise, its descriptions are not without practical significance; indeed, hitting on the right descriptions can be thoroughly transformative, converting us from passive, thing-like beings to lucid, active, fully attentive subjects of experience.

Summary of key points

- Sartre claims, *contra* Husserl, that the ego does not appear in or to consciousness in non-reflective experience.
- The ego appears as a transcendent object in second-degree, reflective consciousness.
- The ego is constituted like other transcendent objects, via adumbrational, incomplete appearances.
- "The ego is *by nature* fugitive", which means that any attempt at self-knowledge is ultimately futile.
- Human existence, as involving consciousness or the for-itself, is the source of nothingness, of whatever negative features reality possesses.
- As involving nothingness and indeterminacy, human existence is prone to anguish.
- To alleviate this anguish, human beings slide into "bad faith", which involves acting either as though who one is was already fixed and determined or as though one's existence was entirely distinct from one's situation and past choices.

four

Merleau-Ponty and the phenomenology of embodiment

Merleau-Ponty: life and works

A close contemporary of Sartre, Maurice Merleau-Ponty was born in 1908, in Rochefort-sur-Mer, France. His early education followed the expected trajectory of an academic: he entered the École Normale Supérieure in 1926, where he studied with the neo-Kantian Léon Brunschvicg and also became acquainted with Sartre and de Beauvoir. In the mid-1930s, after teaching and conducting research under the auspices of a fellowship from the Caisse Nationale de la Recherche Scientifique (CNRS), Merleau-Ponty returned to the École Normale to pursue a doctoral degree. He submitted his preliminary thesis, *The Structure of Behaviour* in 1938, although it was not published until 1942. In this work, Merleau-Ponty developed a critique of then-prevalent conceptions of the conditioned reflex as a purely physiological phenomenon, and he was highly critical as well of behaviourist theories in psychology. The orientation of these criticisms, to the effect that such quasi-mechanical views fail to account for the sense and significance of embodied movements and activity, foreshadowed his more mature phenomenological views.

Following the outbreak of the Second World War, Merleau-Ponty served in the infantry as a lieutenant. He returned to teaching after the demobilization, and began conducting the research that led to the completion of *Phenomenology of Perception*, which was published in 1945. Throughout the 1940s, Merleau-Ponty was closely allied with Sartre and other figures in the emerging existentialist school of thought. He helped Sartre to found and edit *Les Temps modernes* and, like Sartre, he took public positions on social and political issues. As with Sartre, his political views were deeply informed by Marxism. However, political questions, prompted by the Korean War, created a rift between Merleau-Ponty and Sartre, which was made formal in 1953 when Merleau-Ponty resigned from *Les Temps modernes*.

During these politically charged debates and disagreements, Merleau-Ponty's academic career continued onwards and upwards. In 1945, he began teaching at the University of Lyons, where he was appointed Professor in 1948, and in 1952, he was elected to the Chair of Philosophy at the Collège de France, a position previously held by Henri Bergson. His publications following the appearance of *Phenomenology of Perception* include *Humanism and Terror* (1947), *Sense and Non-Sense* (1948), *Adventures of the Dialectic* (1955), *In Praise of Philosophy and Other Essays* (1960) and *The Prose of the World* (1969), the last an unfinished manuscript published subsequent to his untimely death in 1961. At the time of his death, Merleau-Ponty was also at work on a significant extension and revision of his phenomenology. This similarly unfinished manuscript has been published under the title *The Visible and the Invisible*.

In this chapter, we shall concentrate exclusively on *Phenomenology of Perception*, and even here, we shall confine ourselves largely to the Preface, Introduction and Part One of the book (roughly the first 200 pages). *Phenomenology of Perception* constitutes a thorough rethinking of phenomenology and phenomenological method (as we shall see below, Merleau-Ponty holds that such rethinking is essential to the ongoing practice of phenomenology), although there is no doubt that Merleau-Ponty learned a great deal from Husserl, Heidegger and Sartre, as well as Scheler. Perhaps the most striking feature of Merleau-Ponty's phenomenology, in contrast with Husserl, Heidegger and Sartre, is the extent of its engagement with ongoing empirical research in the natural sciences, especially psychology, physiology and linguistics. Merleau-Ponty was deeply influenced by Gestalt psychology (in the 1930s, he attended Aron Gurwitsch's lectures on the subject), especially its emphasis on the holistic structure of experience.

Merleau-Ponty did not, however, slavishly bow to the empirical findings of the day. On the contrary, a great deal of his attention to empirical research is devoted to exposing the unexamined assumptions concerning the nature of experience and the often Procrustean conceptions of perception, embodiment and human activity at work in the way scientists interpret their findings. These assumptions, tensions and

> **Gestalt psychology**
> A prominent feature of Merleau-Ponty's phenomenology is the influence of the Gestalt movement in psychology. The movement, whose leading figures included Max Wertheimer, Wolfgang Köhler and Kurt Koffka, rejected "sensationalist" accounts of perceptual experience – that is, theories that conceive of perception as involving some kind of sensory atoms or sensations as the basic building blocks – in favour of a theory that emphasizes the priority of the meaningful forms inherent in perceptual experience ("*Gestalt*" = configuration). That is, the Gestaltists argued that perceptual experience is organized into meaningful wholes, for example into figure-and-ground, whose significance cannot be understood as the outcome or product of combining simple, less-than-significant sensory atoms. In experience, the whole is prior to the parts and so is more than their sum (indeed, on the Gestalt view, it is only in terms of the whole that one can delineate any significant parts at all).

distortions serve to underline the need for further phenomenological investigation: for what Merleau-Ponty calls "a return to the phenomena". Before examining this return, however, we shall first return briefly to Husserl.

Husserl on embodiment

The issue of the embodied character of experience is one that we have largely bypassed until now. We saw in *The Transcendence of the Ego* that Sartre, in developing an account of non-reflective occurrences of "I", appeals to the body as the "illusory fulfillment" of these occurrences. Although the body "serves as a visible and tangible symbol of the I", it at the same time also "can consummate the total degradation of the concrete I of reflection" (TE: 90). Apart from these brief, rather disparaging remarks, Sartre is more or less silent on the issue of embodiment in this early work. By the time of *Being and Nothingness*, in keeping with his attention to human existence in its "concrete" manifestations, Sartre's conception of the body becomes far more nuanced and complex. Since the for-itself is, at the same time, always an in-itself, that is, since human existence is always a combination of facticity and transcendence, human existence is always embodied existence. Any particular instance of being-for-itself experiences itself as an embodied being, acting in and on the world. (This idea applies equally to Heidegger and his conception of human existence as Dasein. Heidegger, however, is largely silent on the question of the embodied character of Dasein's existence, alluding only in a cryptic and delegatory fashion to the idea that "Dasein's 'bodily nature' hides a whole problematic of its own", which, Heidegger notes, "will not be treated" in *Being and Time* (BT: §23). For the most part, Heidegger never really takes up the problematic anywhere else.) Thus, Sartre will say in *Being and Nothingness* that "being-for-itself must be wholly body and it must be wholly consciousness" (BN: 404). He quickly adds that being-for-itself "can not be *united* with a body" (BN: 404). Talk of a union between consciousness and the body involves a conflation of two different, mutually exclusive manifestations of the body: my body as experienced by me and my body as experienced by others.

In many of Husserl's works published during his lifetime, the experience of one's body and the body's role in the experience of other kinds of objects receives little, if any, attention, and indeed, his endeavours to isolate and describe "pure" or "absolute" consciousness and the pure, non-empirical ego, along with the requisite procedures of the phenomenological reduction, invite imagery of a kind of ghostly, disembodied field or realm of consciousness. This imagery is further encouraged by Husserl's own characterizations of his investigations as being conducted in the spirit of Descartes (e.g. his work of 1929, titled *Cartesian Meditations*). Descartes, after all, is the author of Cartesian dualism, which conceives of the mind and the body as two distinct, mutually exclusive substances, each of which is capable of existing independently of the other (this is part of what it means to think of each of them as substances). In the Sixth Meditation, as part of the central argument for this separation between mind and body, Descartes claims that he is able "clearly and distinctly" to conceive of himself existing exclusively as a "thinking thing", entirely apart from his body (likewise, he is able to conceive of his body existing entirely apart from his mind). Although Descartes also holds that the mind and body do in fact exist in a state of "substantial union", joined together and capable of mutually affecting one another, their ontological separation remains a cornerstone of his overall view.

Despite his invocations of Descartes and Cartesianism, Husserl does not partake of Descartes's ontological dualism. Indeed, when Husserl does address the issue of embodiment and the bodily character of experience, his conclusions run directly counter to the claims that motivate Descartes's view, namely, the claims concerning the conceivability of the distinction between mind and body. Husserl's most highly developed treatment of the body appears in the second volume of *Ideas*, which was not published during his lifetime. Attention to this work dispels entirely the ghostly image of consciousness that his characterization of the phenomenological reduction often invites, and serves, moreover, to lay the foundation for Merleau-Ponty's later investigations. Merleau-Ponty made a close study of *Ideas* II, when it was still in its unpublished, archival form, and its influence may be discerned in his own *Phenomenology of Perception*. A brief sketch of some of the main theses on the body from this work will help to both give a more developed picture of Husserlian phenomenology and prepare the way for an account of Merleau-Ponty's phenomenology of embodied experience.

Husserl's account of the body in *Ideas* II is oriented around two principal claims:

(a) The body is something that appears in experience as a categorically distinct kind of thing.
(b) The body and bodily self-experience play an essential role with respect to the possibility of different forms of intentionality, that is, to the possibility of experience that is of or about objects other than the body itself.

Let us, as Husserl does, explore claim (b) first. The claim that the body plays an essential role with respect to different forms of intentionality should be understood as a constitutional claim: the constitution in experience of various kinds of objects involves the body. By "involves", Husserl does not mean to be asserting a claim about physiology; he is not making a claim about whatever causal mechanisms are at work in the body that may be productive with respect to various forms of experience. Rather "involves" should also be understood phenomenologically. In order to have experiences that are of or about various kinds of objects, I must experience myself as embodied, as having a body. (In keeping with the strictures of the phenomenological reduction, this latter claim can be true even when I do not "in fact" have a body.)

The objects Husserl has in mind are material, spatiotemporal objects: ordinary things such as rocks and trees, tables and chairs. Thus, his claim is that in order to have experience that is of or about material, spatiotemporal objects, one must experience oneself as embodied. Most broadly, Husserl claims: "The Body is, in the first place, the *medium of all perception*; it is the *organ of perception* and is *necessarily* involved in all perception" (*Ideas* II: §18). To begin to explicate this claim, we must begin with a remark about terminology, since the use of the upper-case for "Body" records an important distinction. In German, all nouns are capitalized, but the translation's use of the capital "B" signals that the

German word being translated is *Leib*, whereas "body" with a lower-case "b" translates *Körper*. The latter term, etymologically related to the English word "corpse", signifies the body understood in material terms, as a physical object of a particular kind, whereas *Leib* specifies the living body and, in the phenomenological context, the experienced body or body-as-lived. As noted in (a) above, one of Husserl's principal points (and one that carries over to Merleau-Ponty) is that the body is not experienced as just one more material object among others, but rather is manifest in a categorically distinct manner. (In the remainder of this section, my citations of passages will preserve this distinction, but I will not myself use it.)

To return to Husserl's broadest claim, that the body is the "medium" and "organ" of perception seems reasonably clear, since many of the most basic descriptions of our perceptual experience involve reference to our bodily existence. We say, for example, that we see with our eyes, hear with our ears, touch and feel with our hands, and so on, and these references in turn refer to the body more generally: eyes and ears are located on the head, hands at the ends of the arms and so on. Although the references to the body in these basic descriptions appear important, in what sense do they refer to the body *necessarily*, as Husserl claims? After all, it would seem that we could imagine perceptual experience, especially visual and auditory experience, that was not in fact mediated by the body, for example in dream-experience or, more drastically, in the machinations of Descartes's "evil demon". Furthermore, does not Husserl's own practice of the phenomenological reduction teach us to "bracket" or "parenthesize" our empirical existence, which would include our existence as embodied beings? Even if we remain within the perspective of the phenomenological reduction, we must still remain faithful to the contours of our experience as experienced, and so even if we bracket the actual existence of our material bodies, our perceptual experience still refers to our bodies just as much as it refers to the various objects perceived (and commitment to the actual existence of the latter has also, of course, been suspended). Moreover, even if we indulge in the more fantastical scenarios of deception, Husserl would claim that a careful explication of our perceptual experience in these scenarios still involves an essential reference to the body, in so far as that experience presents material, spatiotemporal objects.

To get a feel for this, recall what Husserl regards as another essential dimension of the perceptual experience of material objects, namely that it is always perspectival in nature: I always see the rock from one side or other, from one angle or another, at a particular distance and so on.

My perceptual experience of the rock is always oriented, even when I just imagine seeing the rock in my "mind's eye", and the body, Husserl claims, plays an essential role here as what he calls the "zero-point of orientation" (*Ideas* II: §18). That is, the body serves as the reference point that, in conjunction with the location of the object, determines the way in which the object will be perceived. I see this side of the rock because it is the side facing me (my eyes/face/body); it takes up this much of my visual field because it is such and such distance from me (my eyes/face/body). Indeed, if we consider the metrical character of our perceptual experience, that is, that things are manifest as "here" or "there", as "near" or "far", "up" and "down", to the "right" or "left" and so on, all of these locutions presuppose our being located and oriented with respect to the things that are so manifest. Being located and oriented in turn presupposes our bodily inhabitation of the space we experience. If we had no location in the space we perceive, then things would not show up with any perspectival orientation. At the same time, many of these metrical–spatial locutions do not properly apply with respect to our experience of our own bodies. I am neither near nor far from my own body, nor is my body ever anywhere but where I am; that is why Husserl refers to the body as the *zero*-point of orientation.

Further attention to the perspectival, adumbrational character of perceptual experience will implicate the body to an even greater degree. Consider the adumbrational visual presentation of a table. When I see the table, I see it from one side, and from one angle. However, the table is also manifest to me as viewable from other angles and as having other sides to be seen, such that if I were to turn my head, I would see the table from a slightly different angle, and if I were to walk to another place in the room, I would see the side of the table now hidden from me. Embedded in our perceptual experience is an elaborate network of conditionals that record possible, but not currently actual, perceptual experiences: if I turn my head, then I will see the corner of the table; if I reach out my hand, then I will feel the surface of the table; if I lean in closer, then I will smell the lemon oil I used to clean it yesterday. These conditionals, which Husserl calls relations of "motivation", are essential to our experience being of or about material objects. Without these conditionals our experience would not present things with any kind of density, as having sides and aspects to be further explored, and these conditionals refer essentially to our bodies. Two things should be noted here, however. First, Husserl's appeal to these conditionals cannot constitute a complete or sufficient account of the constitution of material objects, since it is perfectly compatible with such conditionals that the "hidden sides" only come into existence when I actually move to observe them. Secondly, this view is not Merleau-Ponty's, since conceiving of the "motivated" character of perception as involving, however implicitly, such conditionals means conceiving of perception as involving, again however implicitly, something having the form of *judgements*. As we shall see, such a view is emphatically rejected by Merleau-Ponty.

The body (or Body) not only plays an essential role with respect to the constitution of other categories of objects, but is itself constituted in experience as a categorically distinct kind of entity. Such an idea is already implicit in the role played by the body in the constitution of the experience of other things, for example, in the body's being manifest as the zero-point of orientation and as the locus of kinaesthetic motivations in motivated–motivating conditionals. But even these characterizations of the body are not sufficient for fully capturing its distinctive place in experience, as indicated by Husserl's provocative claim that a "*subject whose only sense was the sense of vision could not at all have an appearing Body*" (*Ideas* II: §37). Although such a subject might have kinaesthetic motivations, and so see itself as in some way connected to, or bound up with, one material object, this subject would nonetheless lack kinaesthetic sensations. For example, this subject may apprehend the movement of "his" arm visually, by seeing the movement follow in accord with his willing that it move, but he would not feel the movement of his arm. If, on moving this arm, it were to collide abruptly with an obstacle, our imagined subject could also take note of this if he happened still to be looking at this arm, but he would not feel any pain in his arm, nor any sensation of resistance in the face of this obstacle.

Without these kinds of tactile sensations, the subject would think of his arm as, at most, a special kind of instrument, one over which he had a special and exclusive form of control, but he would not think of it as a part of him. His body would still not be a lived-body: "Obviously, the Body is also to be seen just like any other thing, but it becomes a *Body* only by incorporating tactile sensations, pain sensations, etc. – in short, by the localization of these sensations as sensations" (*Ideas* II: §37). Visual experience lacks this kind of "localization". Although I do see with my eyes and so see that location on my body as bound up with my experience of seeing (e.g. I know that if I put my hand over my eyes, I will not be able to see any longer), still I do not locate the experience in or on my eyes. Visual experience presents me with a world "out there", beyond the boundaries of my body (as well as those boundaries themselves, to some degree), and although that experience is oriented with respect to my eyes, it is not experienced as happening there. The sense of touch, by contrast, is localized; I experience touch sensations only when things come in contact with my body and I experience the sensations at the points where I am touched (no such contact is required for visual experience). A lived-body is a "localized field of sensations", not merely a causal conduit of sensations, but the place in and on which those sensations occur. Within the domain of tactile sensations, Husserl places special emphasis on the phenomenon of "double-touch", which signifies the fact that the body is something that both touches things, that is, has localized tactile sensations, and can itself be touched. If I place my right hand on my left arm, I have both the sensation of being touched on my left arm and sensations of touching an object on the inside of my right hand.

The "double constitution" of the lived-body, as something that touches and is touched, establishes both its materiality and its categorical distinctiveness with respect to material objects in general. According to Husserl, the body is not just a material object that I, this ego, have; nor is it something to which I am attached and that causes me to have various experiences. Instead, the lived-body is thoroughly intertwined with my existence as a conscious being, as Husserl makes clear in the following emphatically anti-Cartesian passage:

> To say that this Ego, or the soul, "has" a Body does not merely mean that there exists a physical–material thing which would, through its material processes, present real preconditions for "conscious events" or even, conversely, that in its processes there occur dependencies on conscious events within a "stream of consciousness" …. Soul and psychic Ego "have" a Body; there exists a material thing, of a certain nature, which is not merely a material thing but is a Body, i.e., a material thing which, as localization field for sensations and for stirrings of feelings, as complex of sense organs, and as phenomenal partner and counterpart of all perceptions of things … makes up a fundamental component of the real givenness of the soul and the Ego. (*Ideas* II: §40)

Many of these key ideas in Husserl's phenomenology of embodied experience find their way into Merleau-Ponty's later *Phenomenology of Perception*. The opening pages of Part One, Chapter 2 ("The Experience of the Body and Classical Psychology") recapitulate to a considerable degree Husserl's claims considering the categorical distinctiveness of the body in relation to material objects in general. Merleau-Ponty calls attention to the "permanent presence" of the body in our perceptual experience, sharply distinguishing it from the "*de facto* permanence of certain objects, or the organ compared to a tool which is always available" (PP: 91). The permanence of the body is not *de facto*, but instead is absolute: "The body therefore is not one more among external objects, with the peculiarity of always being there. If it is permanent, the permanence is absolute and is the ground for the relative permanence of disappearing objects, real objects" (PP: 92).

Merleau-Ponty's appeal to the body as the "ground" for the appearance of other objects echoes Husserl's claim that the body serves as the "zero-point of orientation", and so allows for the possibility of having a perspective on the world at all. As such, the body is not itself just one more object revealed within that perspective. Although Merleau-Ponty clearly learned from Husserl and was inspired by him, *Phenomenology of Perception* is no mere appropriation or duplication of Husserl's prior insights and discoveries. Whatever traces of Husserl's phenomenology there are to be found in *Phenomenology of Perception* are located within an original and distinctive conception of phenomenology. To that conception we now turn.

Merleau-Ponty's "return to the phenomena"

The preface to *Phenomenology of Perception* begins with Merleau-Ponty raising anew the question of what phenomenology is. Given its relatively late placement in the phenomenological tradition, subsequent not only to Husserl, but also to Heidegger's *Being and Time* and Sartre's *Being and Nothingness*, beginning with such a question is jarring, to say the least. After all, should we not know by the time of *Phenomenology of Perception* what phenomenology is, how it is done and what it might achieve? Certainly, there have been disagreements and debates, modifications and departures, changes in both methods and conclusions, but does that render the very idea of phenomenology opaque or otherwise open to question? As his subsequent discussion reveals, Merleau-Ponty is well aware of the oddness of his initial question, and he both anticipates and welcomes its unsettling effect. By returning to the question of what phenomenology is, he hopes thereby to initiate a return to the phenomena themselves, and so to reawaken in us a sense both of phenomenology's subject matter and its significance. The idea of "returning" to the phenomena, of "reawakening" our sensitivity to them, pervades the work as a whole. Merleau-Ponty repeatedly depicts his project as one of recovery and recollection; here are some examples:

> We must begin by reawakening the basic experience of the world. (PP: viii)

> To return to the things themselves is to return to that world which precedes knowledge. (PP: ix)

> We must rediscover, as anterior to the ideas of subject and object, the fact of my subjectivity and the nascent object, that primordial layer at which both things and ideas come into being. (PP: 219)

These imperatives of rediscovery, reawakening and returning are bound up with Merleau-Ponty's raising anew the question of just what phenomenology is, since his conception of phenomenology and his call to "return" to the phenomena are bound together. Phenomenology both facilitates that return and records the results. Indeed, the idea of returning, of having one's attention brought back to something now overlooked, is inherent in the very idea of phenomenology and serves as its founding impulse, especially if we consider Husserl's primary procedure: the phenomenological reduction. As Heidegger notes in his *Basic Problems of Phenomenology* lectures, "reduction" owes its etymology to the combination of "*re-*" (back or again) and "*ducere*" (to lead), so that in the performance of the reduction, one is led back to something unavailable from, or obscured by, a non-phenomenological perspective (see BP: 21). Such an idea is also implicit in Husserl's talk of phenomenology's subject matter as "invisible to the naturally oriented points of view", especially when we consider the role of that subject matter with respect to the possibility of precisely those "naturally oriented points of view" (SW: 10). The subject matter of phenomenology is something that precedes and makes possible points of view from which it is no longer readily visible or accessible. Phenomenology has thus throughout been concerned with returning, reawakening and rediscovering, and so Merleau-Ponty's opening question can be read as a reflexive application of that concern; the practice of phenomenology demands a willingness to reopen the question of the nature of phenomenology itself, and so *Phenomenology of Perception* itself opens with just such a reopening.

As Merleau-Ponty envisages phenomenology, its task is purely descriptive, which means that phenomenology in no way engages in speculation; nor does it seek to construct explanations of any sort. In this way, phenomenology is radically distinct from the natural sciences. Not only is phenomenology distinct from the natural sciences, but it has a kind of priority with respect to them, since what phenomenology seeks to describe is our perceptual, embodied experience of the world that makes the natural sciences possible. As we saw with Husserl, the natural sciences are an outgrowth of the natural attitude more generally, which takes for granted an objective world, replete with a variety of material entities and causal relations. What the natural attitude, and so the natural sciences, overlooks are the origins of that conception of the world in experience, and for Merleau-Ponty phenomenology's task is to "return" to those origins: to describe our "pre-objective" perceptual experience that precedes and makes possible an objective conception of the world. In keeping with his sense of the priority relations between them, Merleau-Ponty marks the distinction between phenomenology and its domain (pre-objective perceptual experience) and the natural sciences and their domain (the objective world) as one between first-order and second-order expression, respectively.

To return to the phenomena, to "reveal a 'primary layer' of sense experience" (PP: 227), requires the performance of the phenomenological reduction, again to be understood as having one's attention "led back" to the perceptual origins of our conception of the world. For Merleau-Ponty, what is "put out of play" or bracketed is the objective conception of the world: of the world understood as a completed, determinate and ready-made realm of objects and relations. Merleau-Ponty's insistence on recovering the point of view of conscious experience should not be understood as a retreat into the sphere of "pure consciousness", to experience had by a pure ego that serves as the condition of the possibility of experience. A sphere of pure consciousness, with its sense-constituting processes, is as descriptively inadequate as the perspective on experience afforded by the natural sciences, which conceive of perception as the outcome or end-product of a causal, mechanical process. For Merleau-Ponty, the subject of experience is never in the first instance cut off or detached from the world, and the world it finds itself within is neither the fully determinate, objective world of the natural sciences, nor a product of various subterranean conscious processes, such as synthesis: "When I return to myself from an excursion into the realm of dogmatic common sense or of science, I find, not a source of intrinsic truth, but a subject destined to the world" (PP: xi). That we are, as subjects of experience, "destined to the world" explains why Merleau-Ponty says, regarding Husserl, that "the most important lesson the reduction teaches us is the impossibility of a complete reduction" (PP: xiv). The return to perceptual experience never effaces the worldly character of our existence, nor does it sever the "intentional threads" linking us to a surrounding world.

Merleau-Ponty's phenomenology proceeds under a banner reading "I am open to the world" (PP: xvii), and the task of phenomenology is to recover and preserve this sense of openness, without falsifying it by smuggling in explanatory hypotheses or a conception of things formed at the level of second-order expression. Carrying out this task is difficult, precisely because of the power and pervasiveness of our second-order conception(s) of the world. There is an overwhelming temptation to "read back" features of our second-order conception into accounts of perceptual experience, thereby obscuring the founding role of perceptual experience in the formation of that conception. Just as, for Husserl, the tendency of the natural attitude is to focus on the things experienced rather than the experience of things, for Merleau-Ponty there is a constant tendency to use the results of experience to account for that experience. Doing so cannot but distort the nature of experience, since it involves using a determinate, objective conception of the world to characterize and explain experience, which is pre-objective (but not therefore wholly subjective) and, in important ways to be spelled out, indeterminate.

Overcoming traditional prejudices I: empiricism and the integrity of perception

Consider the following passage, from a central text in the classical empiricist tradition:

By sight I have the ideas of light and colors, with their several degrees and variations. By touch I perceive, for example, hard and soft, heat and cold, motion and resistance, and all these more or less either as to quantity or degree. Smelling furnishes me with odors, the palate with tastes, and hearing conveys sounds to the mind in all their variety of tone and composition. And as several of these are observed to accompany each other, they come to be marked by one name, and so to be reputed as one thing. Thus, for example, a certain color, taste, smell, figure, and consistence having been observed to go together, are accounted one distinct thing signified by the name "*apple*"; other collections of ideas constitute a stone, a tree, a book, and

the like sensible things – which as they are pleasing or disa-
greeable excite the passions of love, hatred, joy, grief, and so
forth.   (Berkeley [1710] 1957: §1)

This passage, although brief, incorporates a very particular theory of
perception that, with various modifications and adjustments, still enjoys
some currency even today. That is, Berkeley's theory of perception can
very easily be "physicalized", which involves replacing his now-antiquated
talk of various kinds of "ideas" with a variety of physical stimuli. Recall,
for example, the passage quoted in the Introduction from W. V. Quine,
a major figure in twentieth-century empiricism, who characterizes his
perceptual experience in terms of light rays striking his retinas and molecules bombarding his eardrums and fingertips. Quine's conception of
perception inherits the most important features of Berkeley's classical
picture, while making it perhaps more scientifically respectable.

This picture of perception, whether in Berkeley's classical, or Quine's
more modern, idiom, involves four main ideas that should be delineated and considered at greater length, as all of these ideas are ones that
Merleau-Ponty opposes:

- Perception involves the receipt or recording of some kind of
  simple sensory units or atoms, for example, ideas of light and
  colour, simple sensations, retinal stimuli, that are in some way
  less than the things we typically say we see, such as apples, tables
  or chairs. These simple sensory units are both qualitatively and
  quantitatively independent of one another.
- Each sensory faculty or modality serves as an independent "chan-
  nel" of such sensory units – the faculty of sight records ideas of light
  and colour, the faculty of touch ideas of hardness and resistance
  and so on – such that what I see is not literally the same thing that
  I touch.
- The perception of the things we typically say we see, hear, smell,
  touch and taste, for example, apples, tables and chairs, is as an
  outcome, product or result of the reception and combining of the
  more basic units of experience. Our perception of ordinary things
  is a matter of our having "observed" that these sensory units "go
  together" or "accompany" one another, and so we "account them
  one distinct thing", such as *an* apple, *a* table and so on.
- Affective, emotional qualities are further additions to, or continuations of, perceptual experience proper that are "excited by"
  perceptual experience but not a part of it.

Now, the first point against this empiricist picture of perception is that our immediate experience does not involve an awareness of any such individual sensory units. Consider visual experience. Here, we do not have, in the first instance, pure sensations of light and colour, but instead we see, and say we see, things, and we do not even see things in isolation, but instead see them within a scene and so against a background. I see, for example, my red-and-white coffee cup, not sensations of red and white, and I see the cup on my desk, so that the surface of the desk and various other things on the desk serve as the backdrop. Merleau-Ponty contends that "the perceptual 'something' is always in the middle of something else, it always forms part of a 'field'" (PP: 4), and this is so even when we are looking only at a bare patch of colour. The most basic description of the most basic perceptual experience involves the ideas of both figure and ground.

This first point is nothing like a knock-down objection to empiricism, since empiricism claims to be offering a theory of perception, which gives the building blocks of perceptual experience. Of course, when we perceive, these building blocks are already, as it were, built up into something more complex (all of the "accounting" Berkeley speaks of has already been done); nonetheless, empiricism claims that careful analysis will show that there are these building blocks, indeed there must be given the separation among the various sensory "inputs". Although this move deflects the initial objection, it should already appear rather strained as a defence of empiricism, since it appeals to unperceived elements of perception, that is, units of perception to which there corresponds no moment of awareness in the act of perceiving. But even leaving this worry aside, Merleau-Ponty's principal claim is that empiricism is not merely descriptively inadequate (although that is a big problem if one is doing phenomenology!), but, more strongly, that its descriptive inadequacies make it theoretically unsalvageable. That is, his claim is that if one were to start with such atomistic building blocks, such simple sensations, ideas or stimuli, then one can never recover ordinary experience, since the latter contains features that are not reducible to empiricism's sensory building blocks and whatever relations are possible among them. In other words, if empiricism were correct about the basic building blocks of perceptual experience, then the kind of perceptual experience we do in fact enjoy would be impossible.

To begin to see this, consider again Merleau-Ponty's contention that even the simplest form of visual experience involves the notions of figure and ground. Even seeing a simple shape or a bare patch of colour involves seeing it against a background from which it is separated. Again, "the perceptual 'something' is always in the middle of something else, it always forms part of a 'field'", as in the following picture:

When we look at this picture, we perceive a particular shape, a dark triangle, against a lighter background. We do not first experience a number (how many?) of independent sensations, darker ones and lighter ones, that then get grouped together. Not only do we not experience the picture in this way, we could not, since we would then be unable to account for how they combine to make up this picture. To see this, consider how the various features of the picture are related to one another: the dark triangle stands out from the background; the triangle has edges that clearly delineate it and separate it from what surrounds it; the edges belong to the shape, not to the background, as does all of the dark area the edges enclose. To perceive the picture as a dark triangle on a white background involves seeing the dark triangle as on the background, so that the white is seen as running underneath the triangle, much as I see the surface of my desk spreading under the coffee cup resting on it. (There are other ways of seeing the picture, for example as a white surface with a triangular hole cut out of it, and here the relation of figure and ground changes, but without disappearing. That things can be seen in more than one way makes the empiricist's project even more challenging.)

The problem for the empiricist is one of accounting for these features of the picture. That is, the empiricist must explain how all of the independent sensory atoms are grouped together in just this way. How, for example, does the empiricist account for the idea of all the dark area belonging together? Why are the edges of the figure not seen as belonging to the surrounding white, rather than to the darker area within? Clearly the edges are seen as so belonging, but what is mysterious on the empiricist account is how this comes about. The notion of the lighter sensory elements forming a background is even more mysterious, since the sense of the background as continuing behind the figure is one for which, necessarily, no sensory atoms can be adduced: such atoms, lying behind the figure, would be unsensed and so could not play a role in the construction of the perceptual experience. If we look again at the passage from Berkeley, we find that "ideas" are "observed to go together" and that they "accompany" one another, and we might try to use these notions to account for our perception of the picture. The dark elements of the picture have been observed to "go together", as do the lighter elements, and that is why we see the picture as a dark figure on a lighter background. But what are we to make of this talk of the elements "having been observed to go together"? It should be clear that this appeal is circular, since to have made such an observation is already to have seen the picture as a darker figure on a lighter background, and the empiricist owes us an account of how this observation comes about, and so how this grouping is made in the particular way it is. Equally circular are any appeals by the empiricist to memory in accounting for the grouping of sensations in a particular way. To say, with respect to a particular experience, that the arrangement is due to the memory of things having been experienced in accord with that arrangement, only pushes further back the problem of explaining the basic idea of experiencing sensations in an arrangement.

To avoid the charge of circularity, the empiricist needs a mechanism that is sensitive to possible relations among independent sensory atoms that do not presuppose the outcome of the mechanism's workings. The empiricist might appeal, for example, to relations of spatial proximity: all of the darker sensory atoms are closer to one another than to any lighter sensory atoms, and so they are grouped together and separated from the lighter ones. Such an appeal to spatial proximity is problematic, and in more than one way. First of all, the claim is simply false, since there are points on the triangle that are equally close to points on the background as to other points on the triangle, namely, along the edges, which, again, belong to the figure, not to the background. But even if the claim were true, it would be insufficient to explain the mechanism's working as it does, since there are many cases where things are perceived as separated from one another despite spatial proximity. That is, parts of what is perceived will not be grouped together despite being spatially closer than they are to the parts with which they are grouped.

At this point, the empiricist might try another relation: all of the black elements are grouped together because they are more similar to one another than they are to any other sensory atoms making up the perception of the picture. Again, this relation is insufficient to account for the experience of the picture, and again for more than one reason. First, similarity is an exceedingly vague relation, and so the empiricist owes us some kind of "similarity metric" in order to account for the mechanism's operation. Moreover, even if we allow the empiricist his notion of similarity, it seems open to counter-example. Consider a second relatively simple picture:

Here, there are dark and light elements making up the figure, which again rests on a lighter background. The light features of the figure are at least as similar to the background as they are to the darker features of the figure (and certainly much more similar with respect to shade), and yet they are seen as belonging to the figure and not to the background. Just why then the mechanism that groups sensory atoms together has grouped them in just this way is left a mystery. Merleau-Ponty says at one point that "an impression can never by itself be associated with another impression" (PP: 17), which means that no mechanism the empiricist might propose will appear as anything more than arbitrary, or, to the extent that it does, the account will lapse into circularity.

For Merleau-Ponty, the problem thus lies not with the candidate relations so far considered, but with the project of trying to reconstruct perceptual experience using the materials available on the empiricist account. This is so because the various features of the picture are internally related to one another, that is, the features of the picture cannot be described or accounted for independently of one another, whereas sensations or sensory atoms, given their independence, can only be externally related to one another. Merleau-Ponty's contention is that one can never recreate or account for internal relations on the basis of external relations. Consider one of Merleau-Ponty's own examples, which is more realistic than the pictures so far presented: seeing a patch of woolly red carpet (see PP: 4–5). Such an experience cannot be construed as the combination of the sensation of red plus the sensation of woolliness, because the red one perceives would not be this red were it not also woolly (and likewise for the woolliness). The features of the perception infuse and inform one another, and so cannot be treated as autonomous elements, standing only in external relations to one another. Succinctly put, the empiricist ignores what we might call the "integrity of perception", which stresses the priority of the whole over the parts, such that the parts are not independent, antecedently given elements, but are internally connected to each other and to the whole that they make up: "When we come back to phenomena we find, as a basic layer of experience, a whole already pregnant with an irreducible meaning, not sensations with gaps between them" (PP: 21–2).

By ignoring what I am here calling the integrity of perception, empiricism commits two principal errors about perception and perceptual qualities. First, empiricism has a tendency to treat perceptual qualities as elements of consciousness, rather than as elements for consciousness, for example, it treats my perceiving of the red carpet as a matter of my having a red sensation. This first error distorts perception by making it overly subjective, construing it as a series of events taking place within the mind or consciousness (recall Berkeley's talk of "ideas of light and colours"). The second error pulls in the opposite direction, treating perception in overly objective terms. This error involves treating the qualities perceived as fully determinate and developed. Here, the empiricist is looking both to the objects perceived, which are, after all, one way rather than another, as well as the stimulations of the sensory organs, which again are one determinate way. Given these kinds of determinations, the empiricist insists that perceptual experience must itself be determinate. Instead, Merleau-Ponty argues that "we must recognize the indeterminate as a positive phenomenon" (PP: 6), as integral to the very idea of perceptual experience. There is a third error to which empiricism is prone that is closely related to its treatment of perception as fully determinate. This error is what Merleau-Ponty, following the Gestalt psychologist Wolfgang Köhler, calls the "constancy hypothesis", which arises from thinking of perceptual experience as primarily involving the reception of determinate stimuli. The constancy hypothesis maintains that perception, as the outcome of receiving definite and determinate stimuli, reproduces, and co-varies with, those stimuli. That is, constancy of stimuli means constancy of perceptual experience, and a change in stimuli means a corresponding change in perceptual experience.

Consider the following example. Suppose I am looking out at a classroom full of students. Objectively, the class has, say, eighteen students. Suppose further that I am standing in such a way that I can see the whole class at once. According to the constancy hypothesis, my visual experience likewise consists of eighteen students; after all, there *are* eighteen students, and all eighteen students are reproduced or represented on my retinal images. But that need not be the case. If, for example, I am focusing on one student, the rest of my visual field is unfocused and indeterminate, so that the other students form only an indistinct backdrop. Although I am visually aware of some number of students, even "many", it is a mistake to say that there must be a determinate number in my visual field. Or consider a variation on the example. I walk into the classroom and want to know if a particular student is present. Again, I take in the whole class at once, but it takes me a few seconds to register that the student in question is indeed there in the room. During that time my retinal images do not change, and so someone looking at the images might see the student I am looking for reflected along with all the other students all along; yet I do not *see* the student until it registers that she is there, and until it does it sounds strained, to say the least, to insist, because of the constancy of the retinal images, that the student was present in my visual field throughout. If the student were present in my visual field all along, how are we to make sense of my having to find her, of her presence registering only at a particular moment in my experience of perceiving the class? At the same time, it is not the case prior to my registering the student's presence that she was wholly absent from my visual experience. The student was both unseen and, in a sense, there to be seen; prior to my noticing, the student's presence is latent in my visual field, and so registering her presence is a possible development of my visual experience.

There is a final consideration concerning the integrity of perception: empiricism, in construing perception as the reception of stimuli and the possession of sensations, treats perceptual experience as involving independent "channels". That is, on the empiricist account, each perceptual modality or faculty supplies its own separate stream of information, and produces its own fund of sensations in the mind. Berkeley, for example, is willing to follow this idea to its logical conclusion and claim that we do not literally see the same things that we touch, hear, smell and taste, so that a statement such as "I hear the orange bird singing and see its soft feathers" is underwritten by a complex process of combining and correlating independently occurring ideas or sensations. Building on the findings of Gestalt psychology, and in keeping with his idea that perceptual experience involves "a whole already pregnant with an irreducible meaning", Merleau-Ponty sees the internal relations at the heart of the integrity of perception as spanning the different perceptual faculties or modalities. Consider again the example of seeing the woolly red carpet. The woolliness that I perceive visually is manifest *as* woolly in part because of my sense of touch. I see the carpet as woolly because of how woolly carpets feel against my skin. The woolly red carpet, in looking woolly, looks soft and inviting to my touch, even when I am looking at it from a distance. Another example that Merleau-Ponty offers is the way the flame of a candle looks to a child before and after she has been burned by it. The heat and pain felt in the latter case inform the visual experience, so that the flame looks hot and looks painful, and therefore looks different than it did before (see PP: 52). (We can see in these ideas a continuation of Husserl's conception of the horizonal character of experience, since the horizon of any particular perceptual experience will involve other perceptual modalities as well. When I see the chair, part of the horizon of the experience is that I can reach out and run my hand along the arm of it.) The example of the candle shows that the integrity of perception extends beyond the perceptual faculties recognized by empiricism. Not only do the modalities of seeing, hearing, touching, smelling and tasting mutually inform one another, but they are also informed by affective, emotional responses to things. The flame of the candle, which looks painful to the burned child, also looks frightening as well. The flame takes on a menacing, threatening appearance that is part of the child's immediate visual experience, as opposed, say, to merely an associative connection or inference.

Overcoming traditional prejudices II: intellectualism and the role of judgement

The empiricist account of perception as a matter of receiving stimuli and possessing sensations renders experience as something altogether passive and inert: a series of events that arise in a causal, quasi-mechanical fashion. Small wonder, then, that what it countenances as the components of perceptual experience are insufficient to capture perception as it is lived. Indeed, empiricism seems to overlook entirely the fact that perceptual experience is lived by someone who perceives. Perceptual experience is not merely the passive recording of stimuli, a faithful reproduction of the surrounding environment, but an activity, as is signalled, for example, by the many active terms we use in connection with perception. Even if we restrict our attention to visual experience, we find, for example, such active notions as looking, watching, scanning, searching, noticing, finding, attending, investigating, focusing, glancing, peeking, peering, staring, and squinting. The second of the twin "traditional prejudices", which Merleau-Ponty dubs "intellectualism", has the virtue of emphasizing the role of the subject who perceives in the act of perception, and its conception of perception as the achievement of an active subject is one to which Merleau-Ponty is not entirely unsympathetic. At the same time, as his labelling of intellectualism as a "prejudice" indicates, its account of perception remains problematic.

We can get a feel for intellectualism's central commitments if we consider a famous dictum from Kant, one of the principal sources of this traditional prejudice, concerning the idea that perception involves both the faculty of receptivity (by which the mind is passively supplied with what Kant calls "intuitions") and the faculty of spontaneity (by which the mind actively applies concepts to what it passively receives). The dictum reads: "Thoughts without content are empty; intuitions without concepts are blind" (Kant [1781] 1965: 93). Experience, which is not blind, thus involves both a passive or receptive dimension and an active one. The receptive dimension ensures that experience is connected with the empirical world, taking in the world "out there", and the active, conceptual dimension ensures that experience can be a source of knowledge, an often hard-won achievement. Given that perception involves the combination of intuitions and concepts, the picture of perception that emerges out of Kant's famous dictum is that perceptual experience centrally and necessarily involves the notion of *judgement*: all perceptual experience involves judgement, and so to perceive anything at all consists of the making of a judgement with respect to that thing. Perceptual experience, as centrally involving judgement, thus centrally involves the subject who does the judging, thereby making perceptual experience active through and through.

We have seen already one phenomenological account of perception that takes issue with the claim that judgements play a central role in perceptual experience. In his account of the origins of nothingness, Sartre insisted that our perceptual experience always involves a negative element and that these experiences are primarily "pre-judicative". When I perceive Pierre's absence from the cafe, I take that in without forming a judgement to the effect that Pierre is absent. Even the simple experience of perceiving a figure against a background, as involving a field divided into figure and non-figure (or background and non-background), includes negativity, but without there necessarily being any judgement on the part of one who perceives. The formation of a judgement is a secondary affair, according to Sartre: the judgement is built on top of perceptual experience, rather than constitutive of it.

Merleau-Ponty shares Sartre's view that judgement is secondary with respect to perceptual experience, and so agrees that it falsifies the character of perceptual experience to see judgement as an ever-present feature. Consider the case of the Müller–Lyer illusion:

Even once we have determined that the lines enclosed by the arrows are indeed equal, and so on seeing them judge that they are equal, it still remains the case that we see the lines as not being equal. If perception and judgement were equivalent, then the lines should appear equal once we have been informed of the illusion. That the illusion remains in effect indicates a distinction between seeing and judging. We can also see this distinction emerging quite clearly in the case of seeing a schematic cube, such as:

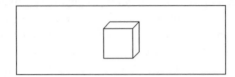

Here we know, and so judge, that this picture is really just nine lines on the paper, a two-dimensional drawing. At the same time, it is extremely difficult actually to see the picture as merely a two-dimensional assemblage of lines. The picture appears immediately and involuntarily as a three-dimensional cube, no matter what judgements, indeed true judgements, we may have formed. Seeing would thus appear to be pre-judicative.

Persistent perceptual illusions are not the only domain where the distinction between perceiving and judging is evident; cases of persistent illusion only help to bring out the distinction in an especially vivid manner. According to Merleau-Ponty, the distinction is quite generally applicable: the "primary layer" of perceptual experience that phenomenology seeks to isolate and describe is, in keeping with its status as pre-objective, pre-judicative through and through. The indeterminacy and incompleteness that are constitutive of perceptual experience signal the secondary role of judgement. When I scan the classroom looking for a particular student, I may, finally, judge explicitly that she is in fact present, but that is only one moment in my perceptual experience; before the judgement, I was seeing the classroom and the students, but my visual experience lacked the kind of determinacy recorded by the eventual judgement. The student I was looking for was both there-to-be-seen and yet not fully present in my visual field. By insisting on the primacy of judgement, the intellectualist effaces these kinds of tensions and indeterminacies in the act of perception, thereby rendering perceptual experience as more frozen and static than it really is and must be. Intellectualism is thus an overreaction to the lifeless, mechanical model offered by the empiricist. As Merleau-Ponty notes, neither view can accommodate the vital character of perceptual experience as it is lived:

In the first case [empiricism] consciousness is too poor, in the second [intellectualism] too rich for any phenomenon to appeal compellingly to it. Empiricism cannot see that we need to know what we are looking for, otherwise we would not be looking for it, and intellectualism fails to see that we need to be ignorant of what we are looking for, or equally again we should not be searching. They are in agreement in that neither can grasp consciousness *in the act of learning*, and that neither attaches due importance to that circumscribed ignorance, that still "empty" but already determinate intention which *is* attention itself. (PP: 28)

Although intellectualism presents itself as, and is in some respects, an antidote to empiricism, correcting the errors and distortions present in the empiricist's conception of perception, part of the problem with the intellectualist position is that it shares too much in common with the empiricist view it claims to reject. Consider again Kant's dictum. That perceptual experience involves, as one of its two components, what Kant calls "intuitions" indicates that the intellectualist retains, and builds on, the empiricist model of perception. As Merleau-Ponty notes: "Judgment is often introduced as *what sensation lacks* to make perception possible" (PP: 32). The problem here is that the introduction of judgement, as making up for what sensation lacks, still shows a commitment to sensations as an ingredient or component of perceptual experience: "Perception becomes an 'interpretation' of the signs that our senses provide in accordance with the bodily stimuli, a 'hypothesis' that the mind evolves to 'explain its impressions to itself'" (PP: 33). By only adding on to the empiricist conception of perception, rather than abandoning it altogether, intellectualism thus inherits the same problems and liabilities inherent in the view it seeks to displace.

The curious case of the phantom limb

Merleau-Ponty's critique of the "traditional prejudices" informing many prevalent (then and now) conceptions of perception in both philosophy and psychology, as well as his insistence on what I have been calling the integrity of perception, opens on to a wider array of phenomena to be described. In particular, what both of the traditional prejudices obscure from view is a proper appreciation of the embodied character of perceptual experience: the integrity of perception is informed by, and founded on, the integrity of bodily self-experience, which neither empiricism nor intellectualism recognizes. We have seen that the empiricist's account of perception treats perception as the endpoint of a causal, mechanical process (the receipt of stimuli, the presence of sensations before the mind), whereas the intellectualist treats perception as a species of judgement. In the case of the empiricist, the body is itself treated as a mechanism, or perhaps an assemblage of mechanisms, causally connected with the surrounding world via the "bombardment" of light rays and molecules, thereby serving as a conduit of sensations. The intellectualist account of perception, bound up as it is with the mental act of judgement, treats the perceiving subject as only accidentally or contingently embodied, with all of the organizing and schematizing work of perceptual experience taking place within the confines of consciousness. Just as the twin prejudices can be shown ultimately to share a picture of perception as involving stimuli or sensations as a key ingredient, so too do the two share a conception of the body as merely one material entity among others, playing only a causal role in the production of perceptual experience. Where they differ is on whether anything more is needed than the workings of such causal mechanisms for there to be perceptual experience. We have already seen how Husserl's phenomenology of embodied experience opens a perspective from which the defects of this underlying conception of the body can be discerned, and Merleau-Ponty continues in this vein, deepening and developing Husserl's insights. Accordingly, Merleau-Ponty's "return to the phenomena", which begins with a description of the integrity of perception, quickly develops into a phenomenology of the body and bodily self-experience.

What a reader new to *Phenomenology of Perception* may find jarring about this development is the amount of attention Merleau-Ponty devotes to the consideration of pathological cases. Part One, which is devoted to the body, opens with a discussion of the phenomenon of phantom limb (along with anosognosia, in which the appendage is still present but "ignored" by the patient), and continues after that with an even longer analysis of a particular case: of a man referred to as Schneider, a brain-damaged veteran of the First World War who has difficulty performing various kinds of movements. I want to look in more detail at these discussions, but it is important first to address the general question of why Merleau-Ponty focuses on these pathological cases, given his desire to "return" to the phenomena of lived experience. After all, most of us do not partake of these pathologies, and so they would not appear to be a fruitful starting-point for understanding non-pathological, "normal" embodied experience. This appearance is misleading, however, and for at least three reasons:

(a) Pathological cases have received considerable attention from theorists and researchers in psychology, physiology and philosophy. Such cases have thus served as the domain in which theoretical, explanatory models of embodied subjectivity have been developed, and which are meant to be applicable more generally, that is, to non-pathological cases as well. How researchers and theorists handle pathological cases is revelatory of their conceptions of ordinary, non-pathological bodily experience, and so their treatment of these cases is a good place to look in developing a critique of their conceptions.

(b) Even leaving aside what researchers and theorists have come up with to explain pathological cases, considering such cases tells us something important about non-pathological experience. By arriving at an adequate account of the pathology in question, one thereby learns something about the corresponding non-pathological mode of experience. For example, if we say that phantom limb involves a patient's continuing to experience the presence of a limb that has been amputated or destroyed, that raises the question of just what it means to experience the presence of a limb.

(c) At one point in the *Phenomenology of Perception*, Merleau-Ponty says that "nothing is more difficult than to know *precisely what we see*" (PP: 58), which signals the difficulty of effecting the desired return to the phenomena. A proper phenomenology of ordinary experience is hard because ordinary experience is transparent to us; we look past our own experience of things, directing our attention instead to the things to which experience affords us access. Pathological cases, by providing a sharp contrast with non-pathological forms of experience, help to delineate the latter forms, making them more vivid and explicit. By inducing in us the thought, "Well, my experience is not like that", pathological cases force on us, and help us to answer, the question of what our experience is like.

With these considerations in mind, let us focus more closely on Merleau-Ponty's treatment of the phenomenon of phantom limb (for the sake of clarity, I shall omit his remarks on the paired case of anosognosia). As mentioned in (ii) above, the most neutral characterization of the phenomenon of phantom limb is that it involves a patient's continuing to experience the presence of a limb that has been amputated. Patients suffering from phantom limb will, for example, report feeling pains and other sensations in the missing limb; moreover, patients will still on occasion act in ways that presuppose the continued presence of the limb, for example getting out of bed or setting out to walk, only to fall to the floor. Merleau-Ponty focuses largely on theories that try to explain or account for the phenomenon of phantom limb. In keeping with his pairing of empiricism and intellectualism, he considers two dominant forms of explanation: physiological explanations (more in keeping with empiricism) and psychological explanations (perhaps more closely allied with intellectualism). Although there are merits to each form of explanation, their inadequacies and mutual antagonisms reveal that neither is sufficient.

Perhaps the more straightforward form of explanation is the physiological model, which accounts for phantom limb largely in terms of the continuation of nervous impulses from the stump remaining after the amputation. These impulses mimic the ones normally received from the limb, and so the patient continues to feel various things as though in the missing limb. There is certainly empirical support for this form of explanation. For example, severing the nerves leading from the stump will effectively discontinue the phenomenon of phantom limb. At the same time, there are problems that arise if one takes the physiological explanation to be complete. For example, phantom limb will often persist even when the stump has been anaesthetized. Furthermore, the phenomenon of phantom limb tends to be suffered by patients only intermittently, rather than continuously, and the occasions when patients suffer bouts of it are often keyed to particular features of the patients' circumstances: the missing limb will be felt when the circumstances of its loss are recalled, or when someone connected with those circumstances is encountered. The role played by such features suggests a psychological form of explanation, as these features serve to remind the patient of his now lost limb. Indeed, it is tempting to describe phantom limb primarily in psychological terms, such that the patient has forgotten the loss of the limb, that he does not remember, or does not want to remember, that the limb is no longer there. In cases of phantom limb, the patient "refuses" his mutilation, represses his knowledge of its absence, as can be seen when the patient continues trying to rise and walk without the aid of crutches or other forms of support. Although these observations lend support to the psychological model, it has a difficult time accommodating the fact that severing the nerves ends the patient's experience of phantom limb.

Given that each form of explanation enjoys some observational and experimental support, it is tempting to seek an explanation that somehow combines the two. Merleau-Ponty contends that such a balancing act is difficult to pull off, since the very form of explanation in each case pulls against the other, making the possibility of a successful combination unlikely. That is, the physiological model ultimately construes phantom limb as the continued representation of the missing limb, occasioned by the continued receipt of nerve impulses, and the psychological model construes the phenomenon as involving the absence, through repression, of a representation of the patient's true condition. In one case, Merleau-Ponty notes, we have the representation of an absence, and in the other, an absence of a representation, and so it is not clear how to combine an absent present with a present absence (see PP: 80).

The underlying problem is that both forms of explanation, physiological and psychological, depict phantom limb, and so the continued experience of a missing limb, as centrally involving the notion of representation, whether present or absent. The patient continues, either through the receipt of the appropriate nervous impulses or via the mechanism of repression, to represent to himself the missing leg and so to represent to himself his body intact, as it was before the loss of the limb. Hence, his continued feelings of pain and his poignant endeavours to engage in activities now rendered more awkward, if not impossible. What is problematic here is that it suggests that even in the normal, non-phantom case, bodily self-experience and bodily knowledge is representational in nature. But if we attend to the ways in which we perform various bodily movements, we will find this not to be the case. For example, when, desiring a cup of coffee, I rise from my desk and head towards the kitchen, I rarely, if ever, give much thought to what my legs are doing. I simply rise from the chair and start walking, without paying much attention to the movements of my legs at all. Indeed, as I think about it and try to picture the exact movements of my legs, I find it quite difficult to do. I cannot say for sure exactly how the series of movements starting with my rising from the chair and ending with my being downstairs in the kitchen look. Thus, it seems implausible, to say the least, to assert that my performing these movements involves my having a representation of them.

Merleau-Ponty says that "the phantom arm is not a representation of the arm, but the ambivalent presence of an arm" (PP: 88). Phantom limb, in other words, involves a kind of clash or conflict between two levels of bodily self-experience: what Merleau-Ponty calls the "habitual body" and the "body at this moment" (see PP: 82). The patient suffering from phantom limb continues to rely on the missing limb, taking its presence for granted in the same thoughtless manner those of us who have all our limbs do. The patient's continued reliance bespeaks the deep-seated character of his or her habitual actions and routines: the repertoire of bodily activities the patient could fluently perform before the loss. These deep-seated habits conflict, however, with the current layout of the patient's body; the habits no longer "mesh" with what the patient is currently capable of doing. Thus, the patient falls when rising from bed or setting out to walk, not because of the presence or absence of a representation but because the shape of the patient's habitual body has not yet conformed to the facts of the situation. (These sorts of clashes are experienced on a smaller scale without the kind of trauma involved in losing a limb: think about what it is like to walk in one's shoes after having spent hours skating, or what it might be like to walk through doorways after having worn an especially tall hat for a considerable length of time. It often takes a while to "catch up" to the body's current layout, so that one will continue to feel slightly elevated, even though the skates have been removed, or one will continue to duck, even though the hat has been put away.)

Rather than a combination of physiological and psychological factors, Merleau-Ponty's description of phantom limb operates at a level prior to these sorts of divisions and dichotomies: bodily self-experience is a dimension of my "being-in-the-world", which resists decomposition into physiological and psychological components. Being-in-the-world instead serves as the foundation for these categorical distinctions: "Man taken as a concrete being is not a psyche joined to an organism, but the movement to and fro of existence which at one time allows itself to take corporeal form and at others moves towards personal acts" (PP: 88).

"I can" and "I think": motor intentionality

Consider, and try performing, the following exercises:

- Say, either aloud or to yourself, how your legs are currently arranged.
- Reach down with your right hand and scratch your right ankle.
- Pretend you are a soldier at attention and make a formal military salute.
- Trace a figure-of-eight in the air with your right index finger.

All of these are likely to be relatively easy exercises to perform, requiring little if anything in the way of effort or deliberation. In particular, the performance of these exercises generally requires little in the way of observation. I can tell, and so tell you, that my legs are crossed right now, without having to confirm this through a visual inspection of my legs. To scratch my ankle, I do not need to find my hand, nor my ankle; I simply reach down and scratch the desired spot. Although I have never been in the military, I played enough "army games" as a boy and I have seen enough films and television programmes to perform the requisite movements more or less automatically. Similarly, no difficulties present themselves when carrying out the tracing exercise; I can usually tell I have traced a figure-of-eight even when I keep my eyes closed throughout. These exercises again suggest that one's relation to one's own body is not in the first instance a matter of representations: "Movement is not thought about movement, and bodily space is not space thought or represented" (PP: 137). I do not need to picture the movements to myself before setting out to make them, and I find no picturing taking place in the act of making them.

Now consider Schneider, the pathological case to which Merleau-Ponty devotes considerable attention in Part One of the *Phenomenology of Perception*. Schneider is a veteran of the First World War who was severely wounded in the head by a shell fragment, resulting in permanent brain damage. Schneider, despite the severity of the damage he has suffered, is still able to lead a relatively normal life in many respects. He manages to engage in many routine activities and he is employed at a factory making wallets, where he performs competently if somewhat more slowly than the other workers. The damage to Schneider's brain does not manifest itself to any great degree, as long as the actions in question are performed in a reflexive, routine fashion. For example, if Schneider feels the need to blow his nose, he can reach for his handkerchief in his shirt pocket and bring it to his nose; if a mosquito lands on his leg, he can slap it away while continuing his conversation. Merleau-Ponty, following the researchers who studied Schneider at great length, calls the class of actions Schneider is competently able to perform "*greifen*", which is German for "grasping". However, there is another large range of actions that Schneider can only perform with great difficulty, if at all. He has a great deal of difficulty describing the arrangement of his limbs or the position of his body. If asked to touch his nose or point to a particular spot on his leg, Schneider cannot respond with any kind of immediacy: he must first locate his hand and guide it visually to the spot he has been asked to touch. Merleau-Ponty labels the second class of actions "*zeigen*", which is German for "pointing". He also refers to *zeigen*-actions as "abstract" movements, and *greifen*-actions as "concrete" movements.

Merleau-Ponty's discussions of Schneider and other pathological cases in *Phenomenology of Perception* rely heavily on the research in the early twentieth century of the Gestalt psychologist Adhémar Gelb and the neurologist Kurt Goldstein. As Gelb and Goldstein themselves note, the First World War "brought to the attention of science a large number of cases where young and healthy men were suddenly transformed by brain injury into patients of a type only rarely encountered in times of peace" (Ellis 1938: 315). In studying these patients, Gelb and Goldstein's purpose was "to determine what was contained in the consciousness of these patients" (*ibid.*). Patients such as Schneider were given numerous tests and exercises to limn the contours of their disabilities and to understand more clearly what their experience was like. For example, in the case of Schneider, it was discovered that the recognition of words and other pictures displayed on a screen depended on his ability to trace the pictures, either with his finger or by moving his head. When such movements were prevented, recognition became impossible. Part of what Gelb and Goldstein wanted to understand was just what Schneider's visual experience was like: "That the patient 'sees' cannot be doubted, but this statement says no more than that he does have some kind of visual impressions; it tells us nothing regarding the phenomenal character of these impressions" (*ibid.*: 318). Based on their experiments, they diagnosed Schneider as suffering from what they call "figural blindness", which denotes an "incapacity to *grasp* purely visual presentations" (*ibid.*: 316). Visual presentations could only be grasped indirectly, via the procedure of tracing and other forms of inference. (Gelb and Goldstein refer to Schneider as "guessing" what everyday objects are, for example inferring dice from seeing black dots on a white surface.)

In keeping with his general strategy, Merleau-Ponty considers both empiricist and intellectualist attempts to make sense of Schneider's deficiencies. The empiricist account of Schneider tries to explain his inabilities causally, by locating the damaged mechanism or physiological function, for example by appealing to damage to his visual system. Because Schneider's vision is impaired, his ability to perform *zeigen*-actions is likewise impaired; he is still able to perform *greifen*-actions because his tactile system, his sense of touch, has been left intact. This proposal is open to objection. For example, "normal" people can perform abstract motions with their eyes closed. I can, on request, touch my knee or the bottom of my foot without having to look. To this, the empiricist might reply that these abilities still rely on an accumulation of visually guided movements, to which it might be further replied that congenitally blind people can also perform abstract movements. The empiricist can accommodate this observation by postulating in the congenitally blind more highly developed kinaesthetic abilities. There is no clear terminus to this back and forth, and Merleau-Ponty does not expect any final, decisive objection to any particular empiricist explanation to be forthcoming.

The problem with the empiricist approach lies deeper than its choice of Schneider's visual system as the cause of his difficulties in engaging in *zeigen*-actions (Merleau-Ponty is equally critical of explanations that appeal to damage to Schneider's tactile abilities). Tests, as well as Schneider's own testimony about his condition, show that he clearly has suffered damage to his sense of vision, as well as to his sense of touch, and no one can doubt that his overall impairment arises from the damage wrought by the shell fragment. His difficulties thus have a physiological origin, but the problem lies in how this physiological damage is conceived with respect to his perceptual capacities. That is, the problem lies in trying to explain Schneider's problems by appeal to any one kind of perceptual impairment (vision versus touch, for example), because doing so involves conceiving of the sensory modalities as independent "systems" whose respective causal contributions might be isolated from one another. If, however, the sensory modalities are not isolable, which, as we have already seen, the integrity of perception suggests, then there can be no decisive considerations in favour of one explanatory hypothesis over another. The anatomical and physiological damage Schneider has suffered cannot be readily translated into hypotheses concerning the organization of his perceptual capacities and its effect on his performance of various kinds of bodily actions. All such hypotheses are "*equally probable* interpretations because 'visual representations', 'abstract movement' and 'sense of potential touch' are only different names for one and the same central phenomenon" (PP: 118). Hence, we do not really have competing hypotheses at all, which indicates, for Merleau-Ponty, "the failure of the inductive method or of causal thinking in the realm of psychology" (*ibid.*).

Rather than proceeding as empiricism does, by means of tracing the physiological damage to the dependency of Schneider's difficulties on damage to one perceptual modality, intellectualism concentrates on Schneider's impairments understood as limitations on his subjectivity. According to intellectualism, Schneider is no longer a genuine subject. His ability to continue to perform *greifen*-actions shows simply that he still has the capacity for reflex actions, which are purely mechanical in nature, devoid of any genuine intentionality. That Schneider has difficulty performing *zeigen*-actions shows that he lacks an understanding of objective spatial relationships. As Merleau-Ponty frames the intellectualist position: "If the patient is no longer able to point to some part of his body which is touched, it is because he is no longer a subject face to face with an objective world, and can no longer take up a 'categorial attitude'" (PP: 121).

According to intellectualism, Schneider's *greifen*-actions, as nothing but conditioned reflexes, are capable of entirely causal, physiological explanations, whereas Schneider's difficulties with respect to *zeigen*-actions require an entirely different explanatory scheme. Merleau-Ponty finds this dichotomy odd, since in many cases the "concrete" and "abstract" movements are physiologically indistinguishable. The mosquito biting Schneider's leg would appear to be no different from the edge of the doctor's ruler bearing down on the same spot, and yet Schneider is able to swat the mosquito handily, while stumbling to fulfil the doctor's request to touch the spot marked by the point of the ruler. If the intellectualist were right that *greifen*-actions are mere reflexes, capable of an entirely physiological explanation, then the same ought to be true for most *zeigen*-actions. Since this is not the case, the intellectualist is wrong to dismiss concrete actions as mere reflex. Such actions constitute instead a different way of relating to objects from the objective attitude championed by the intellectualist, but they are nonetheless intentional: Schneider's swat is directed at the mosquito, not any old physiologically indiscernible impulse; his reaching is directed at his handkerchief, and so on.

There is a further, deeper criticism that shows that the intellectualist has mischaracterized not only *greifen*-actions, but also *zeigen*-actions. Schneider is eventually able to perform the latter kind of actions in many cases, and how he does so would appear to live up to the demands of an intellectualist account. That is, Schneider performs these movements by means of observation, inference, deliberation and effort. Schneider has to find his hand and guide it to his leg or to his nose; he has to look and see, and so judge, how his body is positioned before reporting to the doctor. His relation to his body is more like the relationship one might have with an object, which is precisely how intellectualism conceives of that relation. For the intellectualist, a fully competent subject relates to his own body via a grasp of objective spatial relations, which he can apply as much to the parts of his body as to anything else that occupies a position in objective space. But as our exercises at the outset of this section suggest, our non-pathological performance of these actions is not mediated by a grasp of such objective spatial relations. To perform such actions, we do not need to take the measure of our own bodies, applying objective metrical notions and calculating the results; we do not need to locate our bodies at all, and so any appeals to observation and inference are out of place. If intellectualism were true, we would all be more like Schneider; that we are not shows that intellectualism has fundamentally misconceived the nature of bodily self-experience.

More careful attention to Schneider's repertoire of activities helps to reveal both what is problematic or missing in the case of Schneider and, correlatively, what non-pathological embodiment is like. As we have seen, Schneider's impairment reveals a distinction between *greifen-* and *zeigen*-actions. Schneider is only able to perform the latter with considerable effort, whereas normally embodied human beings are able to perform both more or less equally well. For Schneider, to perform *zeigen*-actions requires either adopting a fully objective attitude towards his body, locating it and guiding it like an external object, or striving to make the action as concrete as possible, thereby engaging his continued ability to perform *greifen*-actions. If Schneider is asked to make a soldier's salute, for example, he cannot do so without making the situation as "soldier-like" as possible, adopting completely the stance and attitude of the soldier on duty. He cannot respond to the request casually, by play-acting or pretending; he can only salute to the extent that he succeeds in being a soldier in that moment. What is missing in the case of Schneider is what Merleau-Ponty refers to as the power of "projection", an ability to confront his present situation not just in terms of actualities, but in terms of possibilities too. Lacking for Schneider is a kind of "free space" into which he might imaginatively project himself via his bodily movements, and so he cannot "transcend" his situation in the manner that abstract movements require.

At the same time, this projective capacity, when present, is not primarily a cognitive capacity, a category of thought, as the intellectualist has it, but something "between" movement and thought:

> What [Schneider] lacks is neither motility nor thought, and we are brought to the recognition of something between movement as a third person process and thought as a representation of movement – something which is an anticipation of, or arrival at, the objective and is ensured by the body itself as a motor power, a "motor project" … a "motor intentionality".
>
> (PP: 110)

For Merleau-Ponty, motor intentionality is the basic phenomenon, which is manifest in non-pathological cases in both concrete and abstract movements ("for the normal person every movement is, indissolubly, movement and consciousness of movement" (PP: 110)). Concrete movements are not purely reflexive and mechanical, but intelligently situated and directed, and abstract movements are not purely representational and objective, but instead draw on and engage the same pool of motor skills.

With respect to both concrete and abstract movements, our bodily abilities outstrip our representational capacities. I can no more report the precise angle, direction and speed of my moving arm when I fulfil the request to touch my right foot than when I reach down unthinkingly to adjust my sock. When I try to represent beforehand the movements to be performed (or, worse, during their performance), doing so very often serves as an impediment to their successful completion; I "get in my own way" when I stop to think about what I am doing, and I can often perform the right action if, instead of thinking about it, I simply begin the movement in the accustomed way and let my body take over. If I were asked, for example, to describe the movements of my hand as I write the word "phenomenology" on a sheet of paper or type it on the keyboard (something I have done many many times!), very little comes to mind as worthy of report. I may try to picture the layout of the keys, recall which finger types each letter and how, and so on, but all of these representations are summoned up only with a great deal of effort and without much in the way of confidence. Give me a pen or sit me at the keyboard, however, and I can show how it is done without any hesitation or deliberation. If I watch my hands for a long enough time, I might be able to break down, analyse, and so eventually represent all of the various movements involved in my writing or typing "phenomenology", but that would be a secondary achievement rather than a revelation of what had been guiding my actions all along. Again, "movement is not thought about movement", to which Merleau-Ponty adds:

> and bodily space is not space thought or represented …. In the action of the hand which is raised towards an object is contained a reference to the object, not as an object represented, but as that highly specific thing towards which we project ourselves, near which we are, in anticipation, and which we haunt. (PP: 137–8)

When I set out to type, my hands and fingers "find" their places on the keyboard without me having to look. I may, on occasion, have to adjust my hands or correct their position, but by and large I type without observing my fingers at all.

When I first learned to type, I did have to think about what I was doing – finding the home keys, remembering the arrangement of the keyboard, and so on – but as I became more adept at typing, the need for any such thinking diminished:

> A movement is learned when the body has understood it, that is, when it has incorporated it into its "world", and to move one's body is to aim at things through it; it is to allow oneself to respond to their call, which is made upon it independently of any representation. Motility, then, is not, as it were, a handmaid of consciousness, transporting the body to that point in space of which we have formed a representation beforehand.
>
> (PP: 139)

When it comes to movement, bodily, muscular incorporation, rather than the storage of representations, constitutes genuine understanding. No matter how well I can recite the series of movements involved in a complicated dance step, a difficult athletic manoeuvre, or an elaborate craft technique, if I cannot perform those actions, then I have not (yet) mastered them; I am not yet competent. And when I do achieve mastery, the ability to recite the series becomes superfluous, and even detrimental, since to be genuinely skilful involves being flexible with respect to the particulars of a situation. To be skilful involves the ability to make adjustments, to respond to the "call" of things in all of their specificity, although in a bodily rather than cognitive way: "The acquisition of a habit is indeed the grasping of a significance, but it is the motor grasping of a motor significance" (PP: 143).

Merleau-Ponty claims, provocatively, that "consciousness is in the first place not a matter of 'I think that' but of 'I can'" (PP: 137), which points to the fundamental role of motor intentionality with respect to all forms of intentionality: "Consciousness is being towards the thing through the intermediary of the body" (PP: 138–9). Descartes had conceived of consciousness primarily in terms of thinking ("I think, therefore I am"), which he understood as the mind having within itself a stock of ideas or representations, all of which could be considered apart from the mind's being related to a body, or indeed any engagement with the world. In this way, "I think that" is both independent of, and prior to, any sense of "I can", understood in terms of any ability to make one's way about in the world. Merleau-Ponty's claims concerning motor intentionality, like many of Husserl's concerning the essential bodily dimension of perceptual experience, can be understood as directed at this kind of Cartesian conception of the mind and experience. According to Merleau-Ponty, the world is manifest in experience in accordance with our bodily structure and skills. Things are manifest as near or far, here or there, in reach or out of reach, above or below, available or unavailable, usable or unusable, inviting or repulsive, and so on in relation to our ways of inhabiting the world, and such inhabitation is always bodily in nature. Things are not encountered primarily in terms of a detached gaze, as though our main relation to the world was one of staring. On the contrary, things are manifest, arrayed before and around us, in relation to our bodily abilities, our many ways of getting a grip on the things we encounter. I use the word "grip" here both literally and figuratively, as when I grip the pen, coffee cup, hammer, steering wheel and so on in my hands (literal) and when I "get a grip" on things and situations, putting things in order, getting things under control and optimizing my perceptual access (figurative). The latter, more figurative, kind of grip involves myriad bodily skills. When looking at things, we variously bring them or ourselves closer or otherwise increase our distance, depending on the thing (compare looking at a coin versus looking at the façade of a building), in order to get the best view:

> If I draw the object closer to me or turn it round in my fingers in order "to see it better", this is because each attitude of my body is for me, immediately, the power of achieving a certain spectacle, and because each spectacle is what it is for me in a certain kinaesthetic situation. In other words, because my body is permanently stationed before things in order to perceive them and, conversely, appearances are always enveloped for me in a certain bodily attitude. In so far, therefore, as I know the relation of appearances to the kinaesthetic situation, this is not in virtue of any law or in terms of any formula, but to the extent that I have a body, and that through that body I am at grips with the world. (PP: 303)

To be conscious, to be embodied, to be "at grips with the world" are not three separate or separable notions for Merleau-Ponty, but are three overlapping, interconnected, internally related aspects of our existence. The "return to the phenomena" reveals this overlapping and interconnected unity of consciousness, embodiment and the world made manifest through our embodied experience. Merleau-Ponty calls this unity the "intentional arc", which informs every aspect of our experience:

Let us therefore say … that the life of consciousness – cognitive life, the life of desire or perceptual life – is subtended by an "intentional arc" which projects round about us our past, our future, our human setting, our physical, ideological and moral situation, or rather results in our being situated in all these respects. It is this intentional arc which brings about the unity of the senses, of intelligence, of sensibility and motility.

(PP: 136)

Summary of key points

- Despite the ghostly imagery invited by talk of "pure consciousness", Husserl offers a richly textured phenomenology of embodiment in *Ideas* II.
- The body (or Body) is manifest in experience as a categorically distinct kind of thing and as essential to the possibility of other kinds of intentionality, namely, perceptual experience of spatiotemporal objects.
- For Merleau-Ponty, phenomenology is concerned with primary, pre-objective experience, as opposed to the secondary, objective conception of the world articulated and explored by the natural sciences.
- Perceptual experience primarily involves a meaningful whole, a "perceptual 'something' … in the middle of something else", that cannot be understood as constructed out of some more basic experiential units.
- Perceptual experience, owing to its essential indeterminacy and incompleteness, cannot be understood solely on the model of judgement.
- The intentionality of bodily activity cannot be understood either in terms of physiological reflexes or in terms of representational thoughts or judgements.
- Bodily activity is instead informed by "motor intentionality": a pre-reflective engagement with specific things and situations.

five

Problems and prospects: phenomenology and its critics

Beyond phenomenology?

Over the past four chapters, we have considered the four main figures in the phenomenological tradition. Although, as we have seen, the phenomenological tradition is hardly monolithic, replete as it is with intramural debates and in some cases wholesale changes in orientation (consider the divide between Husserl's and Heidegger's respective conceptions of phenomenology), there is nonetheless among these figures a shared sense of there being a distinctive philosophical discipline worthy of the name "phenomenology", and so a shared sense that phenomenology is both possible and, indeed, philosophically indispensable. Despite many differences both at the programmatic level and at the level of detail, all four figures – Husserl, Heidegger, Sartre and Merleau-Ponty – agree that phenomenology is not only worth doing, but that it aspires to be the method for philosophy.

In presenting the views of these four figures, I have taken something of a "used-car salesman" approach, highlighting the strengths of each position and downplaying the weaknesses, except where outright incompatibilities among the positions prevented my doing so. I have thus served more or less as an advocate for each position, all the while realizing that one could not embrace all four simultaneously. Although one must pick and choose among these positions in phenomenology, there remains the option of opting out of phenomenology altogether, and not just out of personal interest and inclination, but because of more principled philosophical considerations. That is, perhaps it is the case that the shared sensibility among our four figures that phenomenology is both possible and valuable is itself open to dispute. Perhaps the very idea of phenomenology is somehow limited, intrinsically flawed or ill-conceived, and so rather than choosing among the viewpoints canvassed over the last four chapters, we should instead remain more aloof, withholding our wholehearted acceptance or even rejecting them in their entirety.

In this final chapter, we shall examine phenomenology from a more critical perspective, exploring a number of views that try, variously, to expose the limits to phenomenological investigation or, more radically, reveal fatal underlying flaws. We shall consider three such critical perspectives – those of Emmanuel Levinas, Jacques Derrida and Daniel Dennett – that are connected by a number of intransitive similarities (Levinas's position is similar in some respects to Derrida's, and Derrida's is similar in some respects to Dennett's, but one would be hard-pressed to find much of any similarity between Levinas and Dennett). Of the three, Levinas and Derrida are most closely affiliated with the phenomenological tradition. The lines of affiliation are in each case multiple, encompassing cultural, chronological and, most importantly, philosophical affiliations. Levinas was born in Lithuania, but studied and worked in France and wrote in French. Derrida was born in Algeria, but later studied and taught in France as well. Levinas was born a year after Sartre, and two years before Merleau-Ponty. Derrida is of more recent vintage, but studied philosophy at a time when some of the major works of phenomenology were relatively recent. Levinas was a dedicated student of Husserl's philosophy, providing early translations of his work into French and writing an early book-length work and numerous essays on his philosophy, and he was also a close reader of Heidegger. Derrida's early work in philosophy was likewise steeped in Husserl's phenomenology, although always from a more critical perspective, and he wrestled with Heidegger's philosophy throughout his philosophical career (indeed, Derrida's strategy of "deconstruction" was influenced considerably by Heidegger's task, in *Being and Time* and elsewhere, of "destroying the history of ontology" – see e.g. BT: §6).

Dennett, by contrast, occupies a position far more external to the phenomenological tradition. American, trained in England, and possessed of philosophical sensibilities steeped in the kind of science-centered naturalism to which the phenomenological tradition is opposed, Dennett nonetheless sees his own philosophy of mind as emerging in part out of a critical engagement with phenomenology, especially the phenomenology of Husserl (at one point, Dennett modestly describes himself as "no Husserl scholar but an amateur of long standing" (BS: 184)).

Moreover, and perhaps surprisingly, Dennett's critical engagement with phenomenology overlaps with Derrida's, and both use their criticisms as a basis for reconceiving the very idea of consciousness in ways very much at odds with how Husserl (and also Sartre) conceives of it. (Levinas's criticisms, by contrast, are far more tempered: he is concerned not so much with overthrowing phenomenology, as showing where phenomenological method comes up short. These shortcomings are far from trivial, however, so Levinas is certainly offering something more than merely polite disagreement.)

The bulk of this chapter will be devoted to laying out and assessing these critical perspectives on the phenomenological tradition, but in the final part I shall briefly address the question of phenomenology's continued significance for philosophy and suggest that we would do well to view the phenomenological tradition as far more than a museum piece. In this book, at least, phenomenology gets the last word.

Levinas and the epiphany of the face

In the preceding chapters we paid little heed to a theme that runs through the entirety of phenomenology (and really a great deal of philosophy ever since Descartes). Although we have considered many modes and categories of manifestation – spatiotemporal objects (Husserl), equipment and world (Heidegger), the ego or self (Sartre) and the body (Merleau-Ponty) – we have not considered in any detail the distinctive ways in which others, that is, other subjects of experience, show themselves in experience. Two questions immediately present themselves:

- Are there indeed distinctive ways in which others are experienced?
- And, perhaps more pointedly, *can* others be experienced in a distinctive way?

The more pointed version of the question is prompted by the following kind of worry. I have direct or immediate "access" via reflection to my own experience or consciousness, but in what way, and to what extent, can I experience the experience or consciousness of another subject of experience? And if, the worry continues, the consciousness of another subject is not available to me, that is, is not something that I can directly experience, then in what sense can I be said to experience the other as a conscious being at all?

These questions may be familiar from discussions outside the context of phenomenology, as they are the sorts of questions one generally rehearses in raising the sceptical "problem of other minds". The problem in its general form concerns the possibility of ascertaining or knowing that there are other minds besides my own. The existence of my own mind is vouchsafed by the direct and immediate availability of my own experience, but nothing like that is forthcoming with respect to any other minds. Lacking this kind of direct availability, I can never establish or know that there are indeed such other minds. The problem thus treats my relation to "the other" as fundamentally epistemological – as a problem about "access" or knowledge – and very often the worry is raised in order to show that it cannot be assuaged.

In many ways, the phenomenological tradition as a whole is very much alive to the problem of other minds. This is not to say that every figure within the tradition treats the problem as a straightforward problem in need of a solution (Husserl comes closest to holding this view), but all of the figures we have considered in the preceding chapters see it as a problem to be addressed, even if the form of address involves showing why the problem, at least in its epistemological form, is ultimately a bogus one. One way of measuring the importance of Levinas is to see him as attempting to sidestep this problem altogether. The relation to the other is not epistemological, but ethical, and the whole attempt to accommodate or account for the other within the confines of my experience already constitutes a breach of this fundamental ethical relation. The other is precisely that which cannot be the object of my experience in the sense of being completely manifest within it, and so cannot be construed as a phenomenon at all. As something that does not manifest itself in the field of my experience, there cannot be a phenomenology of the other or of otherness: in the encounter with the other, phenomenology has thus reached an impasse.

To work our way further into Levinas, and so understand the nature of these criticisms of phenomenology, we might best begin by considering the title of his most important work, *Totality and Infinity*. The first term in this pair, "totality", is Levinas's name for what he sees as the underlying *telos* of the Western intellectual tradition, namely, the goal of comprehending everything there is within one, all-embracing framework, theory or system. Consider the justly famous opening line of Aristotle's *Metaphysics*: "All men by nature desire to know" (*Metaphysics* I, 1). In Levinas's terms, Aristotle is here naming this desire for totality, which in Aristotle is cashed out as the goal of ordering everything there is so as to be derivable from, and so explained in terms of, a hierarchically organized set of principles. Western philosophy, along with the natural sciences that emerged from it, has throughout its history displayed this longing for totality, for a "grand theory of everything". Levinas refers to this quest for totality as an endeavour to assimilate everything to the same: by rendering everything intelligible according to one comprehensive system of principles, everything is thereby rendered categorically homogenous (there is certainly room for the idea of differentiation, and so heterogeneous categories, but this is all diversity within unity).

The linkage between totality and assimilation indicates a certain kind of orientation on the part of the subject towards the world. Levinas dubs this orientation "enjoyment". Eating is one basic form of enjoyment where the notion of assimilation is particularly vivid. The food that I eat is taken in and digested, and thereby incorporated into my body, and no matter how many different kinds of food I eat, they are all inevitably chewed and mixed into one amalgam in the interior of my one body. The assimilative act of eating is not the only source of enjoyment; perceptual experience also affords such pleasures. Consider the continuation of Aristotle's opening claim: that all men desire to know is indicated by "the delight we take in our senses; for even apart from their usefulness they are loved for themselves; and above all others the sense of sight" (*Metaphysics* I, 1). Although vision serves many practical purposes, very often we simply enjoy looking at things, taking them in with our eyes, even when we have no further purpose beyond the pleasure of gazing. Note the phrase "taking them in" in the previous sentence, which indicates that seeing, and perceiving more generally, is also a kind of assimilation, although in a less straightforward way than eating. In the act of perception, I apprehend (a synonym for "take") the object; I bring it within the field of my experience, and so in that sense make it mine, or even a part of me. When I perceive, the thing I perceive is open to view, available to me, and so under my dominion: "Inasmuch as the access to beings concerns vision, it dominates those beings, exercises a power over them. A thing is *given*, offers itself to me. In gaining access to it I maintain myself within the same" (TI: 194). Vision is commonly referred to as a "power", and to have things in view is already to exercise a kind of control over them. Looking at something is often the first step in investigating it, getting to know it and figuring out what it is and how it works. This kind of control is itself also pleasurable.

Although Levinas sees these themes of totality and assimilation running through the entirety of Western philosophy, the phenomenological tradition is his more immediate target. Indeed, one of Levinas's principal claims is that these themes are no less present in phenomenology than elsewhere in Western philosophical tradition, despite phenomenology's self-understanding as an enlightened response to that larger tradition (consider, for example, Heidegger's critique of philosophy's preoccupation with substance and actuality, or Merleau-Ponty's rejection of both intellectualism and empiricism). The very idea of phenomenology, of the phenomenon as what "shows itself" or as given, betrays the continued presence of these themes. Phenomenology's defining demand that things be made manifest is both totalizing (phenomenology treats everything as a phenomenon to be described and categorized) and assimilating (by treating everything as a phenomenon, as something manifest, phenomenology both treats everything as ultimately the same and pulls everything within the dominating gaze of the subject). Husserl's conception of transcendental consciousness as the all-encompassing field of intelligibility in which intentional objects are constituted provides a vivid example of these totalizing and assimilative tendencies of phenomenology, but Heidegger too is not immune to Levinas's criticisms, despite Heidegger's own criticisms of Husserl. In *Being and Time*, Heidegger characterizes his project as "fundamental ontology", and so as dedicated to answering the question of the meaning of being in general. Heidegger's preoccupation with being manifests a continued striving for totality, and his equating of being with the notion of a phenomenon as "what shows itself" is no less assimilating than Husserl's notion of constitution.

But what do these general criticisms of phenomenology, as no less guilty of certain very general aspirations and ambitions, have to do with a proper conception of the other, or the very idea of otherness? How do these aspirations and ambitions entail any kind of neglect or oversight of the fundamentally ethical character of my relation to the other? Let us begin to answer these questions by looking in more detail at some aspects of phenomenology's approach to the question of the other.

The problem of others is especially acute in Husserl's phenomenology, given the phenomenological reduction and the absolute character of the first-person singular point of view. Although Husserl wants to allay the worry that "solipsism", the view that I am the only genuine subject of experience or sentient being, constitutes a permanent condition, at the same time he is clear that the legitimate starting-point for phenomenology is a solipsistic one. Where Husserl's phenomenology begins is with the reduction to the stream of experience of the transcendental ego, the self, the subject or the "I" of the *cogito*. From this starting-point, the stream of conscious experience, one proceeds outwards, so to speak, via the process of constitution: the constitution of any intentional object, the constitution of actual objects and so on. Given this sort of starting-point, however, it is not difficult to see how there comes to be a problem of other egos, since the appeal to constitution seems unsatisfactory. That is, one cannot be satisfied simply with explaining the constitution of the other as part of my immanent stream of experience, since the very idea of an other involves its being outside my stream of experience, and indeed a possessor of its own stream of experience. The constitution of the other would thus seem to require constituting the other's stream of experience, but doing so would make that stream a part of mine, which undermines the idea that I have succeeded in constituting, and so experiencing, a genuine other, another subject of experience. For Husserl, "the possibility of the being for me of others" is "a very puzzling possibility" (CM: §41), and so a problem very much in need of a solution. For Levinas, by contrast, the problem lies with this very conception of the problem, namely treating the problem of the other as a constitutional one. To constitute the other, in Husserl's sense of constitution, is thereby to assimilate the other to, or within, the field of one's own experience, thereby depriving the other of its very otherness.

We saw in Chapter 2 that Heidegger, in keeping with his rejection of the phenomenological reduction, rejects the problem of other minds as a pseudo-problem. The primacy of Dasein, as being-in-the-world, precludes the kind of solipsistic perspective found in Husserl. For Heidegger, the "being for me of others" is not a "puzzling possibility", as it was for Husserl, since I and others are from the start together, out there in the world. Heidegger thus rejects the kind of explanatory project Husserl thinks phenomenology must confront. Instead, others "are encountered from out of the world, in which concernfully circumspective Dasein essentially dwells", and so Heidegger rejects any "theoretically concocted 'explanations' of the being-present-at-hand of others" (BT: §26). We must, Heidegger insists, "hold fast to the phenomenal facts of the case which we have pointed out, namely, that others are encountered *environmentally*" (*ibid.*).

For Heidegger, self and other are, we might say, co-manifest, and the other shows himself or herself to be an other who is the same as me:

> By "others" we do not mean everyone else but me – those over against whom the "I" stands out. They are rather those from whom, for the most part, one does *not* distinguish oneself – those among whom one is too. This being-there-too with them does not have the ontological character of a being-present-at-

hand-along-"with" them within a world. This "with" is something of the character of Dasein; the "too" means a sameness
of being as circumspectively concernful being-in-the-world.

(BT: §26)

The lack of any sharp distinction in everydayness between self and
other, such that I and others are marked by "a sameness of being", undermines the intelligibility of the problem of other minds. The question
"How can I know that there are other subjects of experience?" fails to
raise any epistemological alarms, when the way of being of the "I" in the
question is revealed to be being-in-the-world. Dasein, as being-in-the-
world, "always already" has an understanding of others (what Heidegger
calls "being-with"), and so there is no general worry about how such
understanding or knowledge is possible (there may, of course, be worries on particular occasions as to what someone is thinking or feeling).
Although Heidegger is dismissive of the epistemological problem of
other minds, condemning it as a pseudo-problem rather than one to be
solved, his stance on the question of others is one that Levinas nonetheless finds problematic. The problem is signalled in the final sentence of
the passage quoted above, where Heidegger essentially assimilates the
other as being or having the same way of being as the "I". For Heidegger,
others are not truly encountered as others, and for Levinas, this means
that the otherness of the other is effaced.

Sartre's phenomenology of the other in *Being and Nothingness* begins
with the idea that if we start from the perspective of our own, individual
experience, there is naturally a kind of privileging of ourselves and that
experience. Each of us, with respect to our own experience, constitutes,
in Husserl's words, a "zero-point of orientation", and so the world that we
experience, its layout and patterning, is for each of us organized around
ourselves. When I am alone, the world I experience is my world, in the
sense that everything manifests itself only to me and only in relation to
me: things are near and far, over here or over there, in front or behind,
solely in relation to the position I occupy. My perspective on the world is
the only perspective there is, again provided that I am alone. For Sartre,
the first effect of the appearance of the other is to disrupt, indeed shatter,
this complacent sense of exclusive ownership and privilege. The appearance of the other marks the appearance of an object in my experience
with its own experience, and so it marks the appearance of someone else
around whom the world is perceptually and perspectivally organized:
"The Other is first the permanent flight of things towards a goal which I
apprehend as an object at a certain distance from me but which escapes

me inasmuch as it unfolds about itself its own distances" (BN: 343). When the other comes on the scene, the world is no longer exclusively mine. Instead, there is "a regrouping of all the objects which people my universe" (*ibid.*) around this new kind of object.

This regrouping "escapes me" in so far as I am unable to inhabit the perspective occupied by the other. Even if I were to move to the precise location of the other and move him out of the way, thereby orienting my body precisely as his was prior to my intrusion, I would still not be having his experience, and indeed, his experience would continue from whatever new location he took up, thereby effecting yet another regrouping to which I am not privy. As Sartre puts it, objects and their qualities turn "toward the Other a face which escapes me. I apprehend the relations of [objects and their qualities] to the Other as an objective relation, but I cannot apprehend [them] *as*" (*ibid.*) they appear to him. The appearance of the other is thus the appearance of an object that "has stolen the world from me" (*ibid.*).

These disruptions caused by the appearance of the other in my experiential field are only the beginning, since with these considerations concerning perspective and orientation, "*the Other* is still an object *for me*" (*ibid.*). The other's subjectivity is most palpable when his experience is directed not towards objects that I too am experiencing, but when his experience is directed towards me, so that "my fundamental connection with the Other-as-subject must be able to be referred back to my permanent possibility of *being seen* by the Other" (BN: 344). The experience of being seen by the other is to be subject to what Sartre calls "the look". When I experience the other as something capable of experiencing me, when, that is, I find myself subjected to the look, I am at that moment transformed from a subject into an object. Recall Sartre's characterization of first-degree consciousness in *The Transcendence of the Ego*: the field of first-degree consciousness is unowned, and so is nothing but pure subjectivity. When I am absorbed in my own experience, there is no me that appears in that experience. The appearance of the other disrupts all of this, suddenly making me aware of myself and so objectifying me. I now feel myself to be an object to be perceived, who is caught up in the perspective opened up by the other's experience. For Sartre, the look is primarily threatening. The other is experienced primarily as a source of shame, self-consciousness (in the ordinary sense) and vulnerability: "What I apprehend immediately when I hear the branches crackling behind me is not that *there is someone there*; it is that I am vulnerable, that I have a body which can be hurt, that I occupy a place in which I am without defense – in short, that I *am seen*" (BN: 347).

Sartre's phenomenology of the other thus does not commit what is for Levinas the sin of assimilating the other to the realm of the same, as Heidegger does. That for Sartre the other occupies a perspective or has a point of view on the world that is in principle unavailable to me is for Levinas a step in the right direction in terms of properly characterizing the relation between self and other. For both Sartre and Levinas, the appearance of the other constitutes a radical disruption of the homogeneity of my experience. Even the appearance of the other-as-object in Sartre marks the appearance of something that resists complete assimilation, as the qualities of the world as they appear to the other "escape me". At the same time, Sartre's overall conception of the self–other relation is still underwritten by the drive for totality and assimilation: the objectifying power of "the look" seeks in each case to deprive the other of his or her subjectivity, thereby making the other just one more thing in my perceptual field. The extent to which Sartre's account of the self–other relation is permeated with notions of hostility, antagonism and threat indicates a failure on Sartre's part to recognize anything beyond this drive towards objectification, anything, that is, beyond the goal of totality. Lacking in Sartre is any sense in which the appearance of the other can be seen as welcoming, as informed by hospitality rather than vulnerability, and so as involving an unqualified acknowledgment of the other's unsurveyable subjectivity. Lacking in Sartre and the rest of the phenomenological tradition is a proper appreciation of what Levinas calls "the face".

The appearance of the other is the appearance of something that exceeds appearance, that cannot, in other words, be assimilated by me into the same:

> The face is present in its refusal to be contained. In this sense it cannot be comprehended, that is, encompassed. It is neither seen nor touched – for in visual or tactile sensation the identity of the I envelops the alterity of the object, which becomes precisely a content.　　　　　　　　　　(TI: 194)

Notice especially the conclusion of this passage. Perception, as a fundamental form of intentionality, always involves intentional content. The object I perceive is the content of my perceptual experience, and so comprehended by that experience. The containment need not be literal, of course. When I look at my coffee cup, the cup is the content of my visual experience, but the cup itself is out there, on my desk. Nonetheless, in offering itself to my gaze, the cup is thereby assimilated by me, incorporated into my visual field.

The disanalogy between objects and the face in Levinas's sense is difficult to characterize adequately. Two worries immediately present themselves, both of which concern the alleged distance between the face and ordinary objects of perception, such as my coffee cup. First, it is unclear what Levinas means by saying that the face can be "neither seen nor touched", since, if we consider real human faces, this just sounds obviously false. The other, including the other's face, is there to be seen, just as the coffee cup he holds is visually present to me. (This remark, on its own, hardly constitutes an objection, since "face" for Levinas need not refer to a literal face; however, his choice of terminology would suggest that what he means by "face" is somehow bound up with, or most centrally attested to in, our face-to-face encounters with one another.) We need to be careful, however, in terms of how we understand the claim that the cup and the other are equally "there to be seen". The range of possibilities is markedly different in the case of the cup. The cup does not, and indeed cannot, refuse or resist my gaze, nor can it turn away from me, hide from me, or in any way prevent my continued inspection. The person holding the cup may of course hide the cup from me, and so in that way the cup resists my gaze, but that is certainly not the cup's doing. The other person is the source of this refusal or resistance, and so what my gaze really fails to contain is him or her, not the cup. In always offering at least the possibility of such resistance, the other always exceeds my perceptual capacities. But this brings us to the second worry. After all, the cup, as a spatiotemporal object, is only presented to me via adumbrations, and so any presentation of the cup always involves the intimation of unseen or hidden sides. Indeed, since the cup is, perceptually speaking, an infinite system of adumbrative presentations, it would seem that my perceptual experience could never fully contain or comprehend the cup. Thus, the disanalogy between the face and ordinary objects is still found wanting.

Although it is indeed the case that the perception of ordinary spatiotemporal objects involves the notion of hidden sides, such that no one presentation (or even many) will fully contain or comprehend the object, there are nonetheless several ways in which the disanalogy between such objects and the face might be sustained. We may begin by noting that in the case of spatiotemporal objects the hidden sides are only contingently hidden from me. For example, if I am looking at the front of my coffee cup, I cannot at the same time see the back of it or the bottom, but I can move myself or the cup whenever I wish so as to reveal those currently hidden aspects. Even if we allow that the presentation of the cup involves an infinite system of adumbrations, so that I, as a finite subject, could never experience all of them, it is still the case that no particular side of the cup is in principle hidden from me; nor is it the case that the cup may in any sense keep a particular side hidden from me. The hidden sides in the case of the face, however, can be hidden in just these two ways. To start with the second, if we consider the power of resistance or refusal, the other may always refuse to reveal a hidden side. I have to allow, in my encounter with another person, that there may be things that I will never know about that person, things that the person may choose to keep secret. Moreover, if we recall Sartre's talk about the other as occupying a point of view that "escapes me", we can see that the other's sides are hidden to a further extent beyond what he or she chooses to reveal. I can never occupy the point of view of the other, take his or place, in the sense of thereby having the other's experience. The other's subjectivity is in this way non-contingently, that is, in principle, hidden from me.

There is still another way in which to sustain the disanalogy, if we think about the relations among the "hidden sides" in the two cases. When I look at the front of my coffee cup, the currently hidden sides are hidden in such a way that they are *predictably* connected with what is present to me now. I know when looking at the front of the cup what will happen when I turn the cup or lift it up, and so what I am seeing now and the hidden sides do indeed make up a series or system. As long as no one has substituted a trick cup while I was out of my study, there is nothing surprising in my visual experience of the cup. The encounter with the other, by contrast, is marked by a lack of any such predictability: even when I feel that I know what someone is going to do or say, I may nonetheless still be surprised by how things develop, by what someone actually says or does. The other opposes me not so much with a "force of resistance, but the very *unforseeableness* of his reaction" (TI: 199). There are, of course, such possibilities for surprise in the case of perceptual experience when we perceive things that are unfamiliar or unusual, but even here, such spectacles hold out the promise of full predictability and so in principle the elimination of any element of surprise. The possibility of surprise in the case of the other is ineliminable.

I have thus far emphasized the notions of resistance and refusal in characterizing the difference between the face and, for example, ordinary spatiotemporal objects, but there is a more positive, happier dimension of this difference as well. Consider the following passage from Levinas's essay "Is Ontology Fundamental?":

A human being is the sole being which I am unable to encounter without expressing this very encounter to him. It is precisely in this that the encounter distinguishes itself from knowledge. In every attitude in regard to the human there is a greeting – if only in the refusal of greeting. (BPW: 7)

Here Levinas is characterizing the way in which the other, another person, engages me in a way that objects do not. Although I may find particular objects interesting, even beautiful, such that I want to look at them further, keep them nearby, and learn more about them, none of those objects are in any way affected by, or responsive to, that interest: it makes no difference to my coffee cup whether I use it or not, clean it lovingly or leave it unwashed, leave it for days on my desk or in the back of the cupboard, or even smash it to pieces. Whatever form my encounter with the cup takes is not something that I can express to the cup, whereas in the case of another human being, I cannot but express my encounter with him. Whenever I encounter another human being, whatever I do "means something", in the sense that what I say and do can be noticed, ignored, answered, taken up, acknowledged, interpreted, understood, misunderstood and so on. In other words, my encounter with another human being is an occasion for speech. Although I may, in my lonelier moments, talk to the many things around me, another human being is distinguished by his ability to talk back. My encounter with the other is thus marked by the possibility of conversation, indeed the inevitability, since even our failing to acknowledge or engage one another is a way of conversing; a "refusal of greeting" is, for all that, a kind of greeting.

The other "remains infinitely transcendent, infinitely foreign", but this "is not to be described negatively" (TI: 194): The negative description is one that emphasizes the lack of comprehension, the failure of predictability, and so on, but "better than comprehension, *discourse* relates with what remains essentially transcendent" (TI: 195). Again, the other is the one to whom I may speak, and who speaks to me, and "speech proceeds from absolute difference" (TI: 194). This last claim may sound especially jarring, since it would seem, anyway, that speaking involves a common language, and so a shared understanding of what is being said. As Merleau-Ponty puts it, "In the experience of dialogue, there is constituted between the other person and myself a common ground", such that in speaking we are "collaborators for each other in consummate reciprocity" (PP: 354). I would not go so far as to say that Levinas wants to deny these aspects and dimensions of dialogue or conversation, but when he says that "speech proceeds from absolute difference", he is pointing to something all of this talk of commonality, collaboration and reciprocity is apt to cover over: in conversing, there is an "absolute difference" with respect to the location of the speakers. What constitutes individuals as speakers, as participants in a conversation, is precisely their separateness. Without that separateness, speech as conversation collapses. A conversation is not a recitation: the rote production and exchange of a set of sentences. If I already know or can predict everything you will say, because what you say is the standard or conventional thing to say, then you fail to occupy a position fully separated from me; your words may be yours in the causal sense of emanating from your body, but their conventionality renders them anonymous. To be conversation, there must again be an element of the unpredictable, the unforeseeable, such that I cannot, at any point, fully sum up my interlocutor.

Any such attempt at summarization forecloses the possibility of conversation, and indeed, marks the ethical violation of the other:

> In discourse the divergence that inevitably opens up between the Other as my theme and the Other as my interlocutor, emancipated from the theme that seemed for a moment to hold him, forthwith contests the meaning I ascribe to my interlocutor. The formal structure of language thereby announces the ethical inviolability of the Other and, without any odor of the "numinous," his "holiness". (TI: 195)

"The ethical relationship", Levinas claims, "subtends discourse" (*ibid.*), which means that speaking to and with the other, as involving the other's "absolute difference", at the same time registers the other's inviolability. By acknowledging the other's separateness, I thereby acknowledge as well my ethical responsibility towards the other, in particular my responsibility not to transgress or violate that separateness. Levinas refers to this inviolability of the other as the "infinity of his transcendence". He explains: "This infinity, stronger than murder, already resists us in his face, is his face, is the primordial *expression*, is the first word: 'you shall not commit murder'" (TI: 199).

"The epiphany of the face is ethical" (TI: 199). It is "ethical" as opposed to ontological: "Preexisting the disclosure of being in general taken as basis of knowledge and as meaning of being is the relation with the existent that expresses himself; preexisting the plane of ontology is the ethical plane" (TI: 201). And note "epiphany" as opposed to manifestation:

> To manifest oneself as a face is to *impose oneself* above and beyond the manifested and purely phenomenal form, to

present oneself in a mode irreducible to manifestation, the very straightforwardness of the face to face, without the intermediary of any image, in one's nudity, in one's destitution and hunger. (TI: 200)

That the face involves a presentation that is ethical rather than ontological and that is "irreducible to manifestation" undermines the primacy and generality of phenomenology. Rather than phenomenon, Levinas sometimes refers to the presentation of the face as an "enigma", a "mystery" of infinite depth or height. No intuition or intuitions, no explication of the meaning of being, no return to phenomena, will ever succeed in dispelling this sense of mystery or in removing this enigma. Husserl was perhaps more correct than he realized in referring to the apprehension of the other as a "puzzling possibility"; where he went wrong, according to Levinas, is in supposing that phenomenology could offer a solution.

Derrida and the mythology of presence

Derrida's critique of Husserl begins at the very beginning of his phenomenology, with a number of distinctions drawn at the outset of his *Logical Investigations*. These preliminary distinctions concern the relation between thought and language, between conscious experience and the spoken and written signs used to express that experience outwardly. Derrida's rather bold contention is that not only the six subsequent investigations but also the entirety of Husserlian phenomenology, including his later "pure" or "transcendental" phenomenology, stand or fall with the validity of these distinctions. To the extent that these distinctions cannot be maintained, then Husserl's phenomenological project fails. In very broad brushstrokes, Derrida argues that Husserl seeks to exclude at the very beginning of his phenomenology anything sign-like at the level of pure consciousness, since pure consciousness, Husserl contends, is immediately available: to the phenomenological investigator without the mediating intervention of signs. Husserl's efforts to maintain this exclusion, however, can be shown to break down, and in such a way as to undercut the very idea of immediacy or presence required by pure phenomenology. What will later be enshrined in Husserl's "principle of all principles" turns out to be an inherited, highly suspect piece of metaphysical baggage, hardly what one would expect from what prides itself as a "presuppositionless" form of enquiry. But if the principle of principles must be abandoned, then Husserl's conception of phenomenology and indeed his entire conception of consciousness must be abandoned too.

The first of Husserl's six "logical investigations" begins with some preliminary but what Husserl considers to be "essential" distinctions, the most fundamental of which is the distinction between expression and indication. At the very beginning of §1, Husserl says "Every sign is a sign for something, but not every sign has 'meaning', a 'sense' that the sign 'expresses'" (LI: 269). What Husserl is saying here at first does not sound too complicated or controversial; certainly it does not sound like anything on which the entirety of a philosophical project might depend. Before trying to assess such a claim of dependence, let us first work through how Husserl explicates this distinction. Husserl (see LI: 270) defines the notion of indication in the following way:

> X *indicates* Y for (or to) A when A's belief or surmise in the reality of X motivates a belief or surmise in the reality of Y.

This general notion of indication covers both signs and what might be called "natural indicators". The former include things such as brands

---

The metaphysics of presence

Derrida sees not just Husserl's phenomenology but the entirety of the Western philosophical tradition as permeated by "the metaphysics of presence". The notion of presence has more than one axis, depending on what it is contrasted with: present as opposed to absent, but also present as opposed to past or future. In Derrida's locution, both senses are in play. The metaphysics of presence involves a privileging of the present, temporally speaking, but there is also a spatial–epistemic dimension, with a conception of presence to the mind or consciousness as the optimal source of knowledge and understanding. The twin notions of presence are actually intertwined, in the sense that the temporal present represents the optimum for epistemic presence: to know or understand something optimally or fully is to have it present before one's mind in the present (all at once). Descartes's *cogito* involves this twin notion of presence. The immediacy of "I am, I exist" vouchsafes Descartes's existence, but only in the moment that this thought is entertained. The *cogito* fails otherwise: "I was in existence" and "I will exist" admit of no certainty whatsoever. Ultimately, one can see in this privileging of presence (and the present) an ultimately theological conception of knowledge and understanding; one way of contrasting divine with merely human understanding is to say that God sees, knows, or understands everything all at once. That human understanding is extended in time is already a mark of its inferiority.

on cattle, which indicate ownership by a particular ranch, flags, which indicate things ranging from nationality to the finish line of a race, and knots in handkerchiefs, which indicate that something needs to be remembered. Some examples of natural indicators are dry lawns, which indicate drought, cracks in the walls of a house, which indicate subsidence, and darkening clouds, which indicate an oncoming storm. The connection between an indicator and what it indicates can thus be a matter of convention, as in the case of signs, or natural, as in the case of natural indicators. Where the connection is not purely conventional, the relation between indicator and indicated could be one of cause and effect (where the "surmise" goes from effect to cause), earlier and later (where there may be a common cause), probability and so on. In both cases, the connection is empirical and contingent, and is underwritten by habit, generalization and custom. In general, the connection is associative: indicators indicate something by our coming to associate the indicator with the thing indicated. As associative, there is in no case an essential or intrinsic connection between indicator and indicated.

Expression, by contrast, brings in the notion of meaning or sense, which, for Husserl, marks an altogether different relation. Expressions are meaningful signs, which Husserl restricts to linguistic signs, thereby excluding things such as facial expressions and bodily gestures. To get a feel for this distinction, consider the difference between the crying of a baby, which indicates, for example, a wet nappy or the need to eat, and the words "My nappy is wet" or "I'm hungry". Although the crying is associated with wetness and hunger, and so points the one hearing the baby's cry towards such things, the crying still only indicates, without actually saying or meaning "My nappy is wet" or "I'm hungry", whereas the expressions in each case do say and mean something: the expressions are *about* wetness and hunger, rather than indicators of them. Unlike the merely associative connection between indicators and what they indicate, the connection between expressions and their meaning is an essential one, as the notion of meaning constitutes what it is for something to be an expression.

Linguistic signs, as meaningful, thus involve the notion of expression, but Husserl's conception of language and linguistic signs is a good deal more complicated than this first pass at distinguishing between expression and indication might suggest. Husserl (see LI: 276) has what I am going to call a two-tiered conception of language, consisting of:

(a) the sensible, physical sign: the articulate, spoken "sound-complex", the written letters, words, and sentence;

(b) the mental states, "associatively linked" with the sensible, physical
     signs, which make them be the expression of something.

For Husserl, (b) is the locus of genuine meaning or sense, whereas (a)
is only meaningful in a derivative sense. Notice that sensible, physical
signs derive their meaning from mental states by being "associatively
linked" with them, which means that linguistic signs involve the notion
of indication: linguistic signs indicate, or point to, the mental states that
are the locus of genuine meaning or sense. The distinction between (a)
and (b) can be further delineated by noting the absence of an essential
connection between the sensible, physical signs and the underlying,
meaningful expressions. Since expressions are only associatively linked
with sensible signs, whatever meaning we accord to sensible signs has a
conventional component. On reflection, we can see that it need not have
been the case that the string of letters "wet" means *wet*; had language
evolved differently, the concatenation of those three letters may have
come to mean something else.

   Given this two-tiered conception, Husserl distinguishes between
communication and what he calls "solitary mental life". The way communication works for Husserl is as follows. Subject *A* has certain
thoughts he wishes to communicate to subject *B*. Accordingly, *A* produces a series of sounds or marks (i.e. words), which *A* intends to be
the outward manifestation (sign, indication) of those thoughts. Subject
B in turn perceives these outward signs or indications, and then sur-
mises the mental states of *A* that *A* wished to communicate. On this
picture of communication, indication plays an essential role; moreover, communication always involves a kind of gap, to be bridged by a
"surmise" of the kind one makes in the move from indicator to indicated. What I am trying to express by means of the indicative signs
I produce is something my interlocutor needs to figure out. Solitary
mental life, by contrast, involves no such gap: "*Expressions* function
meaningfully even in *isolated mental life, where they no longer serve to
indicate anything*" (LI: 269). Such pure expressions, dispensing with
the notion of indication altogether, no longer involve the use of words
as signs. Indeed, there can be no indicative function for words in solitary mental life, since there is no gap between the mental states and the
experience of them. There is nothing to "surmise" or connect by means
of an associative link, because the mental states are fully present to the
one whose states they are, experienced "at that very moment" of their
coming into existence (here we begin to see the way in which Husserl's
initial distinction is bound up with a conception of consciousness as

presence). Without any use of words as signs, there are, Husserl maintains, no "real" words involved in an interior soliloquy, but only "imagined" ones (see LI: 278–80).

From an initial sharp distinction between expression and indication, we are led to a sharp distinction between language understood as a complex of physically articulated signs and the intrinsically meaningful mental states on which the meaning of language depends. This latter distinction leads in turn to a sharp distinction between communication and solitary mental life. According to Derrida, these sorts of distinctions foreshadow, and indeed animate, Husserl's later explicit articulation of the phenomenological reduction. Indication, as bound up with the empirical, even physical, dimension of language, must be eliminable, leaving only an underlying layer of pure expression, whose essential meaning is unaffected by the elimination of associatively formed connections. In a passage that clearly anticipates the later development of the phenomenological reduction, Husserl makes this eliminability explicit:

> It is easily seen that the sense and the epistemological worth of the following analyses [i.e. the six logical investigations] does not depend on the fact *that there really are languages*, and that men really make use of them in their mutual dealings, or that there really are such things as men and a nature, and that they do not merely exist in imagined, possible fashion.
>
> (LI: 266, emphasis added)

If expression and indication cannot be separated in the way Husserl demands, then that will tell against the possibility of the phenomenological reduction. If the very idea of expression, and so the notions of sense and meaning, ultimately involves indication, then any attempt to isolate a layer or domain of "pure expression" that is fully present without any mediating play of signs will be futile, indeed incoherent. Consciousness, in so far as it involves the notion of meaning or sense, cannot be conceived of as fully and immediately present, even to the one whose consciousness it is. The ineliminability of indication, and so of mediation, undermines any privileging of the present, both in the sense of something's being fully present and in the temporal sense of the present moment.

In *Speech and Phenomena*, Derrida's principal argument against the validity of Husserl's "essential distinction" turns on the notion of "representation", and its role both in Husserl's distinction between pure expression and communication and in language and linguistic meaning more generally. Let us begin with the latter domain. Derrida argues here that all of language involves the notion of representation: "A sign is never an event, if by event we mean an irreplaceable and irreversible empirical particular" (SP: 50). In order for a sign to mean or stand for something, it must participate, so to speak, in something beyond itself: the sign, to be a sign, must serve as a representative of a type, and so cannot be "an irreplaceable and irreversible empirical particular". Consider the following set of signs (words):

house **house** *house* house house house **house** *house*

None of these signs is exactly like the others, in the sense that they all vary in size, shape and in some cases darkness; each one occupies its own region of space and has a slightly different history; each can thus be regarded as in some sense an "empirical particular". At the same time, there is also a very definite sense in which each of these signs is the same sign, that is, the sign "house", and this sense is crucial to each of these variously shaped marks being signs. Another way to put this is to say that all of these signs, in so far as they are signs, are tokens of a single type. Language, as a system of signs, requires this type-token structure, whereby different tokens are recognizable as the same. Every sign, as a sign, must stand for, or represent, or instantiate a type; otherwise there would be no words, phrases, sentences and so on that could be repeated, spoken or written on indefinitely many occasions. Repetition (or what Derrida calls "iterability") is essential to language.

But how do these points about representation and repetition affect Husserl and, in particular, the distinction between expression and indication? Recall that one way Husserl distinguishes communication between two subjects (what he sometimes calls "effective" or "genuine" communication) from "solitary mental life" or "mental soliloquy" is that the latter does not involve the production of "real words". Instead, in mental soliloquizing, there are only "imagined" words, fictitious language rather than the real thing, because the subject has nothing to communicate to itself. The critical question Derrida asks us to consider is what exactly the difference is between real and imaginary signs or language, between genuine and fictitious speech. What are real words, and how do we distinguish real ones from ones that are only imagined? Given his observations about representation and repetition, Derrida's point in raising these questions is to show that these distinctions cannot be maintained. All language or speech, as involving representation and repetition, has an element of fiction to it, in so far as any word one produces stands for an ideal type: "*The sign is originally wrought by fiction*" (SP: 56). Any linguistic sign one produces is, in some respects, fictitious and, in some respects, real or genuine: no word-instance has any more claim to reality than any other, since any word-instance, to be a genuine word-instance, must represent, stand for or instantiate a word-type, which is ideal rather than real. These requirements hold to an equal degree in the case of imaginary speech and in the case of "effective" communication, and so there can be no principled distinction between the two: whether "with respect to indicative communication or expression, there is no sure criterion by which to distinguish an outward language from an inward language or, in the hypothesis of an inward language, an effective language from a fictitious language" (SP: 56). Representation and ideality belong to "signification" in general, and so imagined speech and genuine speech are structurally equivalent: "By reason of the primordially repetitive structure of signs in general, there is every likelihood that 'effective' communication is just as imaginary as imaginary speech and that imaginary speech is just as effective as effective speech" (SP: 51). The upshot for Husserl is that "solitary mental life", in so far as it involves signification, involves the use of signs in the same way as in the case of effective communication, and since effective communication involves both expression and indication, so too does solitary mental life.

If Derrida is correct that solitary mental life is pervaded by indication, by the use of signs, then Husserl's appeal to the primacy of presence cannot be sustained. If consciousness is "sign-like", then the very idea of conscious experience involves notions such as representation and repetition, and so anything present to consciousness is bound up with, and depends on, something absent. Whatever there is that is essential to consciousness cannot be grasped, made fully available, within the present, within an "intuition" that is not at the same time founded on what lies beyond it. As developed thus far, Derrida's argument primarily undercuts what we might call the authority of the present in the realm of experience, by showing how any appeal to what is present to consciousness necessarily involves what is absent, and so what is present cannot play any special foundational role. A further consequence of this line of argument is that the very idea of the present moment in experience and, correlatively, of the idea of presence to consciousness, needs to be reconceived, because the way in which the present lacks authority means that it also lacks any kind of autonomy. As Derrida puts it:

If the punctuality of the instant is a myth, a spatial or mechanical metaphor, an inherited metaphysical concept, or all that at once, and if the present of self-presence is not *simple*, if it is constituted in a primordial and irreducible synthesis, then the whole of Husserl's argumentation is threatened in its very principle.   (SP: 61)

The mythological character of the present moment is already revealed in Derrida's critique of Husserl's characterization of solitary mental life. Solitary mental life was to be understood as the locus of "pure expression" because anything that might be indicated by signs would be understood at the very moment the experience occurred. One cannot tell oneself anything, because there is nothing hidden from oneself that needs pointing out. However, the entanglement of expression and indication means that the present is not a simple given, but is instead a complex compound, an intersection of past and future that is dependent on both: the "presence of the perceived present can appear as such only inasmuch as it is *continuously compounded* with a non presence and non perception, with primary memory and expectation (retention and protention)" (SP: 64).

Although the "punctuality of the instant" is already shown up by Derrida's arguments concerning expression and indication, a particularly intriguing and ironic feature of his subsequent argumentation is the extent to which, according to Derrida, Husserl himself debunks this myth of presence. That is, one strand of Derrida's argument is dedicated to showing how many of Husserl's phenomenological insights, especially those concerning the structure of time-consciousness, tell against his own appeals to the founding role of presence. Hence the idea that Derrida's argument is one that "deconstructs" Husserlian phenomenology, by revealing the ways in which it pulls itself apart. This deconstructive element can be seen in the previous quotation, since "retention" and "protention" are, after all, Husserlian terms; indeed, they are essential dimensions of his account of the temporal structure of experience. Derrida's point is that Husserl cannot have it both ways. The phenomenological descriptions of the structure of experience Husserl himself provides tell against his very own "principle of all principles". There is no pure experience, either temporally or spatially speaking. Any moment of experience is informed by, refers to, carries traces of or points ahead to other experiences within the ongoing flow. Husserl himself demonstrates this, despite his own continued allegiance to the mythology of presence.

On Derrida's account, consciousness is, we might say, "sign-like", in that whatever is present at any given time is always at the same time indicative of what is non-present. The structure of language, as well as the structure of signification more generally, involves this interplay of presence and non-presence. We can see this in the indicative dimension of signs, which stand for or represent something beyond themselves, their ideal types, but also in the temporally extended character of language use. Speaking, reading and writing all take place over time; sentences have a beginning, a middle and an end, such that what is said and understood is not something that happens all at once. Derrida calls this extended, representational dimension of signification "differance", which incorporates both the idea of differing and that of deferring. All signs involve difference, in the sense that signs are both empirical particulars and yet stand for something other than themselves (signs are, paradoxically, cases of sameness-in-difference), and the use of signs always involves some kind of delay or deferral, again in keeping with the idea that sense or meaning is never grasped in an instant, but only over time. The play of differance pervades language, but also, in so far as it involves signification, consciousness.

We might also put Derrida's view this way: consciousness is, or is like, a text. In one place, Derrida writes that "there is no domain of the psychic without text" (WD, 199), which underlines what I have been calling the "sign-like" character of conscious experience. As text, consciousness consists of an extended flow, any moment of which is informed by, or carries, traces of what lies elsewhere. Consciousness is, in this way, mediated, never immediate, since what is happening now in my experience can never be fully determined or evaluated at the time of that experience; the content and significance of my experience is continually open to revision and reinterpretation.

Derrida's debunking of the mythology of presence, and his correlative championing of a textual model of consciousness, signals his allegiance to certain ideas in Freud. That is, the essential role of non-presence and the sign-like nature of any present experience points to a fundamental role for the unconscious in the constitution of consciousness. What is present to consciousness, what is open to me about my own mental life at the moment, is not something free-standing or self-sufficient. What is present are symptoms, which point to or indicate some underlying tendencies, conditions or events. The indicative relation here has just been spelled out in spatial terms, as though the unconscious were lurking beneath the level of conscious experience. There is also, however, a temporal dimension, since what has been repressed, according to Freud, are often childhood wishes, fantasies and fears (usually of a sexual nature). The quotation above concerning the textual character of the psychic comes from Derrida's essay, "Freud and the Scene of Writing", wherein he both celebrates and interrogates Freud's use of writing as the dominant metaphor for consciousness. For Derrida, Freud, in his discernment of the domain of the unconscious, is the first to appreciate the textual nature of consciousness. We need to be careful here, though, if we are to appreciate just how radical Freud's ideas are (at least as Derrida understands them), since the metaphors of writing and texts still allow for the idea of a kind of "all-at-once" in the sense that the entirety of the text is somehow present and fully formed, even though it is only accessible or available piecemeal. To say that consciousness is a text or text-like does not mean that our experiences are like a big book, where the previous chapters are there, behind the current one, to be returned to as they were at the time they were read. The unconscious does not have that kind of static determinacy, but is itself a dynamic text, to be revised and reinterpreted. The real lesson of Freud, as Derrida reads him, is that:

> There is no present text in general, and there is not even a past present text, a text which is past as having been present. The text is not conceivable in an originary or modified form of presence. The unconscious text is already a weave of pure traces, differences in which meaning and force are united – a text nowhere present, consisting of archives which are *always already* transcriptions. Originary prints. Everything begins with reproduction. (WD: 211)

That "everything begins with reproduction" means that there is no recoverable moment of presence, no experience that can be inspected and dissected "just as it is", since experience is "always already" transcribed, mediated, permeated by "pure traces". That "everything begins with reproduction" means that there can be no pure phenomenology. Whether there can still be what Dennett calls "impure phenomenology", however, is another matter altogether. As we shall see, Dennett also develops a textual model of consciousness that, like Derrida's, embraces the idea that "there is no present text in general".

Dennett's heterophenomenology

In Part I of *Consciousness Explained* (and elsewhere), Dennett develops and defends a method for investigating consciousness, what he dubs "heterophenomenology", the principal virtue of which is its adherence to what Dennett sees as scrupulous scientific method. "The challenge is to construct a theory of mental events, using the data that scientific method permits" (CE: 71), and what that method allows as data is what is in principle available to a third-person, neutral investigator. In this sense, Dennett's approach to consciousness employs an "outside-in" strategy: the data deemed reliable are those that can be gleaned from a perspective external to the agent whose "consciousness" is under investigation (the reason for the inverted commas will become apparent as we proceed).

Dennett's cautious approach is fostered by his sense that consciousness is a "perilous phenomenon", which provokes "skepticism, anxiety, and confusion" in those who so much as contemplate its study (HSHC: 159). The dangers attending the study of consciousness are due in large part to the legacy of what Dennett sees as so many failed attempts. Like an imposing, yet alluring, mountain littered with the bodies of those who try to scale its heights, consciousness remains elusive in spite of the many efforts of philosophers, psychologists and neuroscientists. Of these three groups who seek to understand and explain consciousness, the failures of the first, the philosophers, have been especially egregious, primarily because of an entrenched but highly problematic set of assumptions about how consciousness both can and must be studied. For Dennett, the phenomenological tradition quite clearly exemplifies these shortcomings, and Dennett thinks that attention to the failings of phenomenology help to motivate the kind of approach to consciousness he recommends.

Although phenomenologists, principally Husserl, endeavoured "to find a new foundation for all philosophy (indeed, for all knowledge) based on a special technique of introspection in which the outer world and all its implications and presuppositions were supposed to be 'bracketed' in a particular act of mind known as epochē" (CE: 44), the exact nature and results of such a "technique" were never completely determined, and so phenomenology "has failed to find a single, settled method that everyone could agree upon" (CE: 44). Dennett's suspicions concerning the merits of phenomenology are fostered by this failure to secure agreement, prompting him instead to found a method inspired by disciplines where at least some agreement has been secured and more is promised: the natural sciences. In stark contrast to the natural sciences, where practitioners can be confidently ranked in terms of their expertise, the failures of phenomenology allow for no such ranking, which leads Dennett to make the following, striking claim: "So while there are zoologists, there really are no phenomenologists: uncontroversial experts on the nature of the things that swim in the stream of consciousness" (CE: 44–5).

Delimiting just what those "items in conscious experience" are is, for Dennett, a delicate matter, particularly in the wake of phenomenology's demise: the absence of experts means that there is no uncontroversial inventory of what "swims" in the stream of consciousness. Indeed, the persistence of "phenomenological controversies", in spite of the well-entrenched philosophical idea that "we all agree on what we find when we 'look inside' at our own phenomenology" (CE: 66), indicates that we must "be fooling ourselves about something" (CE: 67). In particular, Dennett argues that "what we are fooling ourselves about is the idea that the activity of 'introspection' is ever a matter of just 'looking and seeing'" (*ibid*.). Instead, "we are always actually engaging in a sort of impromptu theorizing – and we are remarkably gullible theorizers, precisely because there is so little to 'observe' and so much to pontificate about without fear of contradiction" (CE: 67–8).

According to Dennett, then, there are far fewer things swimming in the stream of consciousness than has traditionally been thought; indeed, what is taken to be there is not so much ascertained by introspective observation, as it is postulated retrospectively through largely creative acts of interpretation (the "impromptu theorizing" to which Dennett thinks we all are prone). That theorizing, moreover, even when it has the "feel" of observation, is as liable to error as any other, perhaps more so despite the fact that what one is theorizing about is one's own conscious experience. Rather than having the kind of certainty often conferred on it, Dennett sees the process of introspective self-interpretation as fraught with a whole host of pitfalls, due largely to the temporal lags between alleged states of consciousness and the introspective cataloguing and reporting of them. Within those lags, Dennett thinks, there is room for all sorts of errors to occur: "The logical possibility of misremembering is opened up no matter how short the time interval between actual experience and subsequent recall" (CE: 318). Dennett's criticisms apply not just to Husserl, but also to Sartre, at least at the time of *The Transcendence of the Ego*. Recall Sartre's conception of phenomenological method as "conspiring" with one's own conscious experience, which requires recreating the experience while tagging along with it. In his account of this procedure, Sartre claims, without argument, that it is "by definition always possible" to "reconstitute the complete moment" (TE: 46) of unreflected consciousness. Dennett's challenge to Sartre is to provide criteria for adjudicating among different and conflicting attempts at reconstitution. Since the original experience is long gone, how does one know and how can one show that one's current reconstitution of that experience is accurate, let alone "complete"?

The retrospective dimension of introspection creates one possibility of error. What I now think I thought back then may perhaps be different from what I actually thought at the time, although because I now think I thought it then, it will seem exactly as if I did back then as well. Such errors are thus highly recalcitrant when one is restricted to a first-person perspective. Misremembering, however, is not the only way in which one can get things wrong about one's own experience. That conscious (and other mental) states admit of the possibility of embedding, such that I can, for example, form judgements about how things seem and so forth, provides ample opportunity for mistakes to arise: "Might it not be the case that I believe one proposition, but, due to a faulty transition between states, come to think a different proposition? (If you can 'misspeak', can't you also 'misthink'?)" (CE: 317). As there is so much room for speculation, fabrication and misperception, introspection provides little in the way of a solid foundation for a properly scientific investigation of consciousness. Hence Dennett's preference for heterophenomenology, rather than the traditional auto- variety; consciousness is best approached from the outside, standing on the banks of the stream, as it were, rather than swimming along introspectively.

In many ways, Dennett's method is the mirror image of the Husserlian one. Whereas Husserl's phenomenology begins with the *epochē*, wherein commitment to the reality of the external world, including oneself as a denizen of that world, is suspended or "bracketed", the heterophenomenological method begins by bracketing any commitment to the reality of consciousness. The scientific investigator is to adopt as neutral an attitude as possible with respect to his subjects: "Officially, we have to keep an open mind about whether our apparent subjects are liars, zombies, parrots dressed up in people suits, but we don't have to risk upsetting them by advertising the fact" (CE: 83). Strictly speaking, then, heterophenomenology does not study conscious phenomena, since it is neutral with respect to the question of whether there are any. Its subject matter is instead reports of conscious phenomena: the actual transcripts produced in a laboratory setting recording what the "apparent subjects" say about their "experience". Indeed, even taking the noises emitted by these apparent subjects to amount to things they say is already a bold leap beyond the given: "The transcript or text is not, strictly speaking, given as data, for … it is created by putting the raw data through a process of interpretation" (CE: 75).

Having worked up the raw data into reports, the heterophenomenologist proceeds by exploring the possible relations between those reports and other data that are likewise accessible (at least in principle) from this external vantage-point, namely, the goings-on in the apparent subject's brain and nervous system. Dennett likens the investigator's approach here to one we might take towards a straightforwardly fictional text. Although we regard the "world" of that text as fictional, we might nonetheless look for "real-life" correlates of the text, for example, contemporaries of the author who may be considered the inspiration for characters in the work,

---

The intentional stance

A key feature of Dennett's heterophenomenological method is his notion of the "intentional stance", which the heterophenomenological investigator adopts when he chooses to treat the "noises" emitted by his subjects as meaningful words and reports. Rather than thinking of intentionality as a property or feature of an organism (or machine) in and of itself, Dennett instead recommends thinking of intentionality as a feature of how we view an entity, of what attitude or stance we take towards it and what it does. Very often, adopting the intentional stance towards an entity or range of events will yield far more in the way of predictive success, while another, such as the physical stance, will afford little in the way of useful insights. For example, someone who had adopted the intentional stance would detect a connection between someone's emitting the noise "Hello" and someone's waving his or her arm. Although the physics of these two events is wildly different, from the intentional stance they can both be located as forms of greeting, and will accordingly generate reliable predictions that the physicist can scarcely imagine. What the intentional stance renders discernible are very often "real patterns", but considerable care is needed in cashing out this idea. Some of these "patterns" are cases where we are reluctant to identify them as involving genuine intentionality. For example, one can take up the intentional stance towards a simple thermostat, attributing to it a small array of "beliefs" about the room (such as "too hot", "too cold" and "just right"), along with another small array of "desires" to change the temperature of the room in one direction or another. While one can take such a stance towards the thermostat, and even though we do often talk this way about things like machines and plants, such talk usually strikes us as loose, figurative or even metaphorical. These are cases of "as-if" intentionality, and so we stop short of treating them as instances of the "real thing". Although we can often feel confident about identifying a pattern as an instance of only "as-if" intentionality, and equally confident with respect to some instances of the "real thing", the thorny issue, according to Dennett, is one of how to make a principled demarcation between the two. There is, he contends, no clean and clear dividing line between the "as-if" cases and the genuine ones, and he suggests instead that we should see the difference as one of (admittedly very great) degree rather than kind.

---

or events in the author's biography that have been reworked to play a role in the dramatic narrative. Dennett's investigator likewise treats all of his worked-up reports as portrayals of "heterophenomenological worlds", populated by a range of fascinating characters: all those putative phenomena of consciousness. In so treating the reports, the heterophenomenologist regards these phenomena as strictly analogous to the characters in fiction. He does not take them as standing for real-life denizens of the world, at least not in any straightforward sense. At best, he regards them as cleverly disguised, reinterpreted versions of what is really going on in the brain. To the extent that Dennett's investigator can find sufficient connections between the population of the heterophenomenological world and the goings-on in the brain, he will (always tentatively) see the latter as the real topic of the reports.

Given this further articulation of Dennett's method, we can grasp more fully the reasons behind his distrust of introspection, as well as see more clearly the diagnosis of the weaknesses of people's "impromptu theorizing". If introspection is really a matter of theorizing, and if the proper objects of this theorizing are really objects and events in the brain, then small wonder that people's reports are unreliable, indeed often wildly inaccurate. After all, very few of us, even those of us who are well educated in other respects, have detailed knowledge of the workings of the brain and nervous system. Moreover, our usual predicament is such that those workings are generally obscured from view, that is, we are not in general well positioned to observe the workings of our own brain in any direct fashion. Thus, "what it is like to [us] is at best an uncertain guide to what is going on in [us]" (CE: 94). The indirect route of introspection is all each of us usually has to go on, and if Dennett is right it is a circuitous route indeed, much like the approach of reading Victorian novels, say, as a means for learning the historical facts of that era. The standard first-person authority championed by the philosophical, and especially the phenomenological, tradition is thus severely restricted:

> If you want us to *believe* everything you say about your phenomenology, you are asking not just to be taken seriously but to be granted papal infallibility, and that is asking too much. You are not authoritative about what is happening in you, but only about what seems to be happening in you.   (CE: 96)

The results of Dennett's heterophenomenology are at least as radical as the method, if not more so. Indeed, Dennett acknowledges that his view is "initially deeply counterintuitive", as it "requires a radical rethinking of the familiar idea of 'the stream of consciousness'" (CE: 17). In keeping with Dennett's speculation that there is less to introspect than has standardly been thought, the "stream of consciousness" is perhaps better understood as a scattered system of rivulets. What Dennett dubs the "Multiple Drafts" model of consciousness maintains that "at any point in time there are multiple 'drafts' of narrative fragments at various stages of editing in various places in the brain" (CE: 113). There is, on this model, a constant process of "additions, incorporations, emendations, and overwritings of content [which] occur, in various orders", and what "we actually experience is a product of many processes of interpretation – editorial processes, in effect" (CE: 112). Although talk of "multiple drafts" carries connotations of a series of processes culminating in a finished product, as takes place in the writing process from which Dennett borrows his terminology, the radicality of the model is precisely the denial of this suggestion: "Most important, the Multiple Drafts model avoids the tempting mistake of supposing that there must be a single narrative (the 'final' or 'published' draft, you might say) that is canonical – that is the actual stream of consciousness of the subject" (CE: 113).

Dennett thinks the virtues of the Multiple Drafts model are especially evident in its ability to accommodate otherwise intractable experimental findings. Dennett devotes considerable attention to cases of apparent movement, or the "phi phenomenon", which is familiar to most of us from watching films and television programmes. A projected film actually consists of numerous still images, but if these images are displayed at a fast enough rate the experience is one of continuous motion. A particularly striking case of the phi phenomenon involves the projection, in rapid succession, of two circles of light, separated by no more than 4 degrees of visual angle. Provided that the two circles are flashed rapidly enough, the viewer will have the experience of a single circle moving backwards and forwards. More interesting is the case where the two circles are of different colours. Here, subjects report experiencing the circle change colour along its apparent trajectory from one spot to another. What is puzzling about this experience is that the change of colour is experienced as taking place *before* the second circle is projected. How can the subject experience the change in colour before the second, differently coloured circle even makes an appearance? It would seem that the viewer would have to wait for the second circle to appear, but by then it would be too late to "go back" and "fill in" the movement from the first circle to the second.

Dennett argues that there are two apparently rival hypotheses to account for the colour phi phenomenon. First, there is the hypothesis that there is a kind of delay in the entire experience: the viewer is only consciously aware of the two circles, along with the apparent movement, following the receipt of both stimuli, that is, both flashing circles. Somehow, the mind or brain "waits" to "display" this "edited" version of events. (Dennett dubs this hypothesis "Stalinesque", in keeping with Stalin's notorious show trials, with their elaborately concocted pseudo-histories.) A second hypothesis contends that both circles are experienced, in the order they are projected, but what happens is that this experience is almost immediately forgotten; this more-or-less accurate version of events is replaced with the (false) memory of the circle's moving and changing colour along the way. Dennett dubs this hypothesis "Orwellian", in honour of the novel *1984*, in which George Orwell depicts an authoritarian regime that revises the historical record, including newspaper stories, photographs, and monuments, to suit its current agenda.

These two hypotheses offer markedly different explanations of the colour phi phenomenon and so it would seem that we should have to choose between them. Dennett contends, however, that there are no criteria, introspective or experimental, for choosing between these two hypotheses. Each hypothesis is equally able to explain the results of experiments that would appear to support the other. Given this, Dennett concludes that there is no "fact of the matter" with respect to the Orwellian and Stalinesque hypotheses, and so they are not ultimately genuine alternatives. Underlying the impulse to try to decide between the two, Dennett thinks, is a commitment to the idea of there being an authoritative moment or episode of consciousness that is the real experience. The Multiple Drafts model is distinguished precisely by its abandonment of this commitment. Given its postulation of multiple processes of input, revision and overwriting, there is no privileged moment of consciousness that counts as how something is really experienced. The real lesson is that: "There seems to be phenomenology. That's a fact that the heterophenomenologist enthusiastically concedes. But it does not follow from this undeniable, universally attested fact that there really is phenomenology. This is the crux" (CE: 366).

Phenomenological rejoinders

The criticisms canvassed in the previous three sections should not be taken as decisive in terms of limiting or, worse, foreclosing the possibility of phenomenology. One very broad consideration is that the criticisms tend to be highly selective. Levinas's criticisms, as we saw, focus only on phenomenology's treatment of the problem of the other, and so do nothing to impugn many of phenomenology's central ideas and insights about intentionality. Moreover, even the criticisms Levinas offers are, in many ways, phenomenological in spirit, in the sense that he proceeds by means of rich descriptions of the experiences through which the other is at least intimated, if not made manifest. Levinas, that is, details the ways in which the other "resists" and "refuses" my gaze. This resistance and refusal are dimensions of my experience and so are amenable to phenomenological treatment. (Similar considerations apply to Levinas's many characterizations of the epiphany of the face, both with respect to its ethical import and the ways in which it is bound up with experience of conversation.) Thus, we may be led to the conclusion that Levinas does not so much criticize phenomenology as offer us a more liberal conception of it.

The other two criticisms are equally selective, focusing on just one conception (or sometimes two) of phenomenology. It is not clear, for example, just how Derrida's criticisms of Husserlian phenomenology as betraying an unwitting reliance on a "metaphysics of presence" apply, say, to Merleau-Ponty. (Derrida, to his credit, does offer arguments to extend his critique to Heidegger, despite Heidegger's own criticisms of the concepts of presence and actuality in traditional philosophy.) Does anything Merleau-Ponty reveals about the integrity of perception or motor intentionality stand or fall on a commitment to the primacy of presence? Similar questions arise with respect to Dennett's criticisms, which seem to engage Husserl and Sartre most directly (Heidegger, for example, almost never mentions the notion of consciousness), but even their conceptions of phenomenology have the resources to mount a response to Dennett. Such a cause is aided by the fact that Husserl did respond to such criticisms in the first volume of *Ideas*, which indicates that scepticism about phenomenology is nothing especially new. It is instructive, I think, to look more closely at how Husserl handles these sorts of criticisms, both as a way of defending Husserl and displaying what is novel about Dennett's heterophenomenology. (Husserl has also been knocked about considerably in this book (and over the years), even by his fellow phenomenologists. Thus, it seems only fair to consider at the greatest length how his position might be defended.)

In sharp contrast to Dennett, Husserl wants to maintain "the absolute legitimacy of reflection" (*Ideas* I: §78), which he sharply distinguishes from introspection. Husserl characterizes reflection as involving the "includedness" of the first-order act within the second-order act, such that the two form an "unmediated unity" (recall our discussion in Chapter 1 concerning the disanalogy between phenomena and, for example, material objects). Given this, we can begin to understand his hostility towards the equating of phenomenological reflection with the notion of introspection, and so understand why he says in "Philosophy as Rigorous Science", which heralded the first volume of *Ideas*, that a proper comprehension of the character and significance of phenomenological method "depends on one's ... not confounding phenomenological intuition with 'introspection,' with interior experience" (PCP: 115). The legitimacy Husserl insists on actually has two dimensions, both of which Dennett would question. First, reflection reveals first-degree conscious acts, which do not need to be reflected on in order to be what they are. Husserl would thus reject Dennett's "first-person operationalism", which "brusquely denies the possibility in principle of consciousness of a stimulus in the absence of the subject's belief in that consciousness" (CE: 132). (It should be noted here that Sartre and Merleau-Ponty would likewise reject Dennett's position. Recall Sartre's account of the experience of nothingness as "pre-judicative", as in the case of seeing Pierre's absence from the cafe, and also Merleau-Ponty's critique of intellectualism, which mistakenly assimilates perceptual experience in general to the category of judgement.) Secondly, reflection does reveal (and so does not distort, nor simply create) those first-degree experiences, so that they become available to the phenomenological investigator for systematic study. It is thus wrong, Husserl insists, "to doubt whether experiences which become the object of a regard are not, as a consequence, converted *toto coelo* into something different" (*Ideas* I: §78). Although Husserl maintains that, with respect to the legitimacy of reflection, it "is only necessary here not to let oneself be confused by arguments which, in all formal precision, allow that conformity to the primal source, to that of pure intuition, be confounded" (*Ideas* I: §78), in §79 of *Ideas* I he nonetheless deigns to consider in some detail some of those arguments. These arguments are not ones of Husserl's own devising: they come instead from contemporaries, who, although as temporally remote from Dennett as Husserl is, are philosophically proximate to an astonishing degree.

In §79, Husserl quotes at length from a 1907 tract by the psychologist H. J. Watt. Husserl cites the following passage as especially illustrative:

> [Watt writes:] "It is scarcely possible even to form opinions concerning the way in which one comes to a knowledge of immediate experience. For it is neither knowledge nor the

object of knowledge; it is rather something else. One cannot see how a record concerning the experience of experience, even if it has been taken, could be put on paper." "But this is always the ultimate question of the fundamental problem of self-observation." "Today one designates this absolute description as phenomenology." (*Ideas* I: §79)

What Watt refers to here as "the fundamental problem of self-observation" is the problem of ascertaining the characteristics of "immediate experience". Drawing a sharp distinction between living through one's own experiences and knowing them, Watt sees the problem to lie mainly in the fact that self-observation is "ever retrospective", and so "is always knowledge about experiences just had as objects" (*Ideas* I: §79). There always arises the question of how one can "know that his experience is in actuality absolutely thus as he thinks it is" (*ibid.*). As Watt sees it, in self-observation "the relation to something objective pertaining to the experiences to be described changes. Perhaps this change has a much greater significance than one is inclined to believe" (*ibid.*). One can never, as it were, catch one's awareness unawares. How one's awareness shows itself in the act of reflection is no guarantee, Watt thinks, of how it was before, and so independently of, the reflective act. Alterations of various kinds might take place, and since the pre-reflective, lived experience has now receded into the past, there is no real possibility of factoring out any such alterations so as to determine what the experience at the time, that is, pre-reflectively, was really like.

Husserl's response to Watt's scepticism about phenomenology is governed by the sense that "all genuine scepticism of whatever kind and persuasion can be recognized by the fundamentally necessary absurdity that, in its argumentation, it implicitly presupposes as conditions of the possibility of its validity precisely what it denies in its theses" (*ibid.*). In other words, Husserl wants to argue that Watt's scepticism about the legitimacy of reflection is ultimately self-refuting in the sense that it presupposes precisely the kind of knowledge the possibility of which Watt denies: "He who says: I doubt the cognitive signification of reflection, asserts an absurdity" (*ibid.*). The absurdity Husserl sees as inherent in the sceptic's pronouncement is akin to the kind of manifest absurdity involved in someone's saying aloud "I am not speaking". This is so because the declaration "I doubt the cognitive signification of reflection" is itself a product of reflection, namely a reflective apprehension of the sceptic's own state of doubt. By confidently announcing his doubt, and by thus taking it for granted that his announcement is an announcement of that doubt, the sceptic thereby displays his reliance on reflection. In other words, the would-be sceptic's act of announcing his doubts undermines the legitimacy of the doubts so announced.

Husserl's point can be generalized beyond the sceptic's declaration of doubt. The problem facing the sceptic more generally is that he helps himself to so much in the way of talking about "immediate experience". In raising worries about the potential for reflection to distort these experiences, the sceptic thereby displays a certain amount of knowledge concerning the domain in question: he knows enough to know that there is something that may or may not be distorted by reflection, but even that knowledge is itself gained through reflection. Again, the sceptic is relying on reflection in order to challenge it.

While this response might be effective with respect to Watt's brand of scepticism, this is due to Watt's unreserved appeal to "immediate experience". In so far as Watt helps himself to such a notion while questioning reflection's capacity to reveal its nature, he is vulnerable to Husserl's charge of implicitly relying on the kind of knowledge his official position denies. Dennett's scepticism, however, is perhaps cagier in its conception of error. Although, as we have seen, he does occasionally state the problem as one of ascertaining now how things seemed then, another, deeper strand of his scepticism is not so much sceptical as eliminativist, in that it asserts that there is, in many respects, simply no such thing as "immediate experience". (Recall his Multiple Drafts model, which rejects the idea of a "final", "published" draft, along with his rejection of the dispute between Orwellian and Stalinesque explanations of the colour phi phenomenon, declaring instead that there is "no fact of the matter" between them.) Thus the problem is not one of error creeping in when trying to ascertain the nature of such experiences, as there is often nothing there to ascertain. This eliminativist tendency in Dennett's position provides another way of construing his otherwise puzzling claim that there only "seems to be phenomenology", namely, that at any moment when I stop to reflect it seems as though there has been a continuous stream of experiences leading up to that present moment. However, Dennett's point is that it does not follow that there really was such a continuous stream, and given that whatever there is of that stream has now flowed into the past, there is really no way of knowing whether or not there was one.

Stated this way, one might begin to sense that Dennett's scepticism carries a faint whiff of hyperbole, similar to the kind found in questions concerning one's entitlement to claiming to know that the world has been in existence for longer than the last ten minutes. If this is right, then he has done nothing to provide any special considerations to impugn our ability to know about our conscious experience. Be that as it may, it is also clear that the charge does little to impugn the general legitimacy of Husserlian reflection, and for two reasons. First, Husserl does not claim for reflection any magical powers such that it can extend any which way with absolute infallibility. Nowhere does Husserl ascribe to reflection the status of infallibility with respect to the entirety of one's conscious existence: the "really inherent includedness" characteristic of reflection is actually quite narrowly circumscribed. To take one example, it is, Husserl says, "lacking even in the case of the remembering of rememberings" (*Ideas* I: §38). He explains:

> The remembered remembering that occurred yesterday does not belong to the present remembering as a really inherent component of its concrete unity. With respect to its own full essence, the present remembering could exist even though in truth the past remembering had never existed.   (*Ibid.*)

Thus, Dennett's withholding of "papal infallibility" concerning phenomenology hardly affects Husserl's claims on behalf of the legitimacy of reflection. At the same time, the lack of such near-divine authority hardly warrants a thoroughgoing scepticism. If that were the basis for one's sceptical dismissal of phenomenology, one must, on pain of inconsistency, be equally dismissive with respect to the experimental sciences, none of which has taken up residency in the Vatican. Secondly, the very way in which Dennett states the problem concerning self-observation, such that there only "seems to be phenomenology" again exploits the idea of reflection, much as Watt's version did before him. Part of what Dennett finds on reflection is that conscious experience has "faded away" into the past in such a way that one might have difficulty determining now what features it might have had then, even to the extent that there were such features, so that now there is the temptation to "make things up" about how it might have been. All of this could very well be construed as insightful phenomenology, and so hardly amounts to a repudiation of such an enterprise.

Phenomenology and contemporary philosophy

In his essay "My Way to Phenomenology", written in the early 1960s, Heidegger writes that "the age of phenomenological philosophy seems to be over. It is already taken as something past which is only recorded historically along with other schools of philosophy" (OTB: 82). The timeframe of our discussion, beginning as it does with Husserl and ending with Merleau-Ponty, would appear to confirm Heidegger's rather dark pronouncement: phenomenology is a movement whose time has come and gone.

Although phenomenology understood as a movement may have peaked several decades ago, especially in terms of the publication of monumental works (*Phenomenology of Perception* perhaps being the last in the line), it would be a mistake to infer from this that phenomenology is no longer philosophically relevant, that philosophers working today have nothing to learn from phenomenological philosophy or that phenomenology does not offer anything of lasting value to students of philosophy in general. Of course, any really great work in the history of philosophy is of continued relevance to the ongoing practice of philosophy: Plato and Aristotle, along with Kant and Hegel, are still read today for more than historical or scholarly interest, despite the fact that whatever "movements" they may have spawned have long since come to an end. The principal texts of phenomenology are no exception. Each of the figures we have considered in the first four chapters has numerous contemporary expositors and devotees: philosophers working today who see ideas in these texts worthy of further articulation and pursuit. I would suggest, however, that phenomenology is important to contemporary philosophy not just in the way any significant works in the history of philosophy are, but in ways that more directly engage contemporary concerns and issues. This is partly due, of course, to the greater historical proximity of phenomenology to contemporary philosophy than other movements or moments in philosophy, but that is only one reason for phenomenology's continued importance.

Consider again phenomenology's rejection of philosophical naturalism, a view that is perhaps even more prominent today than when Husserl railed against it in "Philosophy as Rigorous Science". Dennett is one example of contemporary naturalism, as can be seen in his insistence on studying consciousness "using the data that scientific method permits". The Australian philosophers D. M. Armstrong and J. J. C. Smart are further examples: according to Smart's materialism, "there is nothing in the world over and above those entities which are postulated by physics" (1987: 203), whereas Armstrong maintains that "it is the scientific vision of [human beings], and not the philosophical or religious or artistic or moral vision of [human beings], that is the best clue we have to the nature of" human beings (1981: 4). Although phenomenology by and large does not seek to discredit the natural sciences, exposing them as, say, just one more "interpretation" of reality, nonetheless it rejects the idea, central to naturalism, that the natural sciences are the only legitimate form of enquiry, capable of fully accounting for what there is. Husserl, as we saw, argued that the natural sciences, despite their technical rigour and astounding achievements, remain "naive": unable to account for their own possibility. This kind of charge finds its way into later phenomenology, as can be seen in the following pair of passages from the Preface to *Phenomenology of Perception*:

> Science has not and never will have, by its nature, the same significance *qua* form of being as the world which we perceive, for the simple reason that it is a rationale or explanation of that world. (PP: viii–ix)

> Scientific points of view, according to which my existence is a moment of the world's, are always both naive and at the same time dishonest, because they take for granted, without explicitly mentioning it, the other point of view, namely that of consciousness, through which from the outset a world forms itself round me and begins to exist for me. (PP: ix)

These passages give voice to phenomenology's opposition to naturalism and also indicate what it sees as the stakes in mounting that opposition, both intellectually and existentially. That is, phenomenology's critical engagement with naturalism is not offered as merely a kind of intellectual exercise, whereby one demonstrates the superiority of one philosophical theory, method or view over another, although such an exercise is far from uninteresting (especially to philosophers!), but rather is meant to carry practical significance as well.

What I mean here might be seen by recalling Dennett's naturalistic approach to consciousness, wherein the heterophenomenological investigator brackets his commitment to any claims concerning his subjects' actually being conscious. Dennett's resolutely third-person approach to consciousness is indicative of naturalism's general squeamishness with respect to the very idea of experience: a general refusal to treat experience as a legitimate domain of enquiry in and of itself. (Although Dennett himself counsels against any methodology that involves "feigning anaesthesia", his own approach does not always seem to conform to that advice.) And Dennett is but one example. We find in much recent philosophy of mind a tendency towards such "feigning", as more naturalistically inclined philosophers marshal arguments in favour of various kinds of materialism. According to Armstrong's materialism, for example, a human being is "nothing but a physico-chemical mechanism" (1981: 2). So, he maintains, "we can give a complete account [of human beings] *in purely physico-chemical terms*" (1981: 1), and so presumably give an account that fails to describe human beings and their experience in intentional terms. (As "identity theorists", Armstrong and Smart hold that any intentional states we might ascribe to human beings are identical to non-intentional, physical states, and so the intentional can be "reduced" to the non-intentional.) A more recent and radical form of materialism makes this presumption explicit: "eliminative materialism", which, as the philosopher of mind Stephen Stich has put it, holds:

> that the intentional states and processes that are alluded to in our everyday descriptions and explanations of people's mental lives and their actions are *myths*. Like the gods that Homer invoked to explain the outcome of battles, or the witches that Inquisitors invoked to explain local catastrophes, they *do not exist*.   (1996: 115)

The invocation of the notion of mythology is meant quite seriously here. According to eliminative materialism, just as our modern conception of the world finds no place for witches or the gods of Homer, so too will our ultra-modern conception find no place for such soon-to-be antiquated notions as "belief, desire, fear, sensation, joy, pain, and so on" (Churchland 1988: 44). Intentionality may be the mark of the mental, but the whole notion of the mental is an outmoded myth.

Given these tendencies ranging from reduction to outright elimination of the very idea of intentionality, materialism represents a point of view that, in Merleau-Ponty's words, "is not alive to its own existence, and which resides in things" (PP: 23). Materialism constitutes a kind of forgetfulness (a feigning of amnesia, perhaps, rather than anaesthesia), such that the materialist overlooks or ignores the experience by which he acquired a conception of the material world. That experience is discounted, while what experience discloses is accorded a kind of exclusive validity:

> The physicist's atoms will always appear more real than the historical and qualitative face of the world, the physico-chemical

processes more real than the organic forms, the psychological atoms of empiricism more real than perceived phenomena … as long as the attempt is made to build up the shape of the world (life, perception, mind) instead of recognizing, as the source which stares us in the face and as the ultimate court of appeal in our knowledge of these things, our *experience* of them. (PP: 23)

The kind of failure Merleau-Ponty is describing here is evident in Dennett's conception of heterophenomenology, especially if we concentrate on the heterophenomenological investigator who avails himself of Dennett's methods. Although the heterophenomenologist's stinginess in ascribing consciousness to his subjects is the hallmark of his method, he is not especially stingy with respect to the data that he "works up" into texts depicting "heterophenomenological worlds"; nor is he especially cautious with respect to the availability of neurophysiological data, even if he recognizes the technical difficulties involved in their reliable collection. But how is this "availability" to be understood or, even better, how does the heterophenomenologist understand the availability of such data? In collecting and interpreting data, in deciding to take up or withhold the "intentional stance", in constructing and deciphering texts, it would seem that the heterophenomenologist's experience is in evidence throughout these processes, as more or less presupposed. And yet how does the heterophenomenologist conceive of himself? One is tempted to say, on Dennett's behalf, that he takes the intentional stance towards himself, but in that case, how is his "decision" to be understood? Is the taking up of the stance towards himself motivated by considerations of what best explains what he, the heterophenomenologist, would otherwise have to regard as mere noises and bodily movements? If so, then how is his so "regarding" them prior to "deciding" to take up the stance to be accounted for?

As we have seen throughout this book, a principal motive for the practice of phenomenology is to facilitate a return to experience, to reawaken in us a sense of its importance by demonstrating the founding role of experience in our conception of the world, however sophisticated that conception has become through the advancement of the natural sciences. In striving to reawaken us to our own experience, to the phenomena through which our conception of the world is constituted, phenomenology seeks to awaken us to ourselves: to make us alive to our own existence as subjects who bear a kind of ultimate responsibility for that conception. Phenomenology awakens us to the philosophical and existential primacy of experience, of intentionality, of subjectivity: of everything that comes with the assertion of the words "I am". For Husserl, the primacy of "I am" is something that philosophy is obliged to acknowledge and illuminate. To do otherwise, to deny or disregard subjectivity, is the mark of philosophical immaturity:

> First of all, before everything else conceivable, *I* am. This "I am" is for me, the subject who says it, and says it in the right sense, the *primitive intentional basis for my world*; and, at the same time, it must not be overlooked that likewise the "Objective" world, the "world for all of us" as accepted with this sense by me, is also "my" world. But "I am" is the primitive intentional basis, not only for "the" world, the one I consider real, but also for any "ideal world" that I accept; and this holds, without exception, for anything and everything of which I am conscious as something existent in any sense whatever that I understand or accept – for everything that I show, sometimes legitimately, sometimes illegitimately, to be existent – including me myself, my life, my believing, and all this consciousness-of. Whether convenient or inconvenient, and even though (because of no matter what prejudices) it may sound monstrous to me, it is the *primal matter-of-fact to which I must hold fast*, which I, as a philosopher, must not disregard for a single instant. For children in philosophy, this may be the dark corner haunted by the spectres of solipsism and, perhaps, of psychologism, of relativism. The true philosopher, instead of running away, will prefer to fill the dark corner with light. (FTL: §95)

The intertwining of the kind of philosophical illumination Husserl envisages and the achievement of a kind of self-discovery resonate throughout the phenomenological tradition, from Heidegger's conception of authenticity through Sartre's descriptions of bad faith to Merleau-Ponty's return to phenomena, and this intertwining signals the lasting value of phenomenology. Inherent to consciousness is a tendency towards forgetfulness, and this tendency is both manifest in, and exacerbated by, the staggering successes of the natural sciences, as well as philosophy's own recent tendency to interpret that success as sounding the death knell for any non-scientific form of enquiry. Phenomenology, as an antidote to these tendencies, retains its importance, even as the founding texts of phenomenology recede further into the past. As Merleau-Ponty already recognized, the texts of phenomenology are ultimately of secondary importance, subsidiary to the return to phenomena that each individual must enact on his or her own:

> We shall find in ourselves, and nowhere else, the unity and true meaning of phenomenology. It is less a question of counting up quotations than of determining and expressing in concrete form this *phenomenology for ourselves* which has given a number of present-day readers the impression, on reading Husserl or Heidegger, not so much of encountering a new philosophy as of recognizing what they had been waiting for.
>
> (PP: viii)

Summary of key points

- According to Levinas, phenomenology exemplifies the assimilative tendencies inherent in the Western intellectual tradition, and so fails to preserve the otherness of the other.
- Levinas argues that the other is intimated (rather than manifest) in the epiphany of the face, as something that resists or refuses any attempt at assimilation or containment.
- While Husserl maintains that solitary mental life is marked by the absence of indicative signs, Derrida contends that attention to the representational-repetitive structure of language shows that *all* meaning involves both indication and expression.
- Derrida argues that the content of consciousness, as sign-like, is never fully and immediately present to the one whose consciousness it is, but instead is permeated by indicative relations, deferrals, and delay.
- Against the phenomenological tradition, Dennett argues that consciousness is best approached from the outside, via the method of "heterophenomenology".
- Dennett's Multiple Drafts model of consciousness denies that there is one well-defined stream of consciousness.
- Criticisms of phenomenology tend to be piecemeal, attacking only one conception of phenomenology (namely Husserl's) rather than the movement as a whole.
- Against sceptics, Husserl argues that general doubts concerning the validity of reflection are ultimately self-refuting.
- The continued value and relevance of phenomenology do not depend on its continuation as a movement or school of thought.
- Phenomenology remains important as a *practice* that insists on the general validity of the category of experience.

Questions for discussion and revision

The following questions are designed to facilitate discussion and may also be appropriate as paper topics.

one Husserl and the project of pure phenomenology

1. How and why does Husserl argue against naturalism? What is the relation between his arguments against a naturalistic conception of *logic* and his conception of phenomenology? Why does he think that the phenomena of phenomenology cannot be understood as natural entities, akin to material objects?
2. In what way(s) is phenomenology for Husserl a *transcendental* investigation? What kinds of questions does phenomenology consider, and why does Husserl think that the natural attitude, including the natural sciences, is unable to answer those sorts of questions?
3. What is the phenomenological reduction? How does it work and why does Husserl think it is necessary for phenomenology? What, according to Husserl, does the phenomenological reduction reveal?
4. Consider your own perceptual experience, a particular episode of visual or auditory experience, and try to describe it using Husserl's structural concepts, such as retention and protention, horizon and synthesis, noesis and noema. How might one argue that these structures are *essential* to your experience being what it is?
5. What is the *eidetic* reduction? How does it work? How is it different from the phenomenological reduction? Why is the eidetic reduction essential to Husserl's overall project of transcendental phenomenology?

two Heidegger and the existential turn

1. What is the "question of being", and how is it related to phenomenology? Why does Heidegger say that "only as phenomenology, is ontology possible"?

2. Heidegger's phenomenology is a phenomenology of everydayness. Why does he think that phenomenology must proceed in this manner? How accurate or compelling do you find his descriptions of our everyday activity to be? In what ways, if any, do you find his descriptions to be problematic? Is there anything Heidegger seems to be ignoring or omitting that would raise difficulties for his account?

3. A principal feature of Husserl's phenomenology is its concern with *intentionality*: all consciousness is consciousness *of* something. In what ways, and to what extent, does Heidegger share this concern? That is, in what ways is his account of Dasein's "everydayness" an account of the notion of intentionality, and in what ways, if any, is Heidegger's account *transcendental* in the way that Husserl's is? If Heidegger *is* interested in intentionality, does that mean that he too is primarily concerned with *consciousness*?

4. Heidegger says that Dasein, that is, the kind of beings we are, is a being "for which, in its being, that being is an issue". What is the significance of this definition with respect to Heidegger's phenomenology, that is, what sort of phenomena crucially depend on, or hang together with, the idea that we are beings whose way of being is something we can confront and determine? Could there be a phenomenology of a being whose own being was *not* an issue for it? Could such a being "have" a world in Heidegger's sense of "world"?

5. What role does the notion of *death* play in Heidegger's project in *Being and Time*? What are some of the peculiarities involved in thinking about death, especially when it comes to thinking about one's own? Why, for Heidegger, is death so important for Dasein's realization of its "authenticity"? Could a being who was immortal, that is, a being for whom death was not an issue or a possibility, be authentic in Heidegger's sense?

three Sartre and subjectivity

1. In *The Transcendence of the Ego*, Sartre's principal aim is to demonstrate that "first-degree consciousness" lacks an ego, and the principal way in which he demonstrates this is via phenomenological description. What sorts of issues arise in trying to describe first-degree consciousness? Why, for example, is Husserl's method of *reflection* problematic? What does Sartre propose instead of reflection? How does one know when one has given an adequate description of non-reflective consciousness?

2. What does Sartre mean when he says in *The Transcendence of the Ego* that "the ego is *by nature* fugitive"? How does this claim affect our understanding of the relationship between consciousness and the ego? What is the significance of this claim for comparing Sartre's phenomenology to Husserl's? What consequences does this claim have for the nature and possibility of

self-knowledge, that is, in what sense is there a self to be known, and what can be known about "it"?

3. A central concept of *Being and Nothingness* is that of *bad faith*. What is bad faith, and why is it significant? That is, what does a consideration of bad faith show about the structure of consciousness (or about the kind of beings we are)?

4. In *Being and Nothingness*, Sartre claims that human beings are a combination of "facticity" and "transcendence". What does Sartre mean in claiming this, and how is this claim related to the idea that human beings are *conscious*?

four Merleau-Ponty and the phenomenology of embodiment

1. A central concept in Husserl's phenomenology is the *phenomenological reduction*. How is this notion developed in Merleau-Ponty? How does his conception of a reduction compare with Husserl's? In what ways is Merleau-Ponty's "return to phenomena" a continuation of Husserl's original project and in what ways is it a departure?

2. What does Merleau-Ponty mean when he claims that "an impression can never by itself be associated with another impression"? How does he argue for this claim? What is the significance of this claim within his attempt to overcome "traditional prejudices" in the domain of perception?

3. How does Merleau-Ponty argue against the idea that all perceptual experience involves *judgement*?

4. Why do Husserl and Merleau-Ponty think that the body cannot be regarded as just one more object among others? What is it about the experience of the body that sets it apart, categorically, from the experience of objects?

5. In Part I of *Phenomenology of Perception*, Merleau-Ponty devotes considerable attention to the case of Schneider, a veteran of the First World War with a curious set of impairments. What conclusions does Merleau-Ponty draw from the case of Schneider? How does he use Schneider to criticize both empiricism and intellectualism?

6. What does Merleau-Ponty mean by "motor intentionality"? In what sense is it, as Merleau-Ponty claims, "basic intentionality", that is, what does he mean in claiming that "consciousness is in the first place not a matter of 'I think that' but of 'I can'"?

five Problems and prospects: phenomenology and its critics

1. What is the problem of other minds? How does the problem arise in phenomenology and how is the problem treated in the conceptions of phenomenology we have explored in Chapters 1–4?

2. What is wrong with the notion of totality, understood as the goal or purpose of intellectual enquiry? What gets ignored or effaced in the quest for totalization? Why does Levinas think that phenomenology exemplifies Western philosophy's striving for totality?

3. What is the significance of Levinas's notion of "the face" for phenomenology? In what sense is his account of "the other" phenomenological? In what ways does it constitute a critique of phenomenology?

4. How does Derrida criticize the notion of *presence*? What is the significance of his criticisms for Husserl's conception of phenomenology? More specifically, if Derrida is right, how must we alter our conception of consciousness, and so the project of describing its content and articulating its structure?

5. What does Derrida mean in claiming that "a sign is never an event, if by event we mean an irreplaceable and irreversible empirical particular"? What is the significance of this claim in his overall argument against Husserl?

6. What is heterophenomenology, according to Dennett, and why does he think it is superior to the more traditional forms of phenomenology (or Phenomenology)? What sorts of problems beset phenomenology and why does Dennett think these problems cannot be overcome?

7. What is the Multiple Drafts model of consciousness and why does Dennett think it is superior to more traditional conceptions of consciousness?

8. How might Husserl and other members of the phenomenological tradition respond to the various criticisms raised by Levinas, Derrida and Dennett?

Further reading

The secondary literature on phenomenology is vast, and the newcomer is apt to be bewildered by the variety. As a way into the wilderness, I have assembled a number of works that are, in most cases, readily available, and, in all cases, likely to be useful to students who are still feeling their way around phenomenology. Many of these volumes have their own bibliographies, which will direct you to further, more specialized reading.

General works on phenomenology

Michael Hammond, Jane Howarth & Russell Keat, *Understanding Phenomenology* (Oxford: Blackwell, 1991) is an introduction to the phenomenology of Husserl, Sartre and Merleau-Ponty that is geared in each case to particular works or portions thereof (*Cartesian Meditations* for Husserl, *The Transcendence of the Ego* and parts of *Being and Nothingness* for Sartre and *Phenomenology of Perception* for Merleau-Ponty). The volume is currently out of print, but should not be too difficult to locate. For a comprehensive introduction to the phenomenological movement, see Dermot Moran, *Introduction to Phenomenology* (London: Routledge, 2000). The book is organized chronologically and biographically, with chapters devoted to the "usual suspects" (Husserl, Heidegger, Sartre, Merleau-Ponty), as well as ones on Brentano, Gadamer, Levinas, Arendt, and Derrida. Dermot Moran & Timothy Mooney (eds), *The Phenomenology Reader* (London: Routledge, 2002) is perhaps the only comprehensive anthology of the phenomenological movement available in English, providing selections from Brentano, Husserl, Heidegger, Sartre and Merleau-Ponty, as well as Reinach, Stein, Gadamer, Arendt, de Beauvoir, Levinas, Derrida and Ricoeur. Many of the primary texts in phenomenology (especially those of Husserl) are, when in print, incredibly expensive, and others by some of the less widely read figures can be hard to find, especially in translation. Herbert Spiegelberg, *The Phenomenological Movement*, 3rd enlarged edn (Dordrecht: Kluwer, 1982) is a work that covers the entirety of the phenomenological movement, including its origins in nineteenth-century philosophy and psychology.

Works about Husserl

Rudolf Bernet, Iso Kern & Eduard Marbach, *An Introduction to Husserlian Phenomenology* (Evanston, IL: Northwestern University Press, 1995) provides a comprehensive introduction to Husserl's philosophy, ranging from his views on mathematics and logic to his conception of the "lifeworld", developed in some of his final works. The second chapter, on the phenomenological and eidetic reductions, is especially helpful, as the authors document the several different motivations for the performance of the reduction. Hubert Dreyfus & Harrison Hall (eds), *Husserl, Intentionality, and Cognitive Science* (Cambridge, MA: MIT Press, 1984) contains a number of essays that are useful in terms of explicating and evaluating Husserl's phenomenology, with an emphasis on his relevance to contemporary cognitive science and philosophy of mind. The pair of papers by Dagfinn Føllesdal ("Husserl's Notion of *Noema*" and "Husserl's Theory of Perception") provides short, clear discussions of some of Husserl's main ideas.

Emmanuel Levinas, *Discovering Existence with Husserl*, R. Cohen & M. Smith (trans.) (Evanston, IL: Northwestern University Press, 1998) is a collection of Levinas's essays on Husserl, ranging from 1929 to 1977. Given their span, the essays allow one to observe Levinas's transition from student of phenomenology to sympathetic critic. His *The Theory of Intuition in Husserl's Phenomenology*, 2nd edn, A. Orianne (trans.) (Evanston, IL: Northwestern University Press, 1995) is a study of Husserl's phenomenology, written by Levinas very early in his philosophical career (in 1930, at the age of 24) shortly after studying with Husserl in Freiburg.

Jan Patočka, *An Introduction to Husserl's Phenomenology* (Chicago, IL: Open Court, 1995) is a helpful introduction, covering a number of central topics, including Husserl's early, formative ideas on logic and arithmetic, the reduction, time-consciousness, and embodiment. Patočka, a Czech philosopher, was one of Husserl's later students. Paul Ricoeur, *Husserl: An Analysis of His Phenomenology* (Evanston, IL: Northwestern University Press, 1967) is a collection of essays on Husserl's phenomenology by one of the great French phenomenological philosophers. The commentaries on *Cartesian Meditations* are especially good for reading alongside the original work. A collection of essays by contemporary philosophers and scholars in Barry Smith and David Woodruff Smith (eds), *The Cambridge Companion to Husserl* (Cambridge: Cambridge University Press, 1995) covers many of the central topics in Husserl's phenomenology.

Works about Heidegger

Hubert Dreyfus, *Being-in-the-world: A Commentary on Heidegger's Being and Time, Division I* (Cambridge, MA: MIT Press, 1991) is a comprehensive commentary on Division I by one of the leading American Heidegger scholars, with an emphasis on Heidegger's relevance to contemporary philosophy of mind and epistemology, as well as current debates about the viability of artificial intelligence. The book also contains an Appendix (co-written with Jane Rubin) on Division II. Most of the essays in the collection edited by Hubert Dreyfus and Harrison Hall (eds), *Heidegger: A Critical Reader* (Oxford: Blackwell, 1992) concentrate on Heidegger's early philosophy, and so will be helpful for working through *Being and Time*. Hubert Dreyfus and Mark A. Wrathall (eds), *A Companion to Heidegger* (Oxford: Blackwell, 2004) is a collection of thirty-one essays, organized topically, with nine essays devoted specifically to topics in *Being and Time*, and their *Heidegger Reexamined* (London: Routledge, 2002) is a four-volume set that gathers together many of the most important essays in English on Heidegger's philosophy.

Charles Guignon (ed.), *Cambridge Companion to Heidegger* (Cambridge: Cambridge University Press, 1993) contains a number of helpful essays on Heidegger's early philosophy (and several on his later thought as well). Theodore Kisiel & John van Buren (eds), *Reading Heidegger from the Start: Essays in His Earliest Thought* (Albany, NY: SUNY Press, 1994) considers Heidegger's philosophical development, with particular emphasis on the influences upon his thinking. Accordingly, several essays are devoted to Heidegger's relation to Husserl. Stephen Mulhall, *Routledge Philosophy Guidebook to Heidegger and Being and Time* (London: Routledge, 1996) is a very readable commentary on *Being and Time*, covering most of the key ideas of both Division I and Division II. Mark A. Wrathall & Jeff Malpas (eds), *Heidegger, Authenticity, and Modernity: Essays in Honor of Hubert L. Dreyfus, Volume 1* (Cambridge, MA: MIT Press, 2000) contains a number of important essays on Heidegger and *Being and Time*, and their *Heidegger, Coping, and Cognitive Science: Essays in Honor of Hubert L. Dreyfus, Volume 2* (Cambridge, MA: MIT Press, 2000) concentrates on "applied" Heidegger, that is, the idea of using Heidegger's philosophy to address philosophical problems in such areas as the philosophy of mind, artificial intelligence, and ethics.

Works about Sartre

Christina Howells (ed.), *The Cambridge Companion to Sartre* (Cambridge: Cambridge University Press, 1992) contains a number of helpful essays on Sartre's philosophy, although not all concern his phenomenology. The Conclusion, subtitled "Sartre and the Deconstruction of the Subject", is especially good in documenting the significance of Sartre's early insights concerning the structure of subjectivity. Paul Arthur Schilpp (ed.), *The Philosophy of Jean-Paul Sartre* (La Salle, IL: Open Court, 1981) contains a number of essays on Sartre's philosophy, including ones by Paul Ricoeur, Hubert Dreyfus, Dagfinn Føllesdal and Hazel Barnes. As a volume in the Library of Living Philosophers series, the book also contains an extended interview with Sartre concerning his philosophical development, as well as replies by Sartre to the essays.

Works about Merleau-Ponty

Taylor Carman, "The Body in Husserl and Merleau-Ponty", *Philosophical Topics* 27(2) (Fall 1999), 205–26 is an account of Husserl and Merleau-Ponty's respective conceptions of embodiment that emphasizes their differences. Carman argues that Merleau-Ponty's conception represents a distinctive improvement over Husserl's prior account. Taylor Carman & Mark B. N. Hansen (eds), *The Cambridge Companion to Merleau-Ponty* (Cambridge: Cambridge University Press, 2005) is a very recent collection of essays, including a number that provide helpful accounts of Merleau-Ponty's conceptions of perception, embodiment and motor intentionality, as well as illustrations of his continued relevance to contemporary philosophy and cognitive science. Hubert Dreyfus & Stuart E. Dreyfus, "The Challenge of Merleau-Ponty's Phenomenology of Embodiment for Cognitive Science", in *Perspectives on Embodiment*, G. Weiss & H. Haber (eds), 103–120 (London: Routledge, 1999) provides a detailed account of Merleau-Ponty's conception of motor intentionality and the intentional arc, as seen through the lens of the authors' longstanding interest in skills and skill acquisition. Sean D. Kelly, "What Do We See (When We Do)?", *Philosophical Topics* 27(2) (Fall 1999), 107–28 rehearses and extends a number of Merleau-Ponty's principal objections to empiricist and intellectualist (or cognitivist) accounts of visual experience.

Works about Levinas

Simon Critchley & Robert Bernasconi (eds), *Cambridge Companion to Levinas* (Cambridge: Cambridge University Press, 2002) is a recent collection of essays on a wide range of issues in Levinas's philosophy. Most relevant perhaps to our discussion is R. Bernet's essay, "Levinas's Critique of Husserl".

Works about Derrida

J. Claude Evans, *Strategies of Deconstruction: Derrida and the Myth of the Voice* (Minneapolis, MN: University of Minnesota Press, 1991) is in large part a meticulous reconstruction of Derrida's arguments against Husserl in *Speech and Phenomena*, along with a vigorous defence of Husserl against them.

Works about Dennett

David R. Cerbone, "Phenomenology: Straight and Hetero" in *A House Divided: Comparing Analytic and Continental Philosophy*, C. G. Prado (ed.), 105–38 (Amherst, MA: Humanity Books, 2003) is a more extensive examination than found in Chapter 5 of Dennett's conception of heterophenomenology, his critique of the phenomenological tradition, and the effectiveness of these criticisms in light of Husserl's own response to scepticism about phenomenology. John McDowell, "The Content of Perceptual Experience", in his *Mind, Value, and Reality*, 341–58 (Cambridge, MA: Harvard University Press, 1998) is an excellent critique of Dennett's account (among others) of perceptual experience that diagnoses his "off-key phenomenology" and emphasizes the importance of the distinction between the personal and the sub-personal in descriptions of perceptual experience.

References

Aristotle 1941. *The Basic Works of Aristotle*, R. McKeon (ed.). New York: Random House.

Armstrong, D. 1981. *The Nature of Mind and Other Essays*. Ithaca, NY: Cornell University Press.

Beauvoir, S. de 1962. *The Prime of Life*. Cleveland, OH: World Publishing.

Berkeley, G. [1710] 1957. *A Treatise Concerning the Principles of Human Knowledge*, C. Turbayne (ed.). Indianapolis, IN: Bobbs-Merrill.

Churchland, P. 1988. *Matter and Consciousness*, rev. edn. Cambridge, MA: MIT Press.

Dennett, D. C. 1981. *Brainstorms*. Cambridge, MA: MIT Press.

Dennett, D. C. 1982. "How to Study Human Consciousness Empirically, or Nothing Comes to Mind". *Synthese* **59** (1982), 159–80.

Dennett, D. C. 1992. *Consciousness Explained*. Boston, MA: Little, Brown.

Derrida, J. 1973. *Speech and Phenomena and Other Essays on Husserl's Theory of Signs*, D. Allison (trans.). Evanston, IL: Northwestern University Press.

Derrida, J. 1978. *Writing and Difference*, A. Bass (trans.). Chicago, IL: University of Chicago Press.

Ellis, W. D. (ed.) 1938. *A Source Book of Gestalt Psychology*. New York: Harcourt, Brace.

Haldane, E. E. & G. R. T. Ross (eds) 1984. *The Philosophical Works of Descartes*, vol. 1. Cambridge: Cambridge University Press.

Heidegger, M. 1962. *Being and Time*, J. Macquarrie & E. Robinson (trans.). New York: Harper & Row.

Heidegger, M. 1972. *On Time and Being*, J. Stambaugh (trans.). New York: Harper & Row.

Heidegger, M. 1977. *Basic Writings*, D. Krell, (ed.). New York: Harper & Row.

Heidegger, M. 1982. *Basic Problems of Phenomenology*, rev. edn., A. Hofstadter (trans.). Bloomington, IN: Indiana University Press.

Heidegger, M. 1985. *The History of the Concept of Time: Prolegomena*, T. Kisiel (trans.). Bloomington, IN: Indiana University Press.

Heidegger, M. 2000. *Introduction to Metaphysics*, G. Fried & R. Polt (trans.). New Haven, CT: Yale University Press.

Hume, D. [1739/40] 1978. *A Treatise of Human Nature*, 2nd edn, L. Selby-Bigge (ed.). Oxford: Oxford University Press, 1978. [Cited by book, part and section number.]

Husserl, E. 1962. *Ideas: General Introduction to Pure Phenomenology*, W. R. B. Gibson (trans.). New York: Collier Books.

Husserl, E. 1965. *Phenomenology and the Crisis of Philosophy*, Q. Lauer (trans.). New York: Harper & Row.

Husserl, E. 1970. *Logical Investigations* [2 vols], J. N. Findlay (trans.). London: Routledge & Kegan Paul.

Husserl, E. 1970. *The Crisis of the European Sciences*, D. Carr (trans.). Evanston, IL: Northwestern University Press.

Husserl, E. 1970. *The Idea of Phenomenology*, W. P. Alston & G. Nakhnikian (trans.). The Hague: Martinus Nijhoff.

Husserl, E. 1978. *Formal and Transcendental Logic*, D. Cairns (trans.). The Hague: Martinus Nijhoff.

Husserl, E. 1981. *Husserl: Shorter Works*, P. McCormick & F. Elliston (eds). Notre Dame, IN: University of Notre Dame Press.

Husserl, E. 1982. *Ideas Pertaining to a Pure Phenomenology and to a Phenomenological Philosophy: First Book*, F. Kersten (trans.). Dordrecht: Kluwer.

Husserl, E. 1989. *Ideas Pertaining to a Pure Phenomenology and to a Phenomenological Philosophy: Second Book*, R. Rojcewicz & A. Schuwer (trans.). Dordrecht: Kluwer.

Husserl, E. 1991. *On the Phenomenology of the Consciousness of Internal Time (1893–1917)*, J. Brough (trans.). Dordrecht: Kluwer.

Husserl, E. 1995. *Cartesian Meditations: An Introduction to Phenomenology*, D. Cairns (trans.). Dordrecht: Kluwer.

Kant, I. [1781] 1965. *Critique of Pure Reason*, N. Kemp-Smith (trans.). New York: St Martin's Press.

Levinas, E. 1969. *Totality and Infinity*, A. Lingis (trans.). Pittsburgh, PA: Duquesne University Press.

Levinas, E. 1996. *Basic Philosophical Writings*, A. Peperzak, S. Critchley, & R. Bernasconi (eds). Bloomington, IN: Indiana University Press.

Merleau-Ponty, M. 1962. *Phenomenology of Perception*, C. Smith (trans.). London: Routledge.

Quine, W. V. 1976. *The Ways of Paradox and Other Essays*, rev. and enlarged edn. Cambridge, MA: Harvard University Press.

Sartre, J.-P. 1992. *Being and Nothingness*, H. Barnes (trans.). New York: Washington Square Press.

Sartre, J.-P. 1997. *The Humanism of Existentialism*. Reprinted in *Essays in Existentialism*, W. Baskin (ed.). Secaucus, NJ: Citadel Press.

Sartre, J.-P. 1997. *The Transcendence of the Ego: An Existentialist Theory of Consciousness*, F. Williams & R. Kirkpatrick (trans.). New York: Hill & Wang.

Smart, J. J. C. 1987. *Essays Metaphysical and Moral: Selected Philosophical Papers*. Oxford: Blackwell.

Stich, S. 1996. *Deconstructing the Mind*. Oxford: Oxford University Press.

Index

referential 47–9
relativism 14, 174
repetition 153–4
representation 123, 125, 130–33, 152–4
repression 91–2, 122–3
resistance 144–5, 165
resoluteness 64–5
responsibility 60, 64, 94, 147, 173
retention 26–7, 155
Ricoeur, Paul 10

Santa Claus 29
scepticism *see* problem of other minds
scepticism about phenomenology 167–8, 175
Scheler, Max 10, 97
Schneider 120, 125–7, 129
Schutz, Alfred 10
    self-consciousness 66, 142
self-deception 90–92
self-knowledge 81–3, 95
self-understanding 47, 61, 90
sensations 98, 103–4, 109–16, 119–20
    kinaesthetic 103
    localization of 103–4
    see also sensory atoms
sense 29, 31, 36, 38, 149–52, 156
    touch 103–4, 115, 126–7
sensory atoms 109, 111–13
separateness 147
signs 148, 151, 153, 155, 156
Smart, J. J. C. 170
solicitude 50–51
solipsism 139–40, 174

solitary mental life 151–5, 175
speech 58, 146–7, 153–4; *see also* idle talk,
    language
spontaneity 117
Stein, Edith 10
substance 46–7, 56, 99, 139
synthesis 27, 29–31, 75–6, 155

temporality 56–7
thrownness 55
time 28, 53, 56
    time-consciousness 26, 155
totality 137–9, 143
trace 155–7
transcendence
    in Husserl 36
    in Sartre 81, 90, 92–3, 98
transcendental enquiry 5, 18, 36, 89
transcendental idealism 36
transcendental questions 17, 21–2, 40

unconscious, the 91–2, 156–7
understanding 53, 55, 57, 67
    as projection 53, 56
    pre-ontological 42–3, 44–5
    see also self-understanding

Watt, H. J. 166–8
Wertheimer, Max 98
world 6, 9, 54, 59; *see also* life-world
world-consciousness 51

zeigen 125–9; *see also* movement